REVOLUTION AND REFLECTION

REVOLUTION AND REFLECTION

Intellectual Change in Germany during the 1850's

by

ANDREW LEES

MARTINUS NIJHOFF / THE HAGUE / 1974

To Lynn

ISBN 90 247 1638 1

PRINTED IN THE NETHERLANDS

CONTENTS

ACKNOWLEDGMENTS

The research on which this book is based was made possible by financial grants from the Woodrow Wilson Foundation and from Harvard University for the year 1966-67 and by the staffs of the British Museum, the Bayerische Staatsbibliothek, and the Robert Frost Library at Amherst College. I first formulated my ideas on the subject of the book in a doctoral dissertation, which I completed in 1968 at Harvard University under the direction of Franklin L. Ford. Since then, I have benefited greatly from the willingness of several scholars to read and to comment in detail upon part or all of what I have written: Heinz Gollwitzer of the University of Münster; Harold L. Poor of Rutgers University; James J. Sheehan of Northwestern University; the late John L. Snell of the University of North Carolina; Mack Walker of Cornell University; and my colleagues at Amherst College, John B. Halsted and John William Ward. I am deeply indebted to Fritz K. Ringer of Boston University, who showed me new ways of thinking about intellectual history before I began my research and patiently argued with me at great length both about the dissertation and about an intermediate version of this book. Our conversations have provided some of the most stimulating moments in my growing awareness of what it means to do historical scholarship well. Lynn read and listened to everything I had to say many times over, offering precise criticism and moral support in equal abundance. She has given everything that could be asked for from a wife who is also a historian.

Amherst, Massachusetts
September 1973

ABBREVIATIONS

Most of the works cited in the reference notes which appeared during the period treated in this study are listed in the Appendix. Citations of these works in the notes therefore include only the author's name and a brief form of the title. The following abbreviations appear in the notes and in the Appendix.

DSW: Johann Caspar Bluntschli and Karl Brater, eds., *Deutsches Staats-Wörterbuch* (11 vols., Stuttgart and Leipzig, 1857-70).

DVS: *Deutsche Vierteljahrs Schrift.*

FP: Frankfurt Parliament.

Gegenwart: August Kurtzel, ed., *Die Gegenwart: Eine encyclopädische Darstellung der neuesten Zeitgeschichte für alle Stände* (12 vols., Leipzig, 1848-56).

Germania: Ernst Moritz Arndt, ed., *Germania: Die Vergangenheit, Gegenwart und Zukunft der deutschen Nation* (2 vols., Leipzig, 1851-52).

HPB: *Historisch-politische Blätter für das katholische Deutschland.*

HZ: *Historische Zeitschrift.*

NCL: Hermann Wagener, ed., *Neues Conversations-Lexikon: Staats- und Gesellschafts-Lexikon* (23 vols., Berlin, 1859-67).

PJ: *Preussische Jahrbücher.*

SL: Karl von Rotteck and Karl Welcker, eds., *Das Staats-Lexikon: Encyklopädie der sämmtlichen Staatswissenschaften für alle Stände* (3rd ed., 14 vols., Leipzig, 1856-66).

I

INTRODUCTION

THE PROBLEM AND THE APPROACH

The abortive revolutions of 1848 have been widely regarded by historians as a watershed not only in the political but also in the intellectual development of modern Europe. Before 1848, according to the traditional view, the prevalent climate of opinion was idealistic, hopeful, humane, and progressive. Afterwards, it was empirical, pessimistic, cynical, and obsessed with power. As Hans Kohn put it in his essay "Mid-century: The Turning Point," "In 1848 the foundations of Western civilization – intellectual belief in the objectivity of truth and justice, ethical faith in mercy and tolerance – were still unshaken. ... In the spring of 1848 mankind was full of glowing hope, but the end of 1848 dashed the hopes, and the century which 1848 inaugurated appears to have led slowly but surely to decay and disaster." [1] Germany, a prime culprit in the debacle which marked the last third of that century, has been seen as the country in which the events of 1848-49 had the most profound impact. Although few historians have gone as far as Kohn in linking the failures experienced by mid-nineteenth-century Germans to the horrors perpetrated by some of their twentieth-century descendants, it has long been common to think of Germany's response to her defeated revolution as a process of attitudinal preparation for Otto von Bismarck's authoritarian solution to the national question in the period between 1864 and 1871 – which in turn was fraught with ominous long-range significance. Nevertheless, the years which immediately followed this supposedly crucial failure of German liberalism are among the least studied in German history.

This book investigates the intellectual history of Germany in the 1850's. It attempts to assess the ways in which the mid-century revolution and its inglorious outcome affected the thinking of Germany's leading professors

[1] Hans Kohn, *The Twentieth Century: The Challenge to the West and Its Response* (New York, 1949), 18.

and university-trained publicists. These men had played a prominent role
in German political controversy both before and during 1848-49, and
they continued to enjoy much higher prestige than their counterparts
elsewhere in Europe. The attitudes they articulated toward the issues
raised by the course of contemporary history and the relations between
these attitudes and later historical developments clearly deserve the close
scrutiny which they have not heretofore received.

Before discussing the assumptions which underlie this study and the
methods which have been employed in constructing it, let us examine
somewhat more closely what has been said on the subject by other historians. One view – voiced most harshly by several historians who wrote
around the turn of the century but still implicit in the general lack of
attention by scholars to the period of the 1850's – has been that the
revolution's failure left an intellectual vacuum. Sheer emotional and
mental exhaustion are thought to have led to a decade of sterility, a period
that was barren of interesting or significant activity in the realm of
thought.[2]

A more interesting line of argument has emphasized the emergence of
new attitudes and ideas. Many historians have contended that the events
of 1848-49 had one or both of the following intellectual consequences:
an accelerated rejection of "idealism" in favor of a mode of thought
which has been variously described as materialistic, positivistic, or simply
empirical; and a new sense of self-doubt, pessimism, and respect for
power among those who had earlier agitated for political change. Such
labels often turn out to be synonyms for sterility in the writings where they
appear, but the men who have applied them have at least attempted to
tell us something about what occurred in postrevolutionary life. They
have not simply dwelled on the supposed absence of significant ideas.

With regard to intellectual change in general, it has frequently been
asserted that frustrated idealists relegated *Geist*, or thought, to a subordinate position as a determinant of human affairs, enthroning material
reality in its place. As Theobald Ziegler wrote in his general history of
nineteenth-century thought, "... the whole mood of the time was a
materialistic one. The year 1848 had, so to speak, reduced idealism and
the idealists to an absurdity and made them appear to be impractical
dreamers: thus, away with everything which recalled this illusion and

---

[2] See Theobald Ziegler, *Die geistigen und socialen Strömungen des neunzehnten
Jahrhunderts* (Berlin, 1899), 306-307. His contention that the 1850's were "the
decade of the nineteenth century which was most impoverished in thought and spirit"
is echoed in Vol. XI, part I, of Karl Lamprecht, *Deutsche Geschichte* (Berlin, 1908);
see esp. 133, 177-181, 306, 310.

had led to it." Along the same lines, other historians, such as Hajo Holborn, have referred to the postrevolutionary years as a period which witnessed declining interest in philosophy and an upsurge of sober specialization in empirical disciplines, such as the natural sciences and history. These changes, it is often asserted, simultaneously bore the imprint of the disappointments encountered in the revolution and helped to create a new climate of opinion concerning specific political problems which still remained on Germany's agenda.[3]

Loss of revolutionary nerve and a marked turn to the right on the part of men who had become more empirical in their outlook on the world and less confident in the power of ideas to shape that world is the second intellectual change which has generally been attributed to the postrevolutionary years. As Veit Valentin put it, "The true master stroke of the counterrevolution was to spread widely among the German people the conviction that they were unsuited for politics." This loss of confidence, in conjunction with the sobering effects of radical agitation by the lower classes for social reform, led many men who had formerly opposed the old order to display new respect for existing authority. It has also been assumed that those who remained dissatisfied with the status quo came to regard monarchical power as the most promising agent for the fulfillment of their desires, which now pointed toward national unity instead of individual freedom. To quote Valentin again: "Force, not reason, had conquered. Many now worshipped force and thought it was indispensable." The liberal intellectuals are said to have experienced an especially acute crisis of confidence. Having absorbed a humiliating defeat, they lost faith in their power and their right to shape political history. And as Kohn put it, "Now the intellectuals seized upon the revelation of power – from the exercise of which they remained excluded – with typical German thoroughness, and with the enthusiasm of converts to a new faith." There are exceptions to these views. William L. Langer has recently rejected the charge that the liberals betrayed the revolution, arguing that they had never been real revolutionaries in the first place. But the prevalent opinion has been that 1848-49 was a critical year in the surrender of German liberalism and that it was especially critical for the intellectuals. To put it another way, the middle of the century is frequently viewed as a dividing line between an idealistic liberalism and

[3] Ziegler, 340; Hajo Holborn, *A History of Modern Germany, 1840-1945* (New York, 1969), 115, 119-121. See also Heinrich Heffter, *Die deutsche Selbstverwaltung im 19. Jahrhundert* (Stuttgart, 1950), 359-363; Leonard Krieger, *The German Idea of Freedom* (Boston, 1957), 346-347; and Friedrich C. Sell, *Die Tragödie des deutschen Liberalismus* (Stuttgart, 1953), 177-182.

an outlook which was both much more empirical and, in large part because of this empiricism, much more conservative.[4]

Several problems arise when one examines these views critically. Some are simply wrong – for instance, the belief that the 1850's were a decade of intellectual barrenness. Even a preliminary survey of the period reveals the inadequacy of such an assessment. Having been deeply involved in the public affairs of their country both before and during the revolution, the intellectuals felt impelled to reflect on what they had witnessed. The result was an extensive body of writing on a wide range of issues which had been raised by the recent experience of turmoil. In short, it quickly becomes apparent that the events surrounding the revolution ought to be regarded as a stimulant rather than as a depressant. In other cases, a partial truth has been greatly exaggerated: there was increased respect for material power, but the change was by no means as pronounced or far-reaching as has generally been supposed; moreover, although the liberals did modify some of their earlier expectations in a variety of ways, they did not sink into despair or indulge in an orgy of self-criticism. Some of the traditional wisdom is basically correct: the events of 1848-49 did encourage a shift from philosophical to historical modes of thought; moreover, liberals were certainly more hostile toward democracy, social- ism, and the lower classes after 1849 than before. But the trouble with almost everything written about the postrevolutionary period, even when essentially correct, is that it fails to establish a context within which the variety of intellectual currents operative at the time can be viewed in relation to one another. What was happening in the academic disciplines has not been tied in any clear way to what was happening to ideas about politics and society, and developments in all of these areas still remain in something of a historiographical limbo as they relate to the revolution which is supposed to have so strongly influenced them. Indeed, almost all the general statements which have been made about the intellectual history of these years have simply not been investigated and substantiated in more than rudimentary detail. We do have a few good monographs on individuals, and there are always the relevant chapters of the histories of particular disciplines, but the general works on nineteenth-century German intellectual history are at best brief and suggestive when they

---

[4] Veit Valentin, *Geschichte der deutschen Revolution von 1848-1849,* II (Berlin, 1931), 549-550; Hans Kohn, *The Mind of Germany* (New York, 1960), 140; William L. Langer, *Political and Social Upheaval, 1832-1852* (New York, 1969), 400. See also Krieger on "political positivism" (341 ff.) and Heffter, 351-352.

come to this period.[5] Moreover, they concentrate almost wholly on the classical liberals, devoting relatively little attention to the liberals' intellectual competitors. There is nothing on these years like Franz Schnabel's great volumes on the first half of the century, or like Jacques Droz's study of the responses by German writers to the French Revolution.[6]

One reason for this state of affairs is that historians of modern Germany have been so strongly attracted to the antecedents of the revolution, the revolution itself, and the decisive events of the 1860's.[7] The relatively quiet interlude of the 1850's has inevitably received short shrift. For German nationalists, these years were a period of humiliation, best consigned to oblivion. For intellectual historians, it is as if the imputations of sterility by some have dissuaded almost everybody from taking a really close look at the postrevolutionary milieu – paradoxically, despite the fact that far-reaching changes are supposed to have occurred within that milieu.

Various ways of assessing the revolution's intellectual impact could be pursued. One could take a small group of prominent individuals and compare what they wrote after 1848-49 with what they had written earlier. One might also compare a few of the more interesting men from the first half of the century with a few from the second half. Concentrating on a limited number of figures is eminently feasible. But the disadvantage of this method is that the historian – at least insofar as he wants his small group to stand for something larger – usually starts his investigation by making the basic decisions about what was truly prevalent in the outlook of the period he is studying. What ought to be one of the most important conclusions is all too often an initial assumption.

The present study was undertaken on the premise that it would be more fruitful to concentrate on a wide range of figures within a relatively short time span, rather than to aim for an expanded temporal dimension at the cost of representativeness. The study does not deal at great length with the decades before 1848, nor does it present more than a sketch of

---

[5] The fullest general treatments are by Ziegler, who wrote about fifty pages on the 1850's, and by Heffter, who wrote about half that.

[6] Franz Schnabel, *Deutsche Geschichte im neunzehnten Jahrhundert* (4 vols., Freiburg im Breisgau, 1929-36); Jacques Droz, *L'Allemagne et la Révolution française* (Paris, 1949).

[7] Two examples will suffice. Karl Griewank's "Ursachen und Folgen des Scheiterns der deutschen Revolution in 1848," *HZ*, Vol. 170 (1950), 395-423, contains twenty-three pages on the causes of the failure and five on its effects. Theodore S. Hamerow's *The Social Foundations of German Unification* (2 vols., Princeton, 1969-72), an admirable departure from the traditional preoccupation with Bismarck, begins in 1858.

what men were thinking during the revolution, subjects which have been amply treated by others. The core of the study begins in the spring of 1849. It spans a decade, permitting consideration not only of immediate responses but also of ones which required more time for their completion. It concludes with the start of the New Era, which was marked by the accession of Prince William as regent and the end of the conservative reaction in Prussia and by the nearly simultaneous reopening of the national question in the wake of war between Austria and Piedmont. These events, together with the constitutional conflict and the wars of unification which followed them, imposed a new set of conditions on political discourse and called forth a host of writings which focused much more on current affairs and future possibilities than on the lessons of the revolutionary past.

The names of the men whose works during the 1850's form the basis for this study were gathered with several ends in mind. In the first place, it was necessary to include as many as possible of the period's leading thinkers whose interests lay in areas which were at all likely to be affected by the revolution – the men whose judgments on the general significance of recent history probably carried the greatest weight with the educated reading public. At the same time, I sought to construct a fairly representative sample of certain sectors within the professional intellectual estate as a whole, which enjoyed enormous prestige and influence as a group quite apart from the capacities and reputations of any of its individual members. The list of men to be investigated thus had to be large enough to afford the possibility of making meaningful statements about what was characteristic and what merely idiosyncratic, and yet not be so large as to prove unmanageable. The criteria used in drawing up this list and the ways in which I went about locating items written by the men on it which were relevant to my purposes are made more explicit in the Appendix. Only a few added remarks on these matters are in order here. The word intellectual refers in this study, for the most part, to professors, free-lance scholars, and university-trained publicists. The total number of such men on the preliminary list was 189. I found books, articles, or letters by seventy of these writers which related to the questions I had in mind. About four fifths of this smaller group had been politically active in some way in 1848-49, slightly more than a third of them having sat at the Frankfurt Parliament. Of the men for whom it is possible to establish a place of residence in Germany in the spring of 1849 (all but a handful of the seventy) more than a third lived in Prussia, close to a third lived in other states north of Frankfurt, and about the same number lived in the South. This spread corresponds roughly to the overall distribution of the German population.

Many of the works written by these men which I have considered in this study treat a wide range of questions, but most of them fall into three broad categories: discussions of the recent history and proper functions of various disciplines and modes of thought; historical accounts of the revolution; and general arguments about matters of political or social controversy. The reason for this selection is very simply that the impact of the revolution on the German intellectuals can best be understood as a process in which men redefined the scope and status of their own activity, interpreted the revolution itself, and reconsidered the great public issues which had recently agitated their country. To put it another way, I have assumed that men's interpretations of themselves and their understandings of their place in history lie at the very heart of the ways they think about politics and society.

A few remarks are in order at this point about the design of the book and the arrangement of its chapters. The rest of Chapter I contains a brief discussion of the 1830's and 1840's (often referred to as the *Vormärz*) and a schematic division of the intellectuals who were concerned with political and social issues during the 1850's into four basic groups. Chapter II serves as a second introduction to the chapters which follow it, by indicating how the intellectuals chose and defined their modes of thought. The first half of that chapter treats the movement from speculative philosophy to politically partisan history; its sequels are Chapter III, which treats the highly partisan historiography of the revolution, and Chapter IV, which examines the new, more historically empirical mode of discourse about matters of postrevolutionary concern. The second half of Chapter II discusses proposals for new ways of studying society and thus finds its most obvious sequel in Chapter V, which explores the heightened concern with and sophistication about social questions.

THE POLITICS OF GERMAN INTELLECTUALS
IN THE *VORMÄRZ* AND THE REVOLUTION

Among the forces pushing for political and social change in Germany before and during 1848, intellectuals in the broad sense of the term played a decisive role. Professors, publicists, lawyers, judges, medical doctors, secondary school teachers, clerics, and higher civil servants, who were intellectuals by virtue of their training in the universities, belonged to a prestigious elite. Their eminence stemmed in part from the exclusiveness of the group to which they belonged, men with university training having comprised only a small fraction of the nation. Other characteristics of early and mid-nineteenth-century German social structure also contributed to their high prestige. Changes in economic life and the growth of the bureaucratic monarchies had greatly diminished the social importance of hereditary titles based on the ownership of landed property. Consequently, the old nobility had been increasingly displaced by a new "learned estate." On the other hand, Germany's low level of industrialization meant that the economic middle class of capitalist entrepreneurs still remained quite weak. Men with university training thus enjoyed far greater social standing in Germany than they did in France or England. The reasons for the adherence of so many – though by no means all – of these men to the various movements of critical opinion during the decades leading up to the middle of the century will emerge more clearly as we proceed. It suffices here to mention a central objective which was entirely comprehensible, given both the training of the intellectuals and the conditions they faced: a greater degree of rationality and predictability in German public life.[8]

Both the status of the intellectuals and their ties to the forces of movement were clearly displayed in 1848 at the Frankfurt Parliament, where one tabulation indicates that 75 per cent of 573 delegates belonged to the academically trained "intelligentsia." A further breakdown shows that intellectuals were especially prominent in the center and on the left. Here, the percentage of intellectuals reached 78 per cent, whereas among the 37 delegates who sat on the far right the corresponding figure fell to 59 per cent. Of the 429 men who belonged to this intelligentsia, 69 per cent sat with the parties of the center and the left. Of course, some intellectuals were not affiliated with any party; if they are subtracted from the total the percentage of leftists and moderates among the remaining intellectuals rises to 93 per cent.[9]

[8] Schnabel, II, 196-210; Fritz K. Ringer, *The Decline of the German Mandarins: The German Academic Community, 1890-1933* (Cambridge, Mass., 1969), 5-11, 14-35. For the best overview of political and social tendencies during the *Vormärz*, see Ernst Rudolf Huber, *Deutsche Verfassungsgeschichte seit 1789*, II (2nd ed., Stuttgart, 1968), 324-434. Other works which I have found especially helpful on this period, besides Schnabel's, have been the ones by Heffter, Krieger, and Holborn referred to above and Wilhelm Mommsen, *Grösse und Versagen des deutschen Bürgertums* (2nd ed., Munich, 1964).

[9] The figures are calculated from tables in G. Schilfert, *Sieg und Niederlage des demokratischen Wahlrechts in der deutschen Revolution* (Berlin, 1952), 406. He uses the term "*Intelligenz*." The total number of delegates varies in different tabulations, from about 550 to 830. The lower figures refer to totals at particular points in time. The higher ones represent attempts to enumerate all the men who sat in the Frankfurt Parliament from the beginning to the end. Schilfert's totals are the only ones divided both by occupations and by parties.

In addition to the intellectuals, there were other participants in the efforts to achieve change who came from nonintellectual walks of life, which comprised the great bulk of the population. Most notable were the increasingly vociferous groups of merchants, bankers, and industrialists in the Prussian Rhineland and in East Prussia. Working through their provincial diets, they began to provide the liberal forces with the wider social base which had heretofore been lacking. Moreover, there were groups of radical artisans, many of whom spent a good part of this period living in Switzerland or France. Nevertheless, the position of men with university training remained much more influential. They certainly occupied most of the leading positions in the liberal movements. Returning to Frankfurt, we note that merchants, manufacturers, and artisans accounted for a little under 8 per cent of the delegates.

Among the progressive elements from the intellectual classes thus broadly defined, professors and publicists – intellectuals in the narrower sense of the term – played an especially significant part, even though they constituted nowhere near a majority of the politically active intellectual estate as a whole. Several factors help explain the political prominence of this more limited group of intellectuals. Quite obviously, these men formulated ideas professionally: their work was scholarship and thought. They served therefore as the natural agents for articulating the basic principles, or ideologies, which animated the various movements in which they participated. Moreover, intellectual activity itself assumed particular importance for the groups seeking change owing to the fact that Germany possessed so little in the way of a living historical tradition to which these movements could refer. The lack of a tradition which progressive writers could credibly invoke for their purposes was most evident in the area of parliamentary institutions, but it could be felt elsewhere as well. Consequently it often seemed necessary to dredge up the remembrance of institutions and rights which had long been suppressed or fallen into disuse, to argue in the abstract language of natural human rights, or to hold up contemporary foreign examples. Men who wrote were clearly crucial to these efforts.[10] More specifically, the most appropriate protagonists were historians, philosophers, specialists in comparative constitutional law, and journalists and other writers who acquainted their readers with France, England, and the United States.

To say all this is of course simply to point out the intellectuals' usefulness to the progressive cause. What was it about their own situation that made so many of them both eager and willing to contribute their efforts

[10] Schnabel, II, 195-196.

to changing the political order? First of all, there was the widespread harassment – and in some cases real persecution – which German intellectuals at the time had to endure. They faced not only widespread preventive censorship but also the very real possibility of finding normal academic careers blocked, losing their jobs, or perhaps going to jail. Indeed, if we look at the seventy men treated in this study, we find that before the revolution at least seventeen of them had suffered some kind of fairly serious official retaliation because of their political activities or their scholarly opinions, seven having actually been brought to trial or sent to prison (see the Appendix).

The publicists nursed special grievances in addition to the ones they shared with other intellectuals. They had been recruited from all of the traditional social estates, but a large number came from relatively poor families, and their social status was generally lower than that of professors or other civil servants. The social status of publicists (like that of most professional writers) was low for another more pressing reason. Quite simply, they were victims of academic and professional overpopulation. Education was much sought after in Germany as a path to higher social standing, but in the middle of the nineteenth century there were too many intellectuals for the society to support. The states could not find positions for all men with university training in the bureaucracies, the universities, and the secondary schools. Publicists were therefore likely to be men who could find no other use for their energies except to become independent writers, even though the economic backwardness of the country made it impossible for most of them to earn an adequate living. Their self-esteem and expectations having been nourished by an advanced education, penniless writers all too often experienced real life as a dismal disappointment.[11]

Professors and publicists, despite the harassments which they encountered, enjoyed much greater autonomy than many other members of the intellectual estate, and this in turn made them more willing to oppose the established authorities. Although members of the administrative and judicial bureaucracies contributed heavily to the forces of the liberal opposition in the constitutional states of southern Germany, elsewhere their conditions of tenure did not give them nearly as much latitude to criticize their employers. But professors, their employment by the state notwith-

[11] Lenore O'Boyle, "The Image of the Journalist in France, Germany, and England, 1815-1848," *Comparative Studies in Society and History*, X (1968), 290-317; Rolf Engelsing, *Massenpublikum und Journalistentum im 19. Jahrhundert in Nordwestdeutschland* (Berlin, 1966), 46-62.

standing, still possessed a traditional independence which permitted them to speak out with a certain degree of freedom. Although their direct criticisms of the political status quo were necessarily limited in intensity and scope, they enjoyed freedom of expression in "academic" matters, which might be broadly construed to permit a good deal of indirect commentary on more controversial subjects. Publicists, unless of course they worked for government-sponsored publications, were not tied to the state at all. To be sure, for publicists as well as for professors, censorship and threats of reprisals provided constant irritation, but they were insufficiently rigorous to prevent these men from declaring their opposition to the old order and playing a principal part in the attempt to force the pace of political change. Again looking at the Frankfurt Parliament, we see a marked disproportion between the percentage of men in the parties of the center and the left who belonged to this narrower group of intellectuals and the corresponding figure for the right: 15 per cent compared to only 5 per cent.[12]

Having considered the general determinants of intellectual politics, we may proceed to the ideas and programs of particular groups as they evolved under the pressure of historical events during the period between 1830 and 1849. The year 1830 witnessed a marked upsurge of interest in public issues and the start of serious opposition to the post-Napoleonic restoration which had prevailed throughout Central Europe under Metternich's guidance during the previous decade and a half. Stimulated by revolutionary events in France, Belgium, and Poland – and shortly thereafter by the English reform bill of 1832 – Germans now began to think much more purposefully about altering the political status quo. There was a spate of popular agitation for reform, which culminated in the mass meeting of about 30,000 people organized by the radical Patriotic Press Association at Hambach in the Palatinate in the spring of 1832. At the governmental level, constitutions were granted in all of the most important northern states, except for Prussia: Brunswick, Hesse-Kassel, Saxony, and Hanover. Baden, which along with other southern states had received its constitution over a decade earlier, saw the shift to a liberal ministry, the election of a liberal majority in the diet, the passage of a less restrictive censorship law, and other reforms as well.

Soon after the meeting at Hambach, reactionary tendencies began

[12] Schnabel, II, 202, 204-210; Heffter, 169-170. In calculating these last percentages, I have counted as publicists not only the men whom Schilfert refers to as "writers," but also the "editors" and those who were simply "Dr. Phil." Schilfert lists only six writers, considerably fewer than appear in most other tabulations.

once again to reassert themselves. Reform from above continued in the economic sphere with the foundation of the *Zollverein* under the leadership of Prussia, but political reform came to a halt. Moreover, many gains made during the decade's earlier years were lost, the most notorious case being the revocation of the Hanoverian constitution in 1837. Popular political activity encountered a new wave of repression, which – as had been the case in the 1820's – again bore the German Confederation's stamp of approval.

Intellectual support for the post-1830 reaction was provided by men whose ideas came from the great conservative theorists of the previous two decades: writers such as Adam Müller, Karl Ludwig von Haller, and Georg Friedrich Wilhelm Hegel. Müller had expounded a romantic attachment to the corporate society of the Christian Middle Ages; Haller, a defense both of monarchical and of aristocratic power based on a patrimonial conception of political authority; and Hegel, a view of the bureaucratic Prussian state as the culmination of a rational historical process. All of these ideas persisted into the period after 1830, when the repercussions of foreign upheaval helped stimulate renewed activity by conservative intellectuals. This activity began in Prussia with the establishment of the *Berlin Political Weekly,* which appeared from 1831 to 1841. Founded on the initiative of the Prussian officer and publicist Joseph Maria von Radowitz, it was soon joined by the *Historical-Political Journal,* which appeared under the editorship of Leopold Ranke from 1832 to 1836. Both publications sought to exorcise the newer revolutionary tendencies. In Bavaria, Friedrich Julius Stahl was writing his *Philosophy of Law,* which earned him a post at Berlin in 1840 and later became one of the major texts for the reaction that followed the revolution of 1848.[13] At the same time other Bavarians founded the *Historical-Political Journal for Catholic Germany,* which established a pendant to the more Protestant conservatism of the North.

Intellectual activity, however, did not assume the same importance for the conservative forces as it did for the movements seeking change. After the new reactionary measures had taken shape, conservatives could seemingly breathe somewhat easier. The major intellectual efforts to deal with political and social issues therefore came from the forces of opposition, for whom the years after 1832 became a time not of active agitation but of literary preparation for more open struggle in the future.

During the years immediately after the 1832 reaction, an assortment

---

[13] Friedrich Julius Stahl, *Die Philosophie des Rechts nach geschichtlicher Ansicht* (2 vols., Heidelberg, 1830-37).

of radical writers known as Young Germany enjoyed great popularity with the German reading public, benefiting at least temporarily from widespread disappointment over the failure to experience significant reform. Led by two Jews, Ludwig Börne and Heinrich Heine, these authors ranged widely in their criticisms of German life. Börne and Heine, who were living in Paris at the time, often compared Germany unfavorably with their newer surroundings. They held up as a model to their countrymen the quality of French literary life, pointing to the prose of men like Hugo and Balzac as an alternative to the less socially aware poetry which predominated in Germany. They also attempted to spread many of the ideas of the French Revolution, though they remained German patriots. Of the two, Börne was the more radical politically, espousing a revolutionary democratic program. Insofar as Heine's radicalism went beyond an attack on the prevailing German literary culture, it focused primarily on social and sexual mores. While admiring the achievements of 1789, he opposed both communism and democratic republicanism. Nevertheless, his writings as well as Börne's and those of the other Young Germans were forbidden in 1835 by the Diet of the German Confederation.

It was during the decade's middle years that the classic intellectual expressions of a more moderate – but more widespread – current of opposition made their appearance. German liberalism now came to the fore. German liberals in the 1830's were inspired both by foreign thinkers and by foreign examples at the level of political practice. The writings of Locke and Blackstone and of Montesquieu and Constant were among the major stimulants to the liberal imagination. The circumstances which had resulted from England's long historical development and from France's revolutions were even more influential. Some German antecedents for liberal politics could be found in the old tradition of a princely-estatist dualism, the reforming efforts of eighteenth-century enlightened absolutists, and the more recent reforms (and especially the hopes) of the Stein-Hardenberg period, but they hardly measured up to what had been accomplished abroad. At the theoretical level, the major German antecedents were the writings of Immanuel Kant and Wilhelm von Humboldt in the 1790's, who were themselves responding to the stimulus of events abroad. Kant had pleaded for the development of what later came to be called the "*Rechtsstaat,*" or the "legal state," whose constituted authorities would proceed in their actions according to the dictates of law rather than according to princely whim. Humboldt, on the other hand, had sought to limit government in the interests not so much of predictability as of the free individual's autonomous cultural development.

The demands common to most German liberals during the 1830's focused both on the form of government and on the rights of citizens not only to participate in the political process but also to pursue their private lives without fear of interference from above. The specifically political part of the liberal program addressed itself to the need for what can loosely be labelled "constitutional" government. Constitutionalism in Germany meant in the first place that the affairs of state should be conducted according to clearly articulated legal norms – that the state should in fact be a *Rechtsstaat*. But it also meant a good deal more than this. The liberals wanted legislative bodies, containing representatives of the "people" as well as of the traditional corporate estates. The management of the state would no longer take place simply by royal or bureaucratic ordinance: a form of popular consent would be required for the validation of laws and the collection of taxes. The ruler's ministers would be legally responsible to the people's representatives, having to answer to the parliament for any infractions against constitutional law. Other demands bearing on the structure of government pointed toward trial by jury (and thus the separation of justice from administration) and the extension of the rights of self-government at the local level. In short, political power would be divided and shared rather than monopolized by the autocrats and their servants.

The political program of constitutional liberalism had at least two ends in view. One, which harked back to the reform period and to the southern constitutions of 1818-19 and became more evident as time went on, was to strengthen the state by enlisting in its behalf a greater measure of popular support. Constitutions were desired in part so as to help solidify a shaky political foundation. More noticeable during the 1830's was a second objective: protecting the civil rights of individuals by securing freedom from arbitrary arrest, inviolability of personal property against illegal seizure, and greater cultural liberties. These last were crucially important. In particular, liberals sought constitutional government as a part of their attempts to win freedom of speech, freedom of the press, and freedom of association – all of which were severely limited at the time. Such demands were of course precisely what one would expect from intellectuals.

Inasmuch as a large measure of the inspiration for German liberalism came from abroad, it is hardly surprising that disagreements as to which foreign country provided the most suitable examples for Germany to follow serve as one of the most convenient ways of distinguishing the main variations within the liberal movement. Roughly speaking, it was the same line which separated admirers of England from admirers of France, northerners from southerners, and "moderates" from the more advanced "dualists." [14]

North German liberals, among whom such highly respected professors as Friedrich Christoph Dahlmann, Johann Gustav Droysen, and Georg Waitz stood out, displayed particular sympathy for England. What attracted them was not really a specific set of institutional arrangements. To be sure, they greatly admired the English jury system and the protection which Englishmen enjoyed against arbitrary interference with their personal freedoms. But the true mark of the "German Whigs" showed itself in a romantically tinged respect for historic institutions in general and a belief in the possibility of achieving their ideals through "organic" development. They came nowhere near endorsing the contemporary English practice of parliamentary government. Instead, they located the essence of English political virtue either in certain formal propositions about monarchical sovereignty which were no longer adhered to in practice or in the customary gradualness and empiricism with which the English embarked on any new departures.

The essential moderation of north German, or "classical," liberalism becomes readily apparent when one considers Dahlmann's attitudes toward the distribution of political power within the state, most of which were expressed in his influential *Politics, Based on the Standard of Existing Conditions.*[15] While insisting on the need for new parliamentary organs, he advocated both the inclusion of some corporate representatives as well as popular ones and an upper house organized along the lines of a hereditary peerage. He of course rejected universal suffrage, which no European state at the time came near practicing. The hereditary monarch was to retain the right of absolute veto over any parliamentary decisions and complete control over the appointment of his ministers. Even though his own protest against the abrogation of the Hanoverian constitution and his subsequent dismissal from Göttingen along with six other professors became the *cause célèbre* of German liberalism during this period, Dahlmann refused to admit the right of active resistance against unlawful monarchical action. Revolution lay completely beyond the pale, since it would weaken the state, whose

---

[14] The terms come from Krieger, 303-322.
[15] Friedrich Christoph Dahlmann, *Die Politik, auf den Grund und das Mass der gegebenen Zustände zurückgeführt* (Göttingen, 1835).

strength and integrity Dahlmann felt were essential to the fulfillment of human destiny.

South German liberalism, more popular and widespread in the *Vormärz* than its northern counterpart, found its most articulate representatives in the circle of men who contributed to the avidly read *Political Lexicon*.[16] In addition to the editors, Karl von Rotteck and Karl Theodor Welcker, this circle included such well-known writers as Robert von Mohl, Paul Pfizer, Karl Mittermaier, and Sylvester Jordan. Although Welcker's sympathies lay more with England than with France, in general the liberals from southern Germany were much more strongly influenced by French example than were those from the North. Again, the evidence of foreign influence lay not so much in a specific political program as in the manner of their approach to the whole range of political questions. Whereas the northerners argued within the empirical framework of historically given institutions, the southerners were more prone to discourse in a rationalistic vein, appealing to the dictates of abstract natural law. They thus revealed a profound debt to Rousseau and the French Revolution, even though they frequently criticized both. Rotteck's writings, which had already begun to assume importance in the 1820's, provided especially good examples of this kind of influence.

Some differences did exist between the political programs of the north and the south German liberals. Men like Rotteck, for instance, were readier than Dahlmann's supporters to assert the prerogatives of the representative body over against those of the crown and to proclaim the ideal desirability of "democracy." But it is important to bear in mind the limitations even of this more progressive or "parliamentary" liberalism. Seldom did its adherents expect the makeup of the governing power to be determined by a parliamentary majority. They did not yet aim at parliamentary government in the sense in which it already operated in England, France, and Belgium. As a consequence, their theories led to a sharply dualistic view of the state, with the monarch on one side and the people's representatives on the other. Rotteck's plans for democracy were also narrowly circumscribed. When he used the term, he tended to equate it with legal equality and the elimination of special privileges for the nobility. The demand for equal suffrage was practically nonexistent in the South as well as in the North.

---

[16] Karl von Rotteck and Karl Theodor Welcker, eds., *Staats-Lexikon, oder Encyklopädie der Staatswissenschaften* (15 vols., Altona, 1834-43). See Hans Zehntner, *Das Staatslexikon von Rotteck und Welcker* (Jena, 1929), esp. 93-95, on the work's influence during the *Vormärz*. Of the fifty-four contributors to the first edition who can be identified, thirty-five came from the South (*ibid.*, 32).

Although Rotteck's interest lay in the development of greater freedom within the existing state and he felt little enthusiasm for national unification, he hardly typified south German liberalism as a whole in this respect. Indeed, southerners differed quite markedly from northerners during these years in their more vocal advocacy of German unity. Men from the South pioneered not only in formulating constitutional demands but also in the avowal of political nationalism, whereas men like Dahlmann – with their respect for the historical state – had little feeling for the national cause until the 1840's. South German nationalism was expressed forcefully in Paul Pfizer's widely read *Correspondence of Two Germans*.[17] The main point of this and other writings by Pfizer on the national question was that in order to secure the cause of freedom Germans had to achieve unity too. The former without the latter could not be realized and maintained. At the level of the particularist state, constitutional government would always remain a prey to local rulers. Only at the national level could the dualism between princes and their subjects be overcome. In addition, Pfizer asserted the need for national unity in order to provide the protection from external enemies without which internal freedom would be meaningless. Convinced that freedom would inevitably follow the achievement of unity, he looked to Prussian power as the indispensable agent for attaining the national goal.

At the start of the 1840's, the accession of Frederick William IV in Prussia gave rise to new hopes for reform from above. But as the decade wore on, both economic development and economic distress combined with disappointment over the Prussian king's actual practice to help create a situation in which the forces seeking change from below experienced steady growth. Whereas the popular agitation of the early 1830's had quickly been succeeded by the activity of an influential but fairly restricted number of intellectuals, during the 1840's the various currents of opposition increased in number and acquired a much wider base. New groups of intellectuals entered the arena of political and social discourse and began to acquire prominence. These included publicists in the Rhineland, such as Karl Brueggemann, who were closely connected with the entrepreneurial interests in that area, the "Prussian" school of historians, the Young Hegelians, and an assortment of other figures who began to deal with social and economic issues. A host of new political periodicals gave the intellectuals additional means of voicing their com-

---

[17] P[aul] A[chatius] Pfizer, *Briefwechsel zweier Deutschen* (Stuttgart and Tübingen, 1831).

plaints.[18] The covertly political nationwide meetings of German academics, which had begun with the scientists and doctors in 1822 and had
come to include the conferences of classical philologists in 1838, now
branched out still further, as specialists in German law, literature, and
history met together for the first time in 1846 and 1847.[19] Members of
the liberal opposition from the diets of southwestern and central Germany, having already begun to confer annually in 1839, continued to
do so in following years. Finally, there were the various movements which
possessed a real mass base: the dissident sects of Protestant *Lichtfreunde,*
or "Illuminati," and of "German Catholics," who implicitly challenged
political authority by aiming at a more democratic form of government
within the church; the political activities of artisans and burghers in many
of Germany's larger cities; and the more inchoate manifestations of
popular unrest, such as the famous rising of rural Silesia's starving weavers
in 1844.

Several changes occurred during these years in the thinking of intellectuals who belonged to the liberal camp. Most noticeable was the steady
rise of interest in the national question, as north German liberals began
to join southerners in advocating greater political unity. Stimulated by
renewed French threats to the left bank of the Rhine in 1840, the national
movement drew added strength from a growing awareness that constitutional government could not be won for the whole country piecemeal,
since there were too many centers of reaction. Closely linked with the
growing national movement was a rising conviction that a new German
state would have to be formed under Prussian leadership and that it
could not include Austria. Prussia's special mission was heralded not only
by publicists but also by such politically motivated historians as Dahlmann, Droysen, and Heinrich von Sybel. Not all liberals agreed on these
matters. Southerners, Pfizer notwithstanding, tended to favor a *Grossdeutschland* which would include Austria, with the main support for a
Kleindeutschland coming from the North. But the difficulties which
militated against the inclusion of two great powers within a single state –
especially when one of them possessed large non-German populations –
seemed more and more formidable; moreover, there remained the older
objection that Austria had instigated and perpetuated the post-1815
restoration.

[18] Kurt Koszyk, *Deutsche Presse im 19. Jahrhundert* (Berlin, 1966), 92-104.
[19] R. Hinton Thomas, *Liberalism, Nationalism, and the German Intellectuals, 1822-
1847: An Analysis of the Academic and Scientific Conferences of the Period* (Cambridge, Eng., 1951).

Another change in liberal thinking during the 1840's appeared in a growing emphasis on social and economic issues. Specific demands differed markedly. One tendency, which Friedrich List displayed in his famous work on *The National System of Political Economy*,[20] pointed toward greater economic integration at the national level. Most liberals did not concur with his plea for higher protective tariffs vis-à-vis foreigners, but they could certainly second his call for an extension of economic liberalism within Germany. For example, liberal publicists in the Rhineland advocated domestic free trade and the end of guild restrictions. Another way in which liberals manifested a growing awareness of social and economic issues related more directly to the endemic conditions of economic hardship which marked the "hungry forties." Instead of simply advocating policies favorable to middle-class economic interests, some liberals did begin to interest themselves in the plight of the working man and the farmer and to propose moderate reforms which would speak particularly to their needs: for instance, protective legislation for factory workers and attempts to promote various self-help and charitable associations. The change in this regard can be traced quite graphically by comparing the first edition of Rotteck and Welcker's *Political Lexicon* with the second one, which appeared from 1845 to 1848 and contained far more articles than did its predecessor on social and economic questions.[21]

Finally, many liberals were beginning to pursue something like the English form of parliamentary – not just constitutional – government. And yet, just as most liberals felt that little in the way of positive measures could be undertaken for the benefit of those who might have to suffer from economic change, so too liberal politics remained for the most part within quite narrowly defined boundaries. Hesitancy and caution can be seen even in the thinking of men who used the language of popular sovereignty. "Only a very few deduced the democratic republic and the political self-rule of a whole people at all its levels from popular sovereignty. In essence, the talk was not of sovereignty but rather of the participation of the people in the government, and by the 'people' almost all of the representatives of the political movement understood not the mass of the population, but rather the educated class." [22]

Although most of the liberals still had a long way to go before they could qualify as exponents of political democracy, other intellectuals did

[20] Friedrich List, *Das nationale System der politischen Oekonomie* (Stuttgart and Tübingen, 1841).
[21] Donald G. Rohr, *The Origins of Social Liberalism in Germany* (Chicago and London, 1963).
[22] Mommsen, 35.

begin to agitate at this time for radically democratic solutions to Germany's political problems. These men were the counterparts in the 1840's of the earlier Young Germany school, one crucial difference being that their strength grew rather than declined as the decade progressed. Their ranks included some of the Young Hegelians, who had begun their attack on existing authority at a second remove in the 1830's by criticizing religious orthodoxy. Among these radical philosophers, the most notable representative of a more explicitly political tendency, which began to appear early in the 1840's, was Arnold Ruge. He edited a number of literary and political journals and – like the Young Germans – spent considerable time in France. His sympathies were not only democratic but also cosmopolitan, and he was not a nationalist, but his outlook in this regard was untypical of democratic thinking in general. Other radical intellectuals, such as the lawyer and publicist Gustav von Struve in Baden and the poets Ferdinand Freiligrath and Georg Herwegh, were adamant in their pursuit both of republicanism and of national unity.

In addition to the liberals and the democrats, there emerged a number of men who were beginning to concern themselves primarily with a wide range of issues which came to be known simply as "the social question": problems related to the effects of economic liberalism and of nascent industrialization on both artisans and factory workers, the growth of a rural proletariat, and overpopulation. For these writers, who resembled the democrats in their lack of organizational strength and surpassed them in their diversity of outlook, the nonpolitical side of public life assumed primary significance. Catholic social thinkers, following the earlier lead of Franz von Baader, combined social concern and political conservatism, urging the Church to take the lead in combatting society's ills. At the other extreme, the revolutionary approach to the social question found in Karl Marx an exponent who subsequently became more famous than any of the other men whom we have encountered, even though his reputation in Germany during the 1840's was almost nonexistent. In between, other writers – many of whom did their most important work after the revolution – advocated programs which appealed for everything from a kind of "state socialism" to organized self-help. The most significant men in this broad middle group, whom we shall treat in detail later, were Lorenz von Stein, Karl Rodbertus, and Viktor Aimé Huber.

The above remarks suggest considerable diversity and the potential for serious conflict among the forces seeking change in Germany at this time. And yet, a great deal of what separated one group from another arose not so much from real doctrinal disagreement as from temperamental differences. During most of the 1840's, men did not yet sense a sharp distinction between liberals and democrats. Similarly, it is often difficult to draw a clear line between democrats and socialists.[23] Because of Germany's political retardation, there had simply not been enough cultivation of what Leonard Krieger calls "that vital theoretical middle ground between metaphysical or ethical preconceptions and practical consequences which makes for clear and firm political systems." [24] Theories about the form of the state, the distribution of power within it, and the modalities of representation still remained nebulous in many cases. What separated a liberal from a radical might accordingly stem more from differing degrees of intensity in the advocacy of common demands than from explicit differences in the nature of the demands themselves. Only later, after men had confronted one another in the revolution, were latent conflicts to emerge clearly and crystallize. In any case, almost all of the men referred to here shared a great many specific demands in common: freedom of the press and of association, trial by jury and public judicial procedure, more local self-government, the end of any remaining manorial bonds, and some kind of popular representation in a national parliament. The demand for national unity was especially vital as a focal point around which all kinds of groups which might disagree on other issues could coalesce. Finally, all of these men were united simply by their opposition to the reactionary forces of the status quo, which offered a steadily more inviting target as the decade progressed.

Only a few salient points need to be made concerning the year of revolution, when the intellectuals found themselves in an honored position on a stage which nevertheless now contained great masses of the German people as well. During most of the spring, the sense of solidarity among the progressive forces was quite strong, as the euphoria of the March days heightened the sense of common purpose throughout a wide segment of the political spectrum. The sharp differences between radicals and moderates which had begun to come into the open late in 1847, with the proclamation of the Offenburg and Heppenheim manifestoes in Baden, were bridged by common exultation over joint victories until around June of 1848. One factor that contributed to the heightened solidarity was the early radicalizing of moderate liberals. The fact that the rulers were everywhere on the defensive emboldened them in their demands; and the role which the masses had played in forcing the rulers to grant

[23] George Lichtheim, *The Origins of Socialism* (New York and Washington, 1969), 164-165.
[24] Krieger, 301.

their concessions made it seem both natural and inevitable that the common people as well as the educated elite should be allowed to participate in the political process. As a result, it was decided that the elections to the Frankfurt Parliament should take place according to what was widely regarded as a system of universal manhood suffrage. But neither the liberals nor very many others for that matter had any desire to get rid of the monarchs. Many men who called themselves republicans assumed that the republic would simply be a democratic monarchy.

As the year progressed, splits among the progressive forces began to surface. One way in which these divisions manifested themselves could be seen in the growing cleavage between the Frankfurt Parliament as a whole and other elements in German society which had provided early support for the revolution, particularly the artisans and peasants, many of whom began to lose faith in both the ability and the desire of the parliamentarians to redress their social and economic complaints. Divisions among the progressive intellectuals appeared most strikingly as the parliament itself splintered into a variety of different parties during the summer of 1848. The gap between progressives and conservatives became more apparent in Berlin as a group of intellectuals who represented forces totally hostile to the aims of the Frankfurt Parliament's majority gained a new forum in the pages of the *Kreuz-zeitung,* or *New Prussian Newspaper.*

During the protracted debates which finally produced the parliament's proposed constitution in March of 1849, the liberal intellectuals were subjected to two contradictory pressures. Their natural inclination was to revert to prerevolutionary positions, particularly on the suffrage question and such matters as the monarchical veto. As they considered the implications of universal suffrage more carefully, they shied away from the generosity they had displayed in the spring. As they witnessed outbreaks of popular violence, their pre-1848 willingness to leave considerable powers in monarchical hands also began to return. But the balance of forces within the parliament during the spring of 1849 was such that a workable solution to the national question could not be attained without the support of avowed democrats for the election of Frederick William IV as emperor. Thus, the constitutional draft which the liberals found themselves forced to accept – with its democratic suffrage, its provision of a merely suspensive veto for the monarch, and its statements on ministerial responsibility – went considerably beyond what they really wanted in the winter and spring of 1849. The unity which had persisted among the forces of opposition during most of the 1840's seemed to have been

re-established when the constitution finally gained parliamentary acceptance and Frederick William's election took place on March 28. But
the community of purpose symbolized by the constitution had emerged
only after months of hard infighting and compromise, and it was not to
survive the Frankfurt Parliament's failure. Indeed, one of the most
striking aspects of German intellectual life during the following decade
was to be a pervasive mood of suspicion and hostility among advocates
of sharply conflicting political and social outlooks.

A TYPOLOGY OF THE INTELLECTUALS IN THE 1850'S

Men who continued to write about public affairs in Germany after
leaving the stage of active politics which so many thinkers had occupied
in 1848-49 faced official harassment just as they had in the *Vormärz*.
They had to contend with a host of new controls over the written expression of opinion, such as the requirement of revocable licenses for
printers and bookdealers and laws making incitement to "resistance
against authority" a crime. But these new controls did not come into
force until several years after the revolution had ended, and in any case
they affected the daily press more than journals or books. It is important
to remember too that they were instituted largely in order to replace
preventive censorship, which had everywhere been abolished in 1848-49.[25]
Moreover, even those intellectuals who did suffer administrative or legal
reprisal for their political views or activities – of whom there were about
ten among the seventy men whom I have listed in the main part of the
Appendix – were not so likely to be tried or sent to prison as they would
have been before the revolution. Georg Gottfried Gervinus' trial on the
charge of high treason for writing an introduction to the history of the
nineteenth century which portrayed the efforts to achieve democratic
government as the central theme of the modern period had no real
counterpart in the lives of the other leading German intellectuals, and
in any case he was acquitted.[26] Ferdinand Lassalle was the only one
among the men treated in this study who actually went to jail, whereas
five of them had been imprisoned earlier. This of course does not take
account of men who would have gone to jail had they not fled the
country, but there does seem nevertheless to have been a general improvement in the position of intellectuals vis-à-vis the political authorities.

---

[25] Huber, III (Stuttgart, 1963), 107-108, 136-138, 171-172; Johann Goldfriedrich,
Geschichte des deutschen Buchhandels, IV (Leipzig, 1913), 300-318.
[26] On the trial, see Walter Boehlich, ed., *Der Hochverratsprozess gegen Gervinus*
(Frankfurt a. M., 1967).

In any case, there was sufficient freedom of expression so that the historian can detect several markedly differing viewpoints on major public questions during the period.

Most of the writers whose ideas will be discussed in the chapters that follow can be subsumed under one of four main categories, depending upon their primary response to the issues posed by 1848 and their very conception of what those issues were. These categories will serve for heuristic purposes as a second analytic framework, to be superimposed upon the thematic structure of the book. They are intended primarily to facilitate comparisons of opinion with regard to particular problems and to provide additional threads of continuity from chapter to chapter. The largest group comprised the defenders of the liberal movement for constitutional reform and national unification. There were two smaller groups at the political extremities: the radical democrats and the staunch conservatives. Finally, there were the analysts and the critics of society. Almost every member of this last group, which by and large included the most interesting and original thinkers of the period, could also be treated as a political liberal, democrat, or conservative. But whatever their politics, they were less concerned to expound these beliefs than to discuss other problems which carried them beyond the political realm.[27]

First, the liberals, whose writing displayed an especially acute sense of public vocation. They insisted that although the movement toward a unified and constitutional Germany had failed, the ideals animating this movement still remained valid. In their view, these ideals were neither unworthy nor impractical. If they remained unfulfilled, it was because the opposition – aided by the radicals' impulsiveness – had temporarily proved too strong. Liberals saw various tactical possibilities in postrevolutionary Germany, sometimes criticizing the ways in which national and constitutional ideals had been pursued in the recent past. But none of these men failed to display admiration for at least the aims – if not always the methods – of what had been the moderate center at the Frankfurt Parliament. Conversely, even though some of these men wrote a fair amount about economic life, none of them felt that economic and social

---

[27] The fact that in some cases a man may have been assigned to a "group" of which he would not have recognized himself as a member at the time is of little consequence for my purposes. When one seeks to impose a set of analytic constructs on historical phenomena, there are always borderline cases. What matters here is not whether a particular individual was "really" a conservative whose primary concerns centered on politics or "really" a social thinker with conservative political views. The point of assigning men to one or another group is simply to convey a general sense of the prevalence of certain broad outlooks and some notion of the characteristics of the men who articulated them.

issues deserved special priority. The problems which really mattered were political.

The group of men who responded to the revolution in such fashion numbers about thirty, or close to half of the figures who can be placed in one of the four main categories. Their average age in 1849 was between forty-two and forty-three. Almost all of them had participated in the revolution, a great number as delegates at Frankfurt, where they frequently played leading roles in key committees. Most of these former delegates had been members of the right-center *Casino*. The others had belonged to one of the two left-center parties, the *Württemberger Hof* or the *Augsburger Hof*. In defending the Frankfurt Parliament's moderate center this group therefore provided not simply disinterested analysis but also a large measure of obvious self-justification. Many of the most eminent liberals were historians, such as Johann Gustav Droysen and Karl Biedermann, but the jurist Johann Caspar Bluntschli, the philosopher Rudolf Haym, and the publicist August Ludwig von Rochau also stood out.[28] During the greater part of the decade the liberals lacked a clear focal point for common political efforts. Only a few of them served in legislative bodies, and until the end of the period there were hardly any general political periodicals through which they could communicate with the educated public at large. But many of them did maintain informal personal contacts with one another (Droysen's voluminous correspondence being a particularly good example of such exchange). And within a year of one another, in 1857 and 1858, Bluntschli's *German Political Dictionary* in the South and Haym's *Prussian Annals* in the North emerged to provide the liberals with new forums for concerted intellectual activity.

The paucity both of the radical democrats' numbers and of their writings – as well as the isolation in which they worked – makes it difficult to define a common outlook toward all the issues which concern us. But they were united both by their allegiance to political democracy and by the feeling they frequently expressed that revolution was essential for achieving the objective they desired. In their view, the growth of constitutional legality and the securing of national independence were not

---

[28] Also, Ernst Moritz Arndt, Theodor von Bernhardi, Friedrich Christoph Dahlmann, Jakob Philipp Fallmerayer, Ludwig Häusser, Max Duncker, Friedrich von Raumer, Wilhelm Adolf Schmidt, Heinrich von Sybel, Heinrich von Treitschke, Georg Waitz, and Heinrich Wuttke (historians); Rudolf von Gneist and Karl Theodor Welcker (jurists); Karl Arnd, Karl Nebenius, and Max Wirth (economists); Carl Fortlage, Constantin Rössler, and Friedrich Theodor Vischer (philosophers); Gustav Freytag, Heinrich Laube, and Paul Achatius Pfizer (publicists).

enough without the establishment of political equality. When they wrote
about the failure by the Frankfurt Parliament to achieve the goals upon
which the assembly's majority had agreed, their emphasis fell on the
vitiating effect of liberal half-heartedness and moderation in opposing
the established powers. The liberals rarely criticized themselves for not
having carried their opposition to the old order far enough. But the
radicals, with their commitment to a democratic revolution, found the
basic reason for the Frankfurt Parliament's defeat in liberal unwillingness
to mount a truly effective attack against the forces of reaction.

Most of the democrats, whose average age in 1849 was thirty-seven,
had participated in the revolution. Those who had sat at the Frankfurt
Parliament had generally belonged to one of the parties on the far left:
the *Donnersberg* or the *Deutscher Hof*. The ideals of such groups continued to find their advocates among these men. But they were scattered,
lonely, and powerless. The only one of any note was a historian, Georg
Gottfried Gervinus. He stood out by virtue both of his writing and his
university post (which he lost in the middle of the decade). Most of the
others were publicists.[29] Intellectual radicals in the 1850's, as at other
times, thus tended to be much more "free-floating" than their moderate
counterparts.[30]

At the other end of the political spectrum from the democrats stood
another small but much more influential group of intellectuals who
rejected not only political and social radicalism but also more moderate
efforts to achieve liberal reform. Their sympathies lay unequivocally with
the forces of order and stability, and when they discussed public issues
they continually sought to buttress the existing regimes. Their view of the
moderates, who saw themselves as having participated in a liberal "movement," was that they had indeed been implicated in a "revolution." Like
the moderates, the conservatives reacted with horror to anything that
smacked of communism or socialism. But they differed from the moderates in viewing extreme economic demands as an inevitable outgrowth of
rather mild political ones. The conservatives saw socialism and communism as the end products of an inexorable progression which had
begun with liberal constitutionalism and whose middle stage had been

[29] Ludwig Bamberger, Hermann Baumgarten, Heinrich Bernhard Oppenheim, Arnold Ruge, and Wilhelm Schulz-Bodmer. Karl Hagen, a historian, lost his teaching
position after the revolution.

[30] In this connection, it ought to be noted that journalists and private lawyers, or
"*Advokaten*" (as opposed to the numerous state attorneys), had constituted a much
greater portion of the left than of the right or the center at the Frankfurt Parliament.
See Lenore O'Boyle, "The Democratic Left in Germany, 1848," *Journal of Modern
History*, XXXIII (1961), 375.

democratic republicanism. When they talked about the possible virtues of constitutional government, what they had in mind was the sort of regime established by the decrees of Frederick William IV. They certainly did not envision the submission of monarchical power to real parliamentary control. They might grudgingly recognize the need for a greater degree of German unity, but they seldom broached the idea with much enthusiasm. It should be added that both their general denunciations of the revolutionary phenomenon and their specific proposals for preventing another revolution in Germany often had a strongly religious flavor. And even if a conservative writer did not specifically invoke the divinity to support his political arguments, he was quite likely in any case to be deeply religious.

Before and during the revolution most of these men could be characterized in one of two ways. Either they had already displayed conservative tendencies (the few who had been at the Frankfurt Parliament having been members of the rightist *Café Milani*), or they had been politically uninvolved and quietist. None had been noted as a vigorous advocate of reform. In 1849, their average age was forty-nine, by far the highest for any of the four groups. Two men stood out from the rest: the historian Leopold Ranke and the jurist Friedrich Julius Stahl. Ranke and Stahl exemplify the fact that the most important conservatives maintained close personal ties to institutional strongholds of the old order: Ranke taught at Berlin, corresponded with the royal family, and lectured privately to King Max of Bavaria; Stahl, also a professor at Berlin, led the far right in the upper chamber of the Prussian Diet, was an active lay member of the Evangelical hierarchy, and frequently wrote for the semi-official *Kreuz-zeitung*. Several other conservatives also held places of honor in the Prussian state.[31] A second stronghold was the Catholic Church, especially in Bavaria, where the anonymous contributors to the *Historical-Political Journal for Catholic Germany* upheld a strongly political conservatism, at least up until Edmund Jörg became editor in 1852 and introduced a more social outlook.[32]

The groups delineated so far held widely varying political beliefs. But

[31] August Böckh (historian) and Johann Eduard Erdmann and Adolf Trendelenburg (philosophers).

[32] Among the political conservatives whom I have identified, the jurist George Phillips and the philosopher-philologist Ernst von Lasaulx can be linked to the Church fairly directly through their connections with the circle around the *Historisch-politische Blätter*. Several other conservatives, who lived and worked in relative isolation, were two theological critics, Bruno Bauer and David Friedrich Strauss, and a philosopher, Arthur Schopenhauer.

whether they reiterated the demands of the moderate center at the Frankfurt Parliament, hauled down the reformist standard only to replace it with the banner of democratic revolution, or condemned both radicalism and liberalism as unwarranted and dangerous assaults against beneficent authority, they all shared in common a frame of reference that was essentially political. They interpreted the events of 1848-49 largely as the product of strivings for national unity and for a reordering of the relationships between the people and those who governed them, and they defined their own ideological positions within the framework of the issues which these demands had raised.

In contrast to this whole range of politically oriented thinking stood a newer set of assumptions according to which the most pressing problems were essentially social and economic. The substantial array of men who appear under this heading did not necessarily deny the importance – or even the primacy – of politics in the recent history of their native land. What linked these men was the notion – sometimes only implicitly revealed by the contents of their works – that political matters had received far more than their fair share of attention and that it was time to redress the balance by raising a completely different set of issues. They emphasized the need for greater understanding of certain aspects of human life which carried them beyond the structure of the state. Moreover, they were likely to urge a variety of changes in the policies pursued in this area, both by the state and by groups of private citizens. At best, they regarded the central aims of the Frankfurt Parliament as only partially relevant to the true needs of the country. Insofar as they supported these aims, they did so in large measure because they saw them as a first step toward another goal of a very different sort: improvement of the conditions facing ordinary people in their daily lives. They tended to trace the recent liberal failure to disharmony between liberalism and the forces seeking social reform. Not all of the social thinkers shared all of these views. Many did, but for the purposes of classification it has proved sufficient if a man's major interests lay in one of two areas: the cultivation of a new attitude toward the study of society or economics, or the development of criticisms of and proposals for the realm of human experience concerning which the desired new knowledge might be expected to provide some enlightenment.

Most of these men, to whom I shall refer as "social thinkers," devoted much less attention to constitutional and national issues than to social and economic ones. Still, they had enough to say – in passing, as it were – so that one can at least make tentative statements about where they

stood politically. The result of subdividing the social thinkers according
to the political categories employed earlier is to stretch them out from
one end of the spectrum to the other. No single political persuasion
claimed an overwhelming share of adherents. Among the four who had
been at Frankfurt (a significantly small number in relation to the total
size of the group, which numbered over twenty), one had sat on the far
right, one on the right center, and two on the left center. Among the
others, several were radical democrats, about the same number were
conservatives, and about as many were political liberals (with somewhat
more of these falling to the left than to the right of center). Statistical
statements about data of this sort are at best imprecise. But it appears that
among the social thinkers the proportion of men whose political sympathies were generally centrist was a good deal smaller than the proportion
of such men within the larger group of intellectuals for whom politics
was the primary concern. In that group, the moderate liberals considerably outnumbered the conservatives and the radicals put together. In
contrast, a little under half of the social thinkers seem to have been located
in the political center. The average age of the social thinkers in 1849 was
a little over thirty-seven, just about the same as that of the democrats.
Several of the most important men in this group held teaching positions
in the areas of *Staatswissenschaft* (a catch-all term comprising most of
what then existed in the way of social science) and/or public law: Wilhelm
Heinrich Riehl, Robert von Mohl, and Lorenz von Stein.[33] Others who
deserve special mention are two economists who did not hold formal
teaching positions in the area of *Staatswissenschaft,* Karl Marlo and
Johann Karl Rodbertus, and a publicist, Viktor Aimé Huber.[34]

[33] Also, Heinrich Ahrens, Eduard Baumstark, Franz Joseph Buss, Karl Knies,
Wilhelm Roscher, Albert Schäffle, and Friedrich Gottlob Schulze.
[34] Also, Immanuel Hermann Fichte, Ferdinand Lassalle, and Carl Ludwig Michelet
(philosophers); Victor Böhmert, Constantin Frantz, Moses Hess, Edmund Jörg, John
Prince-Smith, and Hermann Wagener (publicists).

II

THE PUBLIC ORIENTATIONS OF SCHOLARSHIP

Before examining directly the intellectuals' views on recent and current problems in the areas of politics and society, we shall consider what they had to say about the public relevance of their own activity as thinkers. German writers sought repeatedly to define their proper function in public affairs, primarily by writing about the history and the tasks of certain academic disciplines: philosophy, history, and the "*Staatswissenschaften*," or social sciences. Their reflections on these matters were stimulated in part by the revolutionary experience, and to that extent they will become fully intelligible only in conjunction with the ideas discussed in the next chapter. But they also help explain the ways in which men interpreted the revolution, as well as the ways in which they analyzed contemporary political and social problems. A growing preference for historical modes of thought – more particularly for politically partisan ones – and the emergence of proposals for a more comprehensive study of society established the guidelines for discussion of the issues raised by the revolution.

What the intellectuals wrote about their scholarly vocation exuded a belief that learning should and could be made relevant to political and social controversy. Only a small minority, most of them conservatives, pleaded for a sharp separation between scholarship and politics, and even several of these men ended up by bridging the gap in their own practice.[1] A much larger number of writers made no pretense that neutral objectivity was the only goal of their work and in fact asserted quite the opposite: the scholar was to use his work not just for arriving at universally acceptable truths but also for effecting the realization of what he

---

[1] For some opinions hostile to academic activism, see the following: Strauss, in the *Briefwechsel zwischen Strauss und Vischer*, I, 212-213, 223-224; Schopenhauer, *Parerga und Paralipomena*, I, 149-210; Böckh, "Ueber die Wissenschaft," 93-97; Erdmann, *Philosophische Vorlesungen über den Staat*, 1-15.

and his allies deemed to be right and necessary. This sense of public vocation was predicated on a profound belief that ideas and writers did make a difference: that they could exert real leverage upon the course of public affairs. Seldom do we encounter the disparagement of intellectual activity which is so often said to have prevailed at the time. To be sure, there were occasional statements such as Heinrich von Treitschke's declaration that the world could not be reformed "with cannons which are loaded with *ideas* of right and truth," or Moses Hess's insistence that since all "ideology" was simply a product of social life philosophy could never create a new social world.[2] But the sense of self-doubt which such statements betray came nowhere near to being the majority opinion. Most intellectuals remained convinced that in doing what they knew best they provided vital assistance for the causes they supported. Even the conservatives, who detected a large part of the liberals' weakness in 1848-49 in their "doctrinaire" qualities, often paid homage to the power of thought.

Certainly those men who continued to press for political or social reforms felt just as strongly as they had in the *Vormärz* that the life of the mind occupied a vital place in their efforts. Ernst Moritz Arndt expressed this conviction in representative fashion for the liberals. Arndt based much of his hope for Germany's future on "the German spirit ... on German learning ... and on the spirit of community." He thus appealed to his fellow writers, whose efforts he felt were crucial – perhaps even sufficient – for the attainment of unity. "The German word," he continued, "was always *a sharp sword*; the German spirit and German learning have always been enlivening, refreshing, and liberating for the whole world; their quietest and most sublime power will finally win us a fatherland...." August Ludwig von Rochau supported this view. Although he stressed the weakness of the idea of national unity as it had manifested itself in combat with the existing order in 1848-49, he did not argue against the power of convictions per se. He urged instead that they be clarified and strengthened, an objective which he hoped his own work would help to achieve. Johann Gustav Droysen's assertions of faith in the power of thought were both frequent and passionate. Greatly moved by Arndt's exhortation, he wrote to a friend, "We are at the start of a struggle in which it must be shown how strong our intellectual battalions are against bayonets and diplomatic stilettos." In another letter, concerning a new periodical he was editing, he stated, "To the degree that I consider the universities important for Germany's salvation and to the

[2] Treitschke, *Briefe*, I, 352; Hess, *Briefwechsel*, 239-243, and "Jugement dernier du vieux monde social," 208.

degree that I see in the force of the deeper recognition of what is necessary the final salvation of Germany, I want to see the *ecclesia militans* of this movement stay and work together." At a loftier level of generalization, in his lectures on historical method he proclaimed that "all movement in the historical world is accomplished as the contrasting images of what ought to be (thoughts) develop out of objective conditions, [and] characters infused with them bring them to realization." In short, it was men with ideas who gave direction to history.[3]

Many of the social thinkers displayed similar optimism. His self-confidence having been strengthened all the more by the failings of the men in power, whom he scorned as "political quacks," Immanuel Hermann Fichte proclaimed that ". . . only learning, based on the belief – which they [the rulers] deride – in the eternal efficacy of ideas in the human race, can save us." Robert von Mohl believed that "the future of all European culture" depended on the development of the proper insights into the nature of society. While admitting that force would have to be used against force in a real civil war, he did not feel that social cleavages had become deep enough so as to vitiate improvements based on rational discussion. Moreover, Mohl contended that an eventual improvement in Germany's situation was already presaged by the great energy being devoted to the scholarly discussion of her public problems. Finally, Constantin Frantz wrote that "a spiritual bond and a spiritual power," coupled with well-developed knowledge, were essential for the renewal of society. All of these men, along with numerous others, believed that intellectuals could exercise enormous influence as public educators on the course of history. This confidence, which runs like a leitmotif through the literature of the period, raised both their avowals of civic responsibility and a good part of their more specialized methodological reflections above the level of merely academic interest.[4]

FROM PHILOSOPHY TO HISTORY

A number of philosophers from all four groups continued during this period to express high hopes for specifically philosophical reasoning as a way of preparing men to deal with the great controversies of public life.

[3] Arndt, "Einleitung," vii-viii; Rochau, *Grundsätze der Realpolitik*, 56, 67; Droysen, *Briefwechsel*, I, 682, 776, and "Grundriss der Historik," 355.
[4] Fichte, *System der Ethik*, I, xiv; Mohl, "Gesellschafts-Wissenschaften und Staats-Wissenschaften," 10, 25, and "Neuere deutsche Leistungen auf dem Gebiete der Staatswissenschaften," 76; Frantz, *Die Erneuerung der Gesellschaft und die Mission der Wissenschaft*, v.

They regarded abstract speculation about the nature of man, the state, and society as the best means both for discovering and for inculcating right knowledge. In voicing such hopes, they tried to sustain the great respect which philosophy had enjoyed during the heyday of German idealism, when it had been represented by such giants as Kant, Fichte, Schelling, and Hegel. It bears noting, however, that these expectations were generally expressed only by philosophers and not even by all of these men. Indeed, one of the decade's most influential philosophers, Rudolf Haym, made a particularly searching critique of the whole tradition of philosophical study. Reflections on the uses of philosophy during this period can therefore be seen as part of a debate about a traditionally prestigious discipline whose public usefulness was being increasingly questioned both from without and from within.

Two of the more notable apologists for the Prussian monarchy, Friedrich Julius Stahl and Johann Eduard Erdmann, both spoke quite forcefully for the older viewpoint. Stahl insisted that the time had come for philosophers to undertake a "reversal of scholarship." Even though he took pleasure in noting what he regarded as the sharp decline since 1830 in the prestige of philosophy, he in fact opposed only a certain kind of philosophy: the "rationalist-pantheistic" sort. During the present struggle between "world principles," the need was not to renounce philosophy as such but to find a new philosophy, which would foster "the old positive belief and the old loyalty toward positive historical order" and accept the truths of Christian revelation. For Stahl, philosophic doctrine was too powerful a weapon to be left in the hands of the enemy. Erdmann sought to demonstrate the necessary properties that all states had to possess if they were to fulfill the basic idea of the state in general. In so doing, he sought to lead his listeners out of the dangerous middle position that so many of them occupied, between simple and unthinking piety toward the state and conscious understanding of its essential nature. The strong implication, sustained by the rest or Erdmann's lectures on the state itself, was that the philosopher should and could help reconcile men to existing conditions.[5]

For the moderates, Carl Fortlage urged a return to speculative thinking, arguing that there could be no better cure for the basic evils of the time than clearly recognized principles. After all, he pointed out, the political movement in Germany had originally grown out of the philosophical upsurge at the turn of the century. Constantin Rössler criticized the radicals of the 1840's because they had tried to base every specific

[5] Stahl, *Die Philosophie des Rechts,* II, part I, vii ff.; Erdmann, 3-4, 14-15.

demand on a philosophical principle, but his reason for doing so was that they had discredited philosophy and thus made more difficult the philosopher's essential task of inspiring "the formative spirit" with great thoughts. In Rössler's opinion the public vocation of the philosopher remained vital and intact. Another political moderate, one whose main interests lay in social questions, struck much the same note. Heinrich Ahrens, asserting that the recent revolutions were at least in part the product of a false social philosophy, argued that the wounds in the social body could be healed only by a sounder philosophy.[6]

It was a democratic radical, Arnold Ruge, who made the most impassioned plea on philosophy's behalf, but both the necessity of a defense and the end result of his efforts showed that other men were at least indifferent if not hostile to the intellectual habits of the past. During the mid-1850's, Ruge attempted to found a new journal, the *Annals for Learning and Art,* which would have functioned as a successor to his earlier *Halle Annals* and *German Annals.* The prospectus for the new journal – sent, among others, to Ludwig Feuerbach, Georg Gottfried Gervinus, Alexander Herzen, Alexander von Humboldt, Friedrich Theodor Vischer, and Kuno Fischer – strongly affirmed Ruge's allegiance to philosophy. He assumed that all who wrote for the journal would share a common faith in "the culture of Hegel, Goethe, Schiller, and its realization in the world of thought, action, and desire." Since most men now felt that only "material" interests really mattered, it was all the more necessary "to be serious about philosophy in the conception of life and of knowledge and to hold high and to honor the ideal where it appears in realized form." Ruge called on "the prophets of the spirit" to emerge from their lonely isolation and enter again into daily life. But the prophets did not heed the call. The replies to Ruge's prospectus were at best lukewarm, and the project did not come to anything at all. The whole affair demonstrated not only Ruge's continuing attachment to the tradition of philosophical journalism, but also the decline of that tradition among German intellectuals in general. While Ruge was trying to reinstate the philosopher as the highest judge of worldly affairs, Germany's political and social thinkers were gravitating toward a more historical and empirical outlook, which was to find its journalistic expression in Rudolf Haym's liberal review, the *Prussian Annals.*[7]

---

[6] Fortlage, *Genetische Geschichte der Philosophie seit Kant,* viii, 2-4, 480; Rössler, *System der Staatslehre,* 274-275; Ahrens, *Die organische Staatslehre,* 5.
[7] Ruge, *Briefwechsel und Tagebuchblätter,* II, 177-179, 181-183. On the *Preussische Jahrbücher,* see below, pp. 47-48.

Before he launched his new journal, Haym experienced a reorientation in his own attitudes toward philosophy which pointed to a larger set of changes taking place among a good many other intellectuals at the time – changes which had begun before 1848 but were powerfully stimulated by the events of that year. Haym became increasingly critical of a certain kind of philosophy, namely the methods and the conclusions developed by Hegel, and then he directed his criticisms not simply against Hegelianism but more broadly against philosophical thought in general.[8]

Having been trained in philosophy at Halle during the 1840's, Haym proudly boasted shortly after participating in the Frankfurt Parliament and the Gotha assembly that he had begun to escape from the realm of abstract theory and to discover "the golden tree of life." He cited as evidence of this achievement his historical work on the political events of the preceding year. He continued his active involvement in public affairs as editor of the *Constitutional Newspaper* in Berlin for several months in 1850, until he was exiled from that city for a year because of his opinions. In the meantime, he had succeeded in habilitating at Halle, and he returned there in 1851 to begin a brief career as a university lecturer.[9]

His first set of lectures treated the history of English philosophy since Bacon. The retrospective comments in his memoirs about his motives for picking this theme pointedly summarize his early views concerning the relations between philosophy and politics:

Involvement in practical politics influenced my scholarly way of thinking in such a way that – already free from the Hegelian system of the world and of reason – I considered it desirable to search out the fruitful seed of long-scorned empirical philosophy. Perhaps here the way would be opened to a sounder and higher point of view. The fact that the Englishmen had come much farther in political affairs than we and that their understanding of the world had made them the freest and most powerful nation ... created a favorable attitude toward their scholarly mode of thought.

Two important points emerge. The first is that Haym had reoriented his philosophical interests as a result of his political experience. But he had not yet been forced to re-evaluate philosophy as such. Instead, he had set himself the task of looking for a better philosophy. A particular mode

---

[8] On Haym's pre-1848 thought, see Hans Rosenberg, *Rudolf Haym und die Anfänge des klassischen Liberalismus* (Munich and Berlin, 1933). For a general pre-1848 critique of philosophical abstraction, see Karl Biedermann, *Die deutsche Philosophie von Kant bis auf unsere Zeit, ihre wissenschaftliche Entwicklung und ihre Stellung zu den politischen und sozialen Verhältnissen der Gegenwart* (2 vols., Leipzig, 1842-43).

[9] Haym, *Ausgewählter Briefwechsel*, 86, and *Aus meinem Leben*, 203 ff.

of philosophical thought was still regarded as a key to political success.[10]

Haym worked during the next few years at elucidating the intellectual history of Germany. "As a result," he wrote, "not only of my talents and my inclinations, but also of my desire for orientation in the darkened present and of the need to find in the past a guide and a signal for the tasks of the immediate future, I planned a *realistic history of the development of the German spirit.*" Along with courses on legal philosophy, the philosophy of history, and the history of pedagogy, he gave courses on German thought since Kant and Lessing, which he hoped to turn into his next book. He was unable to comprehend all of modern German intellectual history within a single framework, but he did publish two impressive studies of individuals: his work on Wilhelm von Humboldt, whom he greatly admired both for his breadth of culture and for his political views, and his book on Hegel, the latter of which was "a war cry against speculation and for liberalism and the national policy." [11]

Haym had already broken with Hegel before 1848, but he felt the need to discover why Hegel's system had held a whole generation in its sway. His effort was therefore not that of the philosopher, who would simply criticize the system internally, but that of the historian, who showed how the system had arisen in a particular milieu and then been rendered obsolete by historical change. Using as his point of departure Hegel's own dictum that any philosophy was "its time grasped in thought," Haym undertook to set himself and his readers clearly apart from a *Zeitbewusstsein,* or "time-bound consciousness," whose validity had already been destroyed by a reality which had outgrown its confines. He set Hegel's philosophy in its historical context, reducing it from the status of a dogma to that of a fact. In this sense his work was avowedly "realistic," although Haym took great pains to distinguish his method from the "materialism" of those natural scientists who sought to reduce all intellectual life to physical events.[12]

Haym first located Hegel within the prior tradition of German philosophy and literature, but the basic element in the historical context was Hegel's relation not to his intellectual forbears but to the realities of politics and society. Haym continually sought to explain the Hegelian outlook by focusing on its nonintellectual environment. "The Hegelian system," Haym wrote, "became the scholarly bulwark of the spirit of

[10] *Ibid.,* 211-212.

[11] *Ibid.,* 218, 225, 257; Haym, *Wilhelm von Humboldt* and *Hegel und seine Zeit.*

[12] Haym: *Aus meinem Leben,* 254; *Ausgewählter Briefwechsel,* 169-170; *Hegel,* 2, 7-8, 12-13.

the Prussian restoration." No philosopher before Hegel had undertaken so thorough-going an idealization of existing political reality. The Prussian state, which had treated Hegel so handsomely, left its imprint most clearly on his legal and political writings. But Haym did not think of Hegel's writings on law and the state as the only instances in which Hegel was influenced by his political surroundings. The breadth of Haym's interpretation is revealed in his discussion of Hegel's critical essay on English parliamentary reform. Haym's remarks here suggested a larger relationship between Hegel's world and his thought as a whole. It was clear to him in reading this essay "that to our philosopher the living process of freedom is nothing, that to him the systematization of the concept and objectively constituted, ordered – albeit unfreely, bureaucratically, administratively ordered – freedom are essential. . . . Prussian bureaucratism, allied with German idealism, takes sides against the English form of the state and the practical-empirical understanding of the countrymen of Bacon." Thus –even though he did not explicitly identify the lines of connection all along the way – Haym portrayed the whole Hegelian enterprise as the defense of a political status quo. Hegel's logic and his philosophy of history as well as his political philosophy revealed a pervasive compulsion to subject living reality to the tyranny of abstract concepts. The end result was a "formalism . . . which served the indolence and falseness of a period which exploited the preceding spiritualism of German life for the installation of the very worst practice." [13]

Although Hegel's intentions had been essentially conservative, Haym rightly pointed out that his system had contained numerous internal contradictions. After the master's death in 1831, the Hegelian synthesis fell apart under the pressure of changing historical circumstances. On one side Hegel's followers emphasized those aspects of the system which suggested a critical stance (Strauss and "Young Hegelian journalism"), whereas followers such as Feuerbach picked up those elements which were empirical and "positivistic," reducing the Hegelian metaphysics to man and nature. In Haym's view, however, it was not simply the Hegelian system of philosophy which had suffered. The decline of Hegelianism was part of *"the exhaustion of philosophy in general,"* which Haym contended had been caused by two intersecting developments: the rise of technical invention and the great material changes which followed in its train; and the political events of 1848. As a result of the former, matter

---

[13] *Ibid.*, 359, 386, 457, 328, 449, 462.

itself seemed to have come alive, forcing spiritualism and idealism into the background. The latter had seriously undermined the previously prevailing confidence in the possibility of "an ideal formation of things," since "the idealism which was believed to be omnipotent" had been shown to be powerless.[14]

Haym therefore renounced the effort to replace Hegel's system of thought with a new philosophical system of his own. He felt that a new metaphysics would become possible only after the German people had become immersed in reality and created a new foundation for philosophizing in the form of political freedom. The next task was political. But scholarship still played a central part in this endeavor. Haym's point was simply that speculative philosophy could no longer serve as one of the most effective tools. What the times now demanded was a greater interest in history. Haym employed one of Hegel's basic concepts, that of the dialectic, to state his case as follows: "In a period which has learned to renounce poetic illusions and romantic confusions, in a period which sees itself surrounded by unresolved contradictions and complicated practical tasks, there is only one step. The dialectic of our practical and theoretical development drives us out of absolute idealism toward the rich investigation and treatment of human history." Philosophy would be reborn in the future, but more empirical knowledge had to be accumulated first, and historical study was the richest source of such knowledge for those who were interested in man and society.[15]

The historian Georg Gottfried Gervinus developed a similar critique, although as an outsider to the discipline he was less narrowly concerned with philosophy. Instead, his arguments concerned all branches of literature. Having argued in the late 1830's that Germany's great period of creative writing was over and that men would now have to direct their energies toward political goals if they were to serve a meaningful function, he reiterated this theme and others which closely paralleled it. The beginning of a preface written in April of 1849 to a study of Shakespeare revealed his basic feelings about the intellectual needs of the time:

After the completion of my history of German literature, I felt an urge to resume the pursuit of my earlier interests in the field of political history. My intention was, and still is, to proceed from the conclusion of that his-

---

[14] *Ibid.*, 464, 5-6.
[15] *Ibid.*, 464-470. See Hans Rosenberg, "Zur Geschichte der Hegelauffassung," in a new edition of *Hegel und seine Zeit* (Leipzig, 1927), 543 ff., on the generally favorable response to Haym's work. A similar call for a new "realism" appeared in "Die deutsche Philosophie seit Hegel's Tode" (anon.), in *Gegenwart*, VI (1851), 294, 310, 340.

torical presentation of our literature and to make the attempt to write the history of our time – to show to the German people in this history, as in a mirror, the picture of its present; to portray its humiliation, its vocation, and its hopes; to indicate to it the traits and the nature of the whole body and spirit of this period, which more and more promised to become great and significant and to repay the efforts of the historical observer. Since then events quickly began to fulfill this expectation. They present the historian with a continually more alluring task and become for him a continually more instructive school.[16]

Gervinus' feeling that Germans should turn from the arts to historical study of their country's real problems led him to assert that insofar as they *did* permit themselves to enjoy "the pleasures of the spirit," these pleasures should be "of such a kind that they become an incentive to our action and effectiveness." Literary and philosophical culture could help fulfill these functions only if it was "free from artificiality" and occupied "the practical understanding as well as the soul and the imagination, thus strengthening the will in its resolve." It was Shakespeare's virtue that he combined strength of imagination with "sobriety and maturity of judgment." His greatness was such that he could even make the Germans begin to doubt their own Goethe and Schiller. Along with the philosopher Francis Bacon, he had produced works which taught men to think and act effectively in the affairs of the real world. "Our tame, sometimes romantically and fantastically dissolute, sometimes domestic . . . poetry and spiritualistic philosophy," wrote Gervinus, did not perform this function. Could such writing prepare men for their public responsibilities? The English, masters of the art of politics, would hardly think so. If on the other hand Germans could develop a taste for "that worldly poetry and that empirical philosophy" which had taken root across the channel, this would surely help them to acquire political skill for themselves. But most essential of all was the movement away from literature and philosophy to history.[17]

Exhortations to make use of historical study as a way of coming to grips with the practical problems of contemporary life were much more explicit in numerous other writings. Indeed, an activist rationale for historiography was a major theme in attempts to define the proper role of the intellectual during this period, particularly those written by political liberals. It is no surprise that the historians were particularly concerned with the relationship between learning and public affairs. Among

[16] G. G. Gervinus, *Geschichte der poetischen National-Literatur der Deutschen,* IV (Leipzig, 1838), vii, and *Shakespeare,* I, v-vi.
[17] *Ibid.,* vi-xii.

the fifty-seven professors at the Frankfurt Parliament from non-Austrian Germany, there were seventeen historians. Outnumbered by the twenty-one jurists, they still constituted far and away the largest group of academics from among the "philosophical" disciplines; next in line was philosophy in the narrower sense, with only four or five representatives. Nor is there cause for surprise in the close link between historical activism and specifically moderate politics. According to my calculations, the parties of the center at the Frankfurt Parliament claimed fourteen of the historians (82 per cent), compared with twenty-five of those professors who were not historians (63 per cent). According to another source, the center claimed only 47 per cent of those who were not professors at all. The differences are even more striking if one compares the percentages of these groups who belonged to the influential right center, or *Casino* party: 59 per cent of the historians, 35 per cent of the other professors, and 19 per cent of the nonprofessors. During the 1850's this pattern remained remarkably constant. Eighteen historians are discussed in this study. Fifteen of them can be placed under the heading of moderate liberalism, yielding a far higher percentage than that which obtains for the rest of the intellectuals, only about half of whom fit into this category.[18]

Many historians argued not simply that their field of study could offer a helpful perspective on the present, but that written history ought to promote definite political viewpoints. They rejected the conservative Leopold Ranke's famous assertion during the *Vormärz* that the historian's task was simply to tell "wie es eigentlich gewesen" ("how it really was") – a principle which Ranke again supported in the 1850's by insisting that he would not let his scholarly work become identified with any political party and saying that the historian's proper goal was "that the subject should make itself purely the organ of the object, namely of scholarship itself." [19] In the *Vormärz*, Friedrich Christoph Dahlmann,

[18] These statistics on the professors at the Frankfurt Parliament are based on a list of over fifty of them compiled from Max Schwarz, *MdR: Biographisches Handbuch der Reichstage* (Hannover, 1965) and the *Verzeichniss der Abgeordneten zur ersten deutschen Nationalversammlung in Frankfurt am Main* (Frankfurt a. M., 1848-49). The percentages for the political ties of nonprofessors are taken from G. Schilfert, *Sieg und Niederlage des demokratischen Wahlrechts in der deutschen Revolution* (Berlin, 1952), 406. To facilitate comparisons with the figures for 1848-49, my calculations for the 1850's count as moderate liberals some of the men whom I refer to in the introduction as "social thinkers" – namely, those whose politics were moderately liberal.

[19] Ranke, *Das Briefwerk*, 432. Despite his insistence that the historian's political sympathies had no place in a scholarly work, Ranke's work during the period clearly betrayed his own highly favorable sentiments toward monarchical government. See Heinz-Otto Sieburg, *Deutschland und Frankreich in der Geschichtsschreibung des 19. Jahrhunderts, 1848-1871* (Wiesbaden, 1958), 253-279.

Georg Gottfried Gervinus, Johann Gustav Droysen, and Heinrich von Sybel had sharply criticized this ideal. They all associated themselves with demands for political reform, both as direct commentators on the present and as scholars. Dahlmann no longer wrote after the revolution, even though he still lectured at Bonn before large numbers of students. Gervinus wrote a great deal, but he had little to say about historical method. Droysen and Sybel, however, both developed their earlier views of the historian's vocation. Their endeavors to cultivate greater political commitment among historians and, more specifically, to celebrate the historical achievements of Prussia, were supported by Max Duncker, Ludwig Häusser, and eventually Heinrich von Treitschke. Together, these five men were to form the core of the influential "Prussian" school of historians, for whom scholarship was avowedly an instrument of political partisanship.[20]

Droysen was in many ways the archetype of the political professor. His work constituted a classic example of politically oriented historical scholarship, none of his contemporaries having made such outstanding contributions to the theory and practice of academic political commitment. Droysen was just the right age to have begun his mature work before the revolution and to have continued it afterwards. The use which he made of his opportunity earned him a place as one of the period's most interesting political intellectuals. He had finished his formal training as a classical philologist at Berlin under August Böckh. The other great influence on him at Berlin had been Hegelian philosophy, Droysen having heard almost all of Hegel's important lectures. As his professional interests turned toward the discipline of history, the residual effects of each of these earlier influences were apparent in his early concern with antiquity, his strong sense of history as a developmental process, and his attachment to the state. Like Hegel, he had little interest in the critical-philological method, which Ranke had employed with such expertise. As time went on, however, he became increasingly concerned with details and much less willing to "construct" history philosophically in such a way that it would appear to follow "necessary" lines of development. By the early 1840's, he had come to feel that the historian ought to uncover dynamic living forces, thus pointing the way toward a better future. He now rejected the assumption that what was important for mankind's progress automatically passed from one age to another. With these views, Droysen

---

[20] Two recent works which treat these men over longer periods are Georg G. Iggers, *The German Conception of History* (Middletown, 1968), 90-123, and Charles E. McClelland, *The German Historians and England: A Study in Nineteenth-Century Views* (Cambridge, Eng., 1971), *passim*.

inevitably turned to the modern period. He made the transition in his lectures on the wars of liberation from France, in which he sought primarily to stimulate the patriotism of his listeners and thus engaged not only in the search for historical accuracy but also in present politics.[21]

Droysen dismissed efforts during the 1850's to influence a broad segment of the population by means of political pamphlets, proposing instead that "decisive political interests" should be furthered by means of historical works. He sought to enhance the attractiveness of history with a variety of arguments. In the first place, he defined history very broadly as "humanity's knowledge of itself." The present, he contended, was only the sum total of what had occurred in the past, and knowledge of the past constituted a kind of self-understanding which was essential for further development.[22] This view of history was accompanied by an intense disaffection with the habits of mind which Droysen felt were being fostered by the rise of certain other disciplines. A "crass positivism" had supposedly begun to emerge in the younger generation as a result of attempts to imitate the inductive methods of the physical sciences. Droysen feared too that people no longer believed in "ideal forces." The spirit of the Napoleonic polytechnic institute, he complained, had led to a conviction among many scholars "that only the microscope and scales are scientific and that their materialistic method is the only method." The study of history, which dealt with the growth and development of "the ethical world," stood in strong contrast to this mechanistic "modern method," which reduced everything to matter. It thus afforded a bulwark against what Droysen took to be the newer tendencies in the direction of a materialism that was bereft of ideals, a bulwark which philosophy, having fallen into discredit owing to the dogmatism of Hegel and his pupils, was unable to provide.[23] At the same time, Droysen argued that historical knowledge was a prerequisite for sound political judgment. He contended that political action had to accord with the historically determined characteristics of individual states, that the statesman had to be a "practical historian," and that historical study was therefore the very foundation of a political education.[24]

The thrust of these arguments was that historical study could serve as

---

[21] Felix Gilbert, *Johann Gustav Droysen und die preussisch-deutsche Frage* (Munich and Berlin, 1931), 16-21, 36 ff., 45-48, 57 ff.; Johann Gustav Droysen, *Vorlesungen über die Freiheitskriege* (2 vols., Kiel, 1846).

[22] Droysen: *Briefwechsel*, II, 175, 203-204; "Grundriss," 358; *Geschichte der preussischen Politik*, I, iii.

[23] Droysen, *Briefwechsel*, II, 47, 54-55, 282, and "Grundriss," 331.

[24] *Ibid.*, 363-364; Droysen, *Briefwechsel*, II, 442.

a primary source of instruction about both the vital "ethical" forces in the present and the practical possibilities of bringing them to fuller realization in the future. This belief led to the further contention that history ought not simply to be studied intensively but also to be presented from a definite point of view, so that the lessons to be learned would be boldly spelled out. Droysen spurned Ranke's "cosmopolitanism" and his "lack of ethical anger," as well as the specialized labors of philological criticism toward which he had directed his pupils. In contrast to Ranke, he insisted that the historian should not only bring the fatherland honor through his scholarly excellence but also perform a function of positive usefulness.[25] To paraphrase what Droysen seemed to have in mind but did not clearly spell out, the historian would pass moral and political judgments on the statesmen of the past, assessing their actions in relation to the (supposedly self-evident) national needs of their times and thus helping to mold the political conscience of his own time. Droysen's own contribution to this effort – which he felt had made considerable headway since 1848 – was of course his multivolume history of Prussia, to which we shall return later.

One final point remains to be made about Droysen's prescriptions for historical writing. Of all the activist historians, Droysen alone specifically eschewed wide popularity. Just as he renounced efforts to reach the masses through pamphlets or journal articles, so too he voiced misgivings over attempts to make major historical works lively and readable for a large audience. Indeed, Droysen criticized some of his scholarly allies, such as Duncker and Häusser, on precisely these grounds. Nothing was to be feared as much as the "prettiness" of Macaulay, whom so many German historians admired.[26] One may well ask, of course, how history was to accomplish the great public tasks assigned to it if popularity outside the scholarly community was to be foresworn from the start.

Like Droysen, Heinrich von Sybel had already begun to break away from Ranke's quietism during the *Vormärz*. Dissatisfaction with his teacher's refusal to mix scholarship and politics was quite apparent in an appendix to Sybel's doctoral dissertation in the area of medieval history, written during the 1830's. Again like Droysen, Sybel turned increasingly during the 1840's toward the modern period. Concurrently, he argued that Germany's universities should be more deeply involved in public affairs. Each discipline was to be evaluated in terms of its service to national interests. Sybel contended not only that the movements of

[25] *Ibid.*, 373-374, 425, 442.
[26] *Ibid.*, 451, 533-534.

the present could help ensure their future success through consideration of the past, but also that the historian would himself benefit from a close rapport with the contemporary world. Only in this way could he gain the "ethical warmth" which would enable him to bring the past back to life in his work.[27]

Sybel's importance as a political historian grew considerably after 1848. His account of the French Revolution was intended to provide commentary on the recent as well as on the more distant past. He wrote explicitly in his memoirs that he undertook the study as a result of his own experiences in 1848-49, which caused him to look for earlier examples that would demonstrate the harmful results of radical agitation. The work served as an outstanding example of didactic historiography.[28] In addition, a celebrated speech which Sybel delivered at the University of Marburg provided a classic statement of the activist historian's professional ethos.

Sybel contended in his lecture that modern German historical writing – "like everything great and good in which the nation rejoiced" – had begun in the period of national rebirth and liberation at the start of the century. In the depths of despair, Germans remembered their past, knowledge of which had previously been monopolized by jurists and philologists. History became a source of inspiration for all the people. In turn, contemporary political circumstances had exercised a powerful effect on the discipline: its practitioners increasingly perceived law, language, religion, and politics as related expressions of a common national life. They uncovered new sources and developed new methods of analyzing them. Sybel felt that historians had also become much more willing to take sides in their works on issues of current interest. There were religious and atheistic, liberal and conservative historians, but none of the more significant ones were unaffiliated with a party of some kind. The *Vormärz*, however, had not been conducive to the development of sound political judgment on the part of the professional historian. On the one hand stood the bureaucratic governments, on the other hand a populace which was excluded from any participation in the life of the state. The results could be seen in the extremes represented by the historians Ranke and Friedrich Christoph Schlosser: one a sympathizer with officialdom who

[27] Conrad Varrentrapp,"Biographische Einleitung," in Heinrich von Sybel, *Vorträge und Abhandlungen* (Munich and Leipzig, 1897), 42-45.
[28] Sybel, *Geschichte der Revolutionszeit von 1789 bis 1795;* see the quotations from Sybel's unpublished memoirs in P. Bailleu, "Heinrich von Sybel." *Allgemeine Deutsche Biographie,* LIV (Leipzig, 1908), 653. Sieburg analyzes the work at some length in *Deutschland und Frankreich,* 233-253.

subordinated all moral considerations to purely descriptive judgments, the other a harsh moralizer who could not appreciate the real problems faced by men of affairs.[29]

At the time Sybel was writing, Germans still did not enjoy the kind of political climate which had served, he felt, as the essential background to the balanced and praiseworthy work of Macaulay in England. But after 1848 "blind fanaticism over political theory and formal constitutional questions" had given way to awareness of the importance of selecting truly attainable goals. Sybel perceived a rising level of interest in history as one concomitant of this change in political thinking. Shaken by a great upheaval, men had generally become much more receptive to the lessons of the past, whereas formerly they had framed their arguments in terms of philosophy or theology. In response to this increased demand, historians had grown in number and become more energetic in the practice of their profession. The most important among them belonged to a "liberal-conservative circle . . . of moderate Whigs and liberal Tories," in whose number Sybel included Theodor Mommsen, Max Duncker, Georg Waitz, Wilhelm Giesebrecht, Ludwig Häusser, and of course Droysen. Neither the extreme conservatives nor the extreme democrats were credited with having produced any works of real significance during the preceding decade. What distinguished German historical writing since 1848 from earlier work was not its scholarly method. The novelty lay in the attitudes expressed toward the state, which now were marked by "greater clarity and more intensive energy of national feeling," by "soundness of political judgment and positive warmth . . . of ethical conception." Historians had to display these ethical qualities if their work was not to become soulless and affected, and the only way to develop them was to show an active interest in contemporary affairs. For Sybel, the fact that historians were rising to the challenge held out for the discipline the promise of a bright and hopeful future.[30]

Shortly after delivering this speech, Sybel went to Munich, where he not only taught at the university but also, with Ranke, organized the Historical Commission of the Bavarian Academy of Sciences. Then in 1859 he founded the *Historische Zeitschrift*. His preface to the first issue emphasized scholarly rather than political objectives. The focus, however, was to be on the modern period; also, greater space was to be given to

---

[29] Sybel, *Ueber den Stand der neueren deutschen Geschichtsschreibung*, 4-10. Schlosser was a professor at Heidelberg who published extensive and widely read works on world history and on eighteenth-century Europe.
[30] *Ibid.*, 11-15, 7.

German than to foreign history. Moreover, Sybel did not hesitate to add the following declaration of "general principles":

From a historical perspective, the life of every people appears, governed by the laws of morality, as a natural and individual evolution, which produces political and cultural institutions with intrinsic necessity. This process cannot be obstructed or accelerated, and it cannot be subjected to extrinsic norms. Such a viewpoint precludes feudalism, which forces dead elements on progressive life; radicalism, which sets subjective arbitrariness in the place of organic development; and ultramontanism, which subordinates national and spiritual development to the authority of a foreign church.

Sybel's failure to see any incompatibility between the above statement and his proclamation of the journal's essential nonpartisanship does not alter the fact that the statement did imply a clear political persuasion. It also implied that the historian could serve as a political guide, by pointing out the paths along which a nation's political well-being would most appropriately and naturally be pursued.[31] Political commitment was taken so much for granted that it crept in even when men thought they were eschewing it.

Droysen and Sybel received support from a number of other politically moderate historians, most of whom were explicitly identified by these two as fellow intellectual partisans. In his correspondence with Droysen, Max Duncker asserted that historical study would foster an "ideal realism," mid-way between "the materialism of the natural sciences" and "the fantastic idealism of philosophy ... which filled and warped the heads cf the young before 1848." Ludwig Häusser offered his views on the writing of history in an article on Macaulay, who was belittled by Droysen but highly esteemed by other historians. Häusser stressed the lessons to be learned both from the situations which Macaulay portrayed, so many of which provided parallels to the present, and from the political moderation and patriotism which appeared in the portrayal itself. Häusser also envied Macaulay's opportunity to develop his historical sensitivities within a large and active polity, remarking that he had an advantage which German historians would always lack until their own country was unified. Häusser, like Sybel, thus stressed the benefits which would accrue to historians themselves if their works grew out of – or least along with – deep interest in the problems of their own times. Finally, Wilhelm Adolph Schmidt asserted that the historian's task was "*to recall that* which can

---

[31] Sybel, "Vorwort," iii.

be of *use* to the living generation" and that the scholarship he produced should have the character of "hortatory memory." [32]

Support for the political uses of historiography came from outside as well as inside the ranks of the discipline's professional practitioners. Rudolf Haym, whose concluding lecture on Hegel had referred to historical study as the crucial intellectual requirement which faced the present generation, developed this theme further when he founded the *Prussian Annals,* which began to appear in 1858 as an organ for "the constitutional and national party in Prussia." In contrast to Arnold Ruge's pre-1848 *Halle Annals,* the new journal was to be "more practical, more realistic, and more historical." But the emphasis was not to be on formulating a definite political program. Even aside from the problem of external constraints, Haym felt that cultivating a proper general outlook had first priority. Haym hoped that writers such as Max Duncker, Heinrich von Treitschke, and Theodor von Bernhardi (major contributors to the journal during its early years) would help develop a new practical sensibility by writing about real life, rather than about philosophy or literature. Their essays were also to help develop a new national consciousness. Finally, they were to focus attention both on those elements in German life which seemed to hold out the promise of a better future and on those which revealed that improvement really was needed. Haym mentioned the following as some of the most important subjects which had been treated in the journal's pages during its first year: Schleswig-Holstein, the Prussian Diet, Italian-Austrian relations, German emigration, and the German co-operative movement. Other articles treated Beethoven and Alexander von Humboldt and France, England, and the United States. Many of the essays focused on quite contemporary problems, but Haym repeatedly emphasized a historical perspective, which he deemed to be the exemplary scholarly way of coming to grips with the concrete realities of collective human experience. He favored the historical point of view because it permitted the beholder to see the present as a mid-point between the past from which it had developed and the end points toward which it was moving. At the same time, Haym implied, it prepared him both to accept and to work for those historical developments which were inevitable. [33]

---

[32] Droysen, *Briefwechsel,* II, 200-201; Häusser, "Macaulay's Geschichte Englands," 1-21; Schmidt, *Preussens deutsche Politik,* iii.

[33] Haym: "Aufruf zur Begründung der Preussischen Jahrbücher," 307-308; *Ausgewählter Briefwechsel,* 139-143; "Vorwort," 1-10; "Rundschreiben des Herausgebers an die Mitarbeiter der 'Preussischen Jahrbücher,'" 310-312. Also see the favorable comments on the *Historische Zeitschrift* in Haym's brief notice, "Sybel's historische

It is important to note here that Haym, like the other men we have been discussing, did not perceive a basic conflict between scholarly accuracy and political utility. These men had not yet become "relativists." Instead, they asserted that they were drawing the only correct lessons from human experience. In their view liberal academic partisanship was objectively grounded in historical facts. As Sybel suggested in his preface to the *Historische Zeitschrift,* it was only the presence of an extreme political persuasion which vitiated the search for truth. A centrist persuasion was no obstacle at all.

Most of these writers believed not only that the status of history ought to be enhanced but also that it was already on the rise. Their confidence that they could perform important political tasks, which was doubtless nourished by their belief in history's popularity, was similarly paired with the conviction that they had already written or were in the process of writing politically significant scholarly works. Julian Schmidt, a literary historian but not a professional member of the historical guild, ratified these beliefs in one of the decade's most widely read works by asserting that a new period of the German spirit was opening. Historical scholarship, he observed, was breaking out of its shell and obtaining a place of honor as an important and influential form of literature. "Its tongue," he wrote, "has been loosened, it has the strength to say what it knows. . . . Among all branches of prose literature, historical writing has the most immediate influence on the education of the people – more than philosophy." [34]

What independent evidence is there to support this judgment? Historical studies had made indisputable advances during the first half of the century. New critical methods had been developed by Niebuhr and Ranke and historical courses had attained greater autonomy within the curriculum of the university, where they were increasingly liberated from their former subservience to theology and jurisprudence. During the second half of the century, the scholarly status of history continued to rise, with the further development of a great many of the "auxiliary"

Vierteljahrsschrift," 105-106. He welcomed the journal as "a new ally." The following articles in the first volume of the *Preussische Jahrbücher* (1858) also supported historiographical partisanship: L. K. Aegidi, "Die Aufgabe deutscher Staats- und Rechtsgeschichte" (anon.), 31-45; J. W. Loebell, "Zur Methode neuester Geschichtschreibung" (anon.), 150-165; "Zur Entwicklungsgeschichte des deutschen Geistes" (anon.), 594-617. For a general discussion of the journal, see Otto Westphal, *Welt- und Staatsauffassung des deutschen Liberalismus: Eine Untersuchung über die Preussischen Jahrbücher und den konstitutionellen Liberalismus in Deutschland von 1858 bis 1863* (Munich and Berlin, 1919), esp. 32 ff.
[34] Schmidt, *Geschichte der deutschen Literatur seit Lessing's Tod,* III, 418-419.

disciplines such as numismatics and heraldry leading to the formation of a vast panoply of specialized techniques.[35] Moreover, throughout the century other disciplines – such as jurisprudence, philology, economics, and philosophy itself – were deeply influenced by historical modes of thought. The 1850's seem to have been especially fruitful for historical studies. At the universities, the decade saw the establishment of the first permanent historical seminars. The Royal Prussian Academy of Sciences increased history's share of the studies it published in the 1850's by a greater percentage than it raised the share of any other discipline.[36] Statistics on the German publishing industry point in a similar direction. History was the one field that registered and maintained a substantial gain in its share of the total number of books listed in one of the country's most comprehensive review-journals.[37] And of course in 1859 the *Historische Zeitschrift* was founded. One may finally note the great number of well-known individual works which appeared during the decade. In addition to the ones by Droysen and Sybel which we have already mentioned, there were the works by Biedermann on eighteenth-century Germany, Ranke on seventeenth-century France, Giesebrecht on the medieval empire, and Mommsen on Rome. Outside Germany, powerful examples of historical writing were also provided by Marx, Burckhardt, Macaulay, and Tocqueville, who were all publishing their great works at this time.[38]

---

[35] Josef Engel, "Die deutschen Universitäten und die Geschichtswissenschaft," *HZ*, Vol. 189 (1959), 294 ff., 334 ff.

[36] See *ibid.*, 330-334, on the development of historical seminars. My remarks on the publication of scholarly treatises are based on Otto Köhnke, *Gesamtregister über die in den Schriften der Akademie von 1700-1899 erschienenen wissenschaftlichen Abhandlungen und Festreden* (Berlin, 1900; Vol. III in Adolph Harnack, *Geschichte der königlich preussischen Akademie der Wissenschaften zu Berlin*). Not counting the treatises and speeches which dealt with the affairs of the academy itself, the percentage for historical studies in the period 1851-60 was 13 per cent, compared with 9 per cent during the the earlier decade.

[37] My remarks on the German publishing industry, like most of my statistical statements, are admittedly tentative. They are based on tabulations at three-year intervals over the period 1835-59 of all the German-language titles in both the general listings and the review sections of the *Repertorium der gesammten deutschen Literatur* and its successor, the *Leipziger Repertorium der deutschen und ausländischen Literatur*, both of which made their own topical breakdowns. The percentages of notices and reviews together accounted for by historical works rose during the years for which I counted in the period 1850-59 to an average of about 12 per cent, compared with a little under 8 per cent in the period 1835-47.

[38] Karl Biedermann, *Deutschland im achtzehnten Jahrhundert* (2 vols., Leipzig, 1854-58; Vol. II completed in 1880); Leopold Ranke, *Französische Geschichte, vornehmlich im 16. und 17. Jahrhundert* (5 vols., Stuttgart, 1852-61); Wilhelm von Giesebrecht, *Geschichte der deutschen Kaiserzeit* (6 vols., Braunschweig, 1855-95); Theodor Mommsen, *Römische Geschichte* (3 vols., Berlin, 1854-55); Karl Marx, *Der 18te Brumaire des Louis Napoleon* (New York, 1852); Jacob Burckhardt, *Die Cultur der Renaissance in Italien* (Basel, 1860); Thomas Babington Macaulay, *The*

All of this evidence together suggests that the discipline of history was in a very healthy state indeed. In contrast, philosophical writings did not figure as prominently either in the publishing industry or in general intellectual journalism as they had earlier. Nor did the period produce anything in the way of philosophical literature – apart perhaps from the work of Rudolf Hermann Lotze – which demonstrated sufficient originality to win much of a place in later histories of the subject.[39] As for political partisanship, the extent to which historians cultivated that quality in their work will become abundantly clear in the next chapter.

TRADITION AND DEPARTURES IN THE SOCIAL SCIENCES

While the liberals turned toward partisan historical study, two other groups of intellectuals formulated new ways of thinking about economic and social problems. Each group resembled the historians in at least one important respect. The writers who sought to make economics less abstractly theoretical palpably supported efforts to enthrone the historical outlook as the basic mode of apprehending men in their relationships to one another. Outsiders to the disciplines of history, they nevertheless participated, like Haym, in the campaign to raise its status. The writers who called for a new "science of society" resembled the historians inasmuch as they repeatedly framed their arguments with reference to the intellectual imperatives which had been brought to light by the events of the recent revolution. But both groups differed from the liberal historians by directing their readers toward a much broader segment of human experience than the essentially political events which were still the main concern of men like Droysen and Sybel.

The points of departure for the writers who offered these proposals lay in the academic discipline known as *"Staatswissenschaft"* (literally, "science of the state"), the term most generally used in the mid-nineteenth century to denote what today would be called "the social sciences." Sometimes (as at Munich and Tübingen), there was a separate *Staats-*

History of England, from the Accession of James II (5 vols., London, 1849-61); Alexis de Tocqueville, *L'Ancien régime et la Révolution* (Paris, 1856).
[39] See above, note 37, on publishing. The average for philosophy in the selected years between 1850 and 1859 was a little over 1 per cent, compared with almost 2 per cent in the period 1835-47. Corroborating evidence appeared in a topical index of all the articles published in the influential *Deutsche Vierteljahrs Schrift*, which the magazine's editors put together in 1868. During the period 1850-59, the share of articles on philosophy was half what it had been in the years 1838-47. Lotze's major work was *Mikrokosmos: Ideen zur Naturgeschichte und Geschichte der Menschheit: Versuch einer Anthropologie* (3 vols., Leipzig, 1856-64).

wissenschaft faculty, alongside the faculties of philosophy, theology, law, and medicine. Usually, however, *Staatswissenschaft* lay within the domain of the philosophical faculty, appearing in the university's catalogue of lectures next to such headings as natural science, history, and philology. *Staatswissenschaft* included all but a few disciplines then in existence which might be thought of today as social sciences, the most notable exceptions being jurisprudence, which frequently dealt with general political questions, and history. In addition, it included a good many other subjects which would now count as social science only according to the most generous of definitions.

The offerings in this area for the winter semester of 1850-51 at the two largest universities, Berlin and Munich, vividly illustrate the heterogeneity which *Staatswissenschaft* encompassed. Berlin's offerings were described as follows: "public law and politics, that is, historical and statistical explanation of the institutions presently existing in America and Europe ... statistics of the Prussian state ... bases of administrative science, or the theory of internal administration, combined with economic policy ... financial science, combined with a treatment of the financial administration of the most important European states ... national economy, combined with the history of economic systems and of general knowledge about business ... concerning the so-called social questions ... chemical technology ... agricultural theory for the needs of cameralists and economists ... the natural history of domestic animals ... advanced sheep breeding ... the theory of the diagnosis and cure of the internal and external illnesses of all domestic animals." At Munich, students could choose from among courses such as these: "legal philosophy, or general public, international, private, and criminal law, as an introduction to positive legal study ... theory of internal government, or administrative science and law ... mining law ... financial science ... survey of forestry science ... geognosy, with reference to the study of petrefacts, mining, and soil ... general metallurgy ... national economy ... survey of chemical knowledge ... beer brewing ... differential calculus ... analytical mechanics." In other universities, such widely differing subjects as the "political statements of Goethe and of several other poets" (Bonn) and "technology, joined with excursions to nearby factories" (Heidelberg) fell under the same general heading. In short, "*Staatswissenschaft*" at mid-century could refer to almost anything, from philosophy to applied natural science.[40]

[40] *Verzeichniss der Vorlesungen, welche auf der Friedrich-Wilhelms-Universität zu Berlin im Winter-Semester 1850-51 gehalten werden* (Berlin, 1850), 8-9; *Verzeichniss*

This heterogeneity stemmed in large part from the cameralist tradition within which *Staatswissenschaft* had originated. Cameral studies were developed in the eighteenth century as a means of training administrative officials – men who would face practical tasks requiring a wide range of specific skills. These studies frequently dealt with economic matters, conveying odd bits of knowledge about how to run state-owned forests, estates, and mines, or how to assess and collect taxes. As one modern scholar, discussing an encyclopedic treatment of cameral science written during the 1830's, has put it: "Only the faintest gleams of perception could enter anyone's mind from these catalogues of craft rules to the effect that one craft depends on another, and that they all make up or fail to make up an interacting system which must be understood and estimated as a whole in order to be intelligently operated." [41] In short, the eighteenth-century tradition was primarily utilitarian; men who followed it did not really pursue an academic discipline.

One thread of methodological reflection which emerged in this milieu had to do particularly with economics: the plea that economic science should become less theoretical and more inclusive of historical variety. The men who made this plea – most notably Wilhelm Roscher, Bruno Hildebrand, and Karl Knies – were not really in revolt against the dominant tradition described above. Instead, they drew on certain elements within that tradition in order to criticize newer methods which had been developed by Adam Smith and his followers in Great Britain and introduced into Germany during the first half of the nineteenth century by men such as Karl Hermann Rau and Friedrich Hermann. Roscher, Hildebrand, and Knies insisted on the need to consider the noneconomic factors which impinged upon economic life. In line with the cameralist emphasis on practical specificity, they stressed the social context within which buying, selling, and production took place, arguing that the attempt to understand economic behavior without reference to social institutions and to historically determined trends and traditions was one-sided and fruitless.

The historical economists drew sustenance from several intellectual traditions besides cameralism. Adam Müller and Friedrich List had both anticipated a historical method in their writings on economic matters. List was especially influential in urging that tariff policy be geared to

der Vorlesungen an der königlichen Ludwig-Maximilians-Universität zu München im Sommer-Semester 1850-51 (Munich, 1850), 6-7.
    [41] Albion W. Small, *Origins of Sociology* (Chicago, 1924), 125-126. On this whole subject, see Nathan Glazer, "The Rise of Social Research in Europe," in Daniel Lerner, ed., *The Human Meaning of the Social Sciences* (New York, 1959).

the specific level of economic development which a nation had reached at a particular moment in time. The historical jurisprudence of Savigny and the historical philology of the Grimm brothers were among the many formative influences from areas completely outside the study of economics itself.[42] These influences bore fruit during the 1840's in Roscher's brief *Outline for Lectures on Political Economy According to Historical Method* and Hildebrand's longer *The National Economics of the Present and Future*. After the revolution, the effort was sustained in influential works by Roscher and Knies.[43]

A standard history of economic thought summarizes the objections raised by these writers against the theoretical economists as follows: "Broadly speaking, three charges are levelled against the classical writers. (i) It is pointed out that their belief in the universality of their doctrines is not easily justified. (ii) Their psychology is said to be too crude, based as it is simply upon egoism. (iii) Their use, or rather abuse, of the deductive method is said to be wholly unjustifiable." Knies and Hildebrand articulated the most forceful methodological criticisms. Knies was particularly harsh in his strictures against the narrowness of the English approach, rejecting what he called "the absolutism of theory . . . the claim to reveal in the scholarly works of political economy things that are equally valid for all periods, countries, and nationalities." As Hildebrand pointed out, the English theorists had moved from the particular aspects of one economic system – their own – to general rules for all economic systems, fallaciously assuming that England was a microcosm of the world. All three complained that classical economic theory was afflicted with serious ethical shortcomings. The classical economists, it was argued, had a blind spot for the bitter human consequences of free trade and industrialization: on the one hand, their theoretical preoccupations led them to renounce

---

[42] Franz Schnabel, *Deutsche Geschichte im neunzehnten Jahrhundert*, III (Freiburg im Breisgau, 1934), 126; Gottfried Eisermann, *Die Grundlagen des Historismus in der deutschen Nationalökonomie* (Stuttgart, 1956), 74 ff., 98 ff. Eisermann's study, an excellent essay in the sociology of knowledge, treats this movement in detail, but it does not set historical economics in the context of other writing about social science. See also Albert Müssiggang, *Die soziale Frage in der historischen Schule der deutschen Nationalökonomie* (Tübingen, 1968).

[43] Wilhelm Roscher, *Grundriss zu Vorlesungen über die Staatswirthschaft, nach geschichtlicher Methode* (Göttingen, 1843); Bruno Hildebrand, *Die Nationalökonomie der Gegenwart und Zukunft* (Frankfurt am Main, 1848); Roscher, *Die Grundlagen der Nationalökonomie*; Knies, *Die politische Oekonomie vom Standpunkte der geschichtlichen Methode*. Knies's work was not widely noted in the 1850's, but in later decades it was to be acclaimed as a kind of bible by the "younger historical school," which gained great prominence under the leadership of Gustav Schmoller. Hildebrand, who spent the 1850's in Switzerland, wrote nothing on methodological questions until he returned to Germany in the 1860's. In what follows, he will remain in the background.

ethical judgments; on the other hand, their supposedly objective theory actually ratified private egoism as an essential contributor to the general welfare.[44]

At the same time that they criticized the theoretical predispositions and the moral blindness of the classical writers, Roscher, Hildebrand and Knies were even more critical of the socialists. Men such as Owen and Fourier, they admitted, had delineated the limitations of the Smithian faith in private egoism; but socialist writing about moral issues was still subject to "the absolutism of theory." Although the socialists rightly pointed out many of "the shady sides of higher culture," their thinking was indelibly marked by an affinity for abstract idealism and the construction of utopias. They thus revealed a preoccupation with theory at least equal to that of the liberals, even though the implications of their theories were of course vastly different.[45]

What the German economists proposed instead of either classical or socialist abstraction was a "historical-physiological" method, with far less emphasis on general theory and far more attention to empirical reality. Although they did not all deny the validity of every attempt to discover general economic laws (Roscher's substantive work in fact contained a good deal of classical theory), the historical economists showed more concern than their English counterparts with specific details which could be used to illustrate and to qualify theoretical statements. Every general theory had to be modified according to the individual historical experiences of differing national groups. The institutions and values of each such group were all interrelated, and the sum of these "organic" relationships determined the ways in which its economic affairs would be and ought to be conducted. The economist could not comprehend his subject if he abstracted completely from this complex social reality. Finally, in so far as they *were* concerned with detecting regularities, these men placed greater weight on recurrent patterns of development through time than on the workings of a stable and supposedly immutable system in equilibrium.[46]

[44] Charles Gide and Charles Rist, *A History of Economic Doctrines,* trans. R. Richards (2nd English ed., London, 1948), 393. On theory: Roscher, *Die Grundlagen,* 37; Knies, "Die Wissenschaft der Nationalökonomie seit Adam Smith bis auf die Gegenwart," 117-118, and *Die politische Oekonomie,* 18-19, 156 ff.; Hildebrand, 27 ff. On moral issues: Roscher, "Der gegenwärtige Zustand der wissenschaftlichen Nationalökonomie und die notwendige Reform desselben," 176 ff.; Hildebrand, 31; Knies, "Die Wissenschaft der Nationalökonomie," 117.

[45] Hildebrand, 275 ff.; Knies, *Die politische Oekonomie,* 25, 333; Roscher, "Der gegenwärtige Zustand," 177, and *Die Grundlagen,* 134-135.

[46] *Ibid.,* 42-46; Knies, *Die politische Oekonomie,* 120-121, 346-347, and "Die Wissenschaft der Nationalökonomie," 154; Hildebrand, v.

The historical economists differed on the question of whether economic science should have an "ethical" component. Hildebrand and Knies answered strongly in the affirmative. Knies wrote that his approach to economics "lets the normative viewpoints for the general moral and political life of men and peoples also be the normative influence for economic reasoning and is ready, in the case of a conflict between what is economically more advantageous and what is better for life in general on ethical-political grounds, to subordinate the former to the latter." It was necessary "that the science also seek to solve that task which arises out of the nature of a moral-political discipline and consists in positive and immediate effort toward realizing the highest moral and political goals of popular life." Knies felt that as a result of their reflections on the experiences of many peoples throughout the ages, economists who employed his approach to their subject would surely have a great deal to say about appropriate methods of promoting the nation's welfare in the largest sense. They would be able, he argued, not only to indicate which economic goals were feasible and which were not, thus channeling men's efforts toward objectives which stood some chance of realization and helping to raise the level of national wealth, but also to help strike a balance between purely economic imperatives and other objectives which were essentially noneconomic. Roscher had a negative attitude toward moral judgments. He viewed economics as a science of what was, not of what ought to be. Nevertheless, his argument that the historical approach would serve as a check against the application of socially "inappropriate" measures had a definitely normative aspect, clearly directed against unrestrained economic liberalism.[47]

By helping to create an intellectual framework within which economic problems could be assessed in relation to needs and values outside the purely economic realm, all of these men were laying the groundwork for a critique of *laissez-faire* liberalism, the economic policy that had accompanied classical theorizing about "*homo oeconomicus.*" But their main significance lay in the area of methodology rather than in the area of policy. Although they felt that the new economic science should be policy-oriented, their admonitions had more to do with the ways in which economists ought to think than with what they ought specifically to propose.

The historical economists were joined during the 1850's by another group of men who developed still more ambitious programs for expanding

[47] *Ibid.*, 31-32; Knies, *Die politische Oekonomie*, 320, 350; Roscher, *Die Grundlagen*, 41-42, and "Der gegenwärtige Zustand," 189-190.

men's understanding of social experience. Robert von Mohl, Lorenz von Stein, Wilhelm Heinrich Riehl, and others urged not simply that an old discipline should be reformed but that a new one should be created. They employed various terms for the new discipline – the most popular of which was *"Gesellschaftswissenschaft"* – but they were all translatable as "science of society." In order to understand their efforts, several points need to be added to our earlier discussion of *Staatswissenschaft*. It bears emphasis that this congeries of disciplines and pseudodisciplines approximated modern social science only very roughly. Not only did it include subjects which would be excluded today; it also failed to include modern disciplines such as sociology. The closest existing equivalent to sociology in Germany was a kind of philosophizing about society, with little attempt being made to separate "science" from ethical judgments and prescriptions. In part this situation resulted from Germany's economic backwardness. Germany had not yet felt the full force of industrialization, a process which in England and France had already begun not only to highlight the importance of economic affairs but also to make the sphere in which various social groups experienced growing conflict with one another a necessary object of investigation. A final point brings us back to Germany's intellectual inheritance. German idealism and romanticism had two inhibiting effects on social science. They encouraged men to denigrate concern with "material" problems as a denial of man's essential spirituality; moreover, their emphasis on the uniqueness of the individual militated against scientific generalization.[48]

Not all of the proposals for a "science of society" during the 1850's were new, but the depth and breadth of concern in this area did mark a change since the *Vormärz*. All of the men who proposed a new branch of knowledge about society were united by the sense that the older traditions of study and reflection were inadequate in the contemporary situation. In their view, the events surrounding the revolutions of 1848 strikingly demonstrated that social structures and social problems had to be taken into disciplined consideration. It is therefore possible to identify the movement as one of the phenomena in the intellectual life of the period which had been most strongly stimulated by the mid-century revolutions.[49]

---

[48] Heinz Maus, "Geschichte der Soziologie," in Werner Ziegenfuss, ed., *Handbuch der Soziologie* (Stuttgart, 1956), 13; also see Glazer, cited above in note 41.

[49] On this whole subject, see Erich Angermann, *Robert von Mohl, 1799-1875* (Neuwied, 1962), 330-387 (a chapter on "Gesellschaftswissenschaft"). Angermann treats not only Mohl but also several of his predecessors and contemporaries. See also Eckart Pankoke, *Sociale Bewegung – Sociale Frage – Sociale Politik: Grund-*

Robert von Mohl had already pleaded as early as 1840 for a clearer distinction between the political and the social sciences. But the preface to the famous *Journal for the General Science of the State* which Mohl founded in the middle of the forties contained only the barest suggestions that the older corpus of disciplines should be expanded. Public, international, and administrative law, political economy, administrative science, politics, statistics, and political history were still the staple subjects for discussion. It was in the years directly following the revolution that Mohl became the leading spokesman for the creation of a new social science, which in the meantime had become one of his major concerns. Mohl now asserted in several influential works that after the experiences of 1848-49 the time was overripe for new ways of thinking about the social world.[50]

Mohl argued that historically the great scholarly achievements in the area of *Staatswissenschaft* as a whole had been inspired by acute public turmoil. Although the works had usually been written during periods of relative calm, it was false to assert that such tranquillity was a sufficient precondition of political and social insight. It had to follow a storm if it was to offer a truly congenial setting in which to work. In this regard, the recent sequence of revolution and reaction was highly favorable to intellectual innovation. The other vital stimulus was a change in the general level of moral culture and ethical attitudes, and the recent period had been propitious in this respect too. A livelier sympathy for the lower classes had encouraged the feeling that a whole new science of society had to be founded and developed. Closely intertwined with this moral change were socialism and communism, which demonstrated the most obvious concern of any movements for the plight of the poor. Mohl branded the socialists as "immature" and the communists as "barbaric," but he did not simply disparage them. He also acknowledged that they had forced the practitioners of *Staatswissenschaft* to recognize and think about aspects of human life which they had hitherto almost completely overlooked. The proponents of socialism and communism were at the very least part of the process of suggestive disruption, whatever one might think of their specific ideas. It was imperative, Mohl felt, to pick out what might be valid and practical in the socialist theory according to which

fragen der deutschen "Socialwissenschaft" im 19. Jahrhundert (Stuttgart, 1970), 101-166.
[50] Angermann, 329; [Robert von] Mohl, *et al.*, "Vorwort," *Zeitschrift für die gesammte Staatswissenschaft,* I (1844), 3-4.

the state served merely as a means for improving society. But Mohl did not regret this necessity. He also deemed it an opportunity.[51]

Mohl sensed a need to go beyond the hitherto dominant view that the state was the only subject for investigation in the whole realm outside the individual. He recognized that this step had already been taken by several writers in the recent period, the most noteworthy of whom were Stein and Heinrich Ahrens, both Germans. In his opinion, however, Stein had overemphasized economic factors and neglected intellectual and moral ones, whereas Ahrens had merely outlined a series of social organizations, without defining society itself. Mohl's own efforts were directed toward rectifying these omissions with a new and more explicit program of his own, thus providing the theoretical foundation that was indispensable if the more ominous aspects of contemporary social problems were to be remedied.[52]

Mohl distinguished society from two other entities, one constituted by individuals, the other by the state. "Society" denoted an in-between area, occupied by a variety of groups which were organized around lasting and important interests. In such associations, individuals could pursue their own interests only by seeking the common advantage at the same time. These groups differed from the state in two important ways: they had only a "fragmentary life goal," whereas the state was "the realization of the idea of unity in a people"; and they arose independently from the state, out of natural relations among men, even though they might have formal organizations regulated by the state. The most important of the "social formations" were those determined by racial or family ties, employment, the form and extent of property, the local community, and religion or education.[53]

Mohl's recommendations for the systematic organization of an academic discipline to deal with this area were at best sketchy. He did not go much beyond simply listing the subjects he wished to see treated, which he subsumed under the following headings: general social theory ("establishment of the concept of society, its general laws, its components, its goals, and finally its relation to other spheres of human life"); "dogmatic"

[51] Mohl: *Die Geschichte und Literatur der Staatswissenschaften,* I, 16-19, 71; "Neuere deutsche Leistungen," 12-13; "Gesellschafts-Wissenschaften und Staats-Wissenschaften," 6-7, 10, 13.

[52] *Ibid.,* 21-22, 24-25; Mohl, "Neuere deutsche Leistungen," 8.

[53] Mohl, "Gesellschafts-Wissenschaften," 27-51. Mohl also referred to "employments" as "estates," suggesting the traditional distinctions among nobility, clergy, burghers, and farmers (*ibid.,* 35-38). Later, however, he made it clear that he was moving decisively toward a breakdown of society according to functional occupations (see Angermann, 347-348).

social sciences (including social jurisprudence, social ethics, and social politics); and the historical social sciences. He was more explicit concerning the social benefits to be derived from the new discipline. He attached special significance to the study of social politics, or the "theory of the means for the attainment of the goals of the individual social circles." Knowledge of the ways in which social groups ought to organize and act in "free associations" in order to achieve their ideal purposes or ends (which Mohl seemed to feel could be arrived at scientifically) might well determine "the whole future of European morality." The new perspective as a whole was also intended to alter men's ideas about the state. Mohl felt that given his view of society the state could no longer be regarded simply as an aggregate of atomistic individuals. One had to consider its "social articulation." The state's functions could then be extended, he suggested, to include regulation of and assistance to forces outside itself, since a people's highest goals would be directly ascertainable in the multitude of organizations which served specific interests. As an example, Mohl suggested that it would be easier for the state to intervene in industrial affairs for the purpose of alleviating the conditions of workers. These matters would no longer be thought of simply as an outgrowth of private relations among individuals and could thus be related to the state in a new way. The very existence of the new discipline would have clear implications for the world of practice.[54]

Lorenz von Stein, probably the most important social thinker anywhere in Germany during the 1850's, resembled Mohl in having given preliminary indications during the *Vormärz* of arguments in favor of a new social science which he elaborated after 1848. Early in the 1840's he voiced admiration for socialism as the start of a new science of society. A few years later, he expressed the desire to move beyond what he now felt was the abstract and one-sided ideology of a single class and to develop a science which would speak to society as a whole. At the same time, he was becoming increasingly critical of the men who studied and taught *Staatswissenschaft* for not addressing themselves to social phenomena. After the revolution, Stein developed his ideas considerably. The introduction to a revised edition of his classic work on French socialism and communism, his *History of the Social Movement in France,* provided not only additional remarks on the need for intellectual change but also, in the theoretical introduction, an impressive example of the new mode of thinking which Stein had in mind. Moreover, the rest of

[54] Mohl, "Gesellschafts-Wissenschaften," 56-57, 62, 67-68, 70.

the work revealed a marked reorientation of Stein's earlier methodological presuppositions. The historical sections demonstrate deep concern with the actual conditions of French society, whereas before 1848 Stein's writing had still dealt almost entirely with the history of ideas.[55]

Stein asserted that men had recently begun to observe "a series of phenomena . . . for which there earlier was a place neither in ordinary life nor in science." Although they had always existed, they had not been understood. But the violent events of recent history had demonstrated that a basic force, which determined "the total existence of the peoples," linked these phenomena to one another. They stood together in necessary relationships, constituting "behind the world that was known up until now and its order, yet another imposing organism of energies and elements." This "organism" was society, whose essence Stein would attempt to grasp. The individual facts of human existence, he asserted, had no value unless they were joined together "in the unity of a concept." Rejecting what he regarded as the vague and arbitrary definitions of society previously formulated by others, he insisted that conceptual clarity was the first objective.[56]

Stein wove his definition of society, the entity which the new science was to elucidate, into the fabric of his theories about society (and his prescriptions for it) in such a manner that it is nearly impossible to deal with either the definitions or the theories separately. Since the theories will be discussed at length in another chapter, it suffices here to make two points. It is implicit throughout his major work that Stein thought of society as something which at the same time lay outside the state but also closely interacted with the state. In addition, although he turned later in the decade to an exceedingly abstruse definition of society as an intellectual or spiritual entity, he regarded social life during the early years as a process which centered in large measure on economic problems. The economic orientation of Stein's outlook in the immediate aftermath of the revolution is amply rendered by the following statement, which was as close as he came to a precise definition: ". . . this organic unity of human life, conditioned by the distribution of goods, regulated by the division of

[55] Heinz Nitzschke, Die Geschichtsphilosophie Lorenz von Steins (Munich and Berlin, 1932), 13-14; Lorenz von Stein, Der Socialismus und Communismus des heutigen Frankreichs (1842; 2nd ed., Leipzig, 1848), I, viii, and "Der Begriff der Gesellschaft," in Vol. I of Geschichte der socialen Bewegung in Frankreich. Concerning changes in Stein's views, see Felix Gilbert, "Lorenz von Stein und die Revolution von 1848: Ein Beitrag zur Entstehung der deutschen Gesellschaftswissenschaft," Mitteilungen des Österreichischen Instituts für Geschichtswissenschaft, L (1936), 369-387.
[56] Stein, Geschichte der socialen Bewegung, I, xi-xiii.

labor, set in motion by the system of needs, and linked through time to definite lines of descent by the family and its rights, is the human society." The economic facts of property and work were central to the investigations he had in mind.[57]

Stein wanted the new science ultimately to relate a great number of diverse variables. At one point he urged that it should incorporate "all areas of the so-called *Staatswissenschaften*." At another, he asserted that the study of society could serve as a focal point for "the old economic sciences, the hitherto existing legal history, and history in the broader sense." It was clear in any event that the new discipline which Stein desired would serve to synthesize many of the existing academic specialties.[58]

Stein also expected the science of society to discover dynamic laws of development. He called for a sociology which was to be at the same time systematic in its formulations and historical in its choice of subject matter, casting its gaze backward as a way of determining what the future held in store. The systematic study of society's developmental laws was intended to supersede several intellectual traditions: the older political science, which Stein felt to be narrow and static in its outlook; the accepted form of historical writing, which he criticized for offering "only a description of history," not "a comprehension . . . of the dynamic elements"; and the "subjective" social theorizing of the French. With regard to the last of these traditions, he asserted that the time for merely partisan theories was past. Germany, he believed, could assert its intellectual independence from foreign tutelage only by moving the discussion of the issues raised by the French to a new level: "to the objective and basically true recognition of the social elements and phenomena," i.e., the science of society.[59]

Like Stein, Wilhelm Heinrich Riehl was identified by Mohl as a leading representative of the new interest in society. But both in his practice and in his methodological prescriptions he pursued a very different course from Stein's. He was — and he urged others to be — more empirically descriptive, more popular and down to earth. He did not display the urge to attain conceptual clarity or to discover all-embracing social laws.

[57] *Ibid.*, xxviii; for later definitions of society, see Stein, *System der Staatswissenschaft,* II, 8, 16.
[58] Stein, *Geschichte der socialen Bewegung,* xlii, and *System der Staatswissenschaft,* II, 269.
[59] See *ibid.,* I, vi-vii, 14 ff., and *Geschichte der socialen Bewegung,* I, ii-iii, vii, cxxxiv, for Stein's remarks on social laws; see *ibid.,* xxxii, cxxxii-cxxxiii, for his criticisms of historical writing and of socialism; comments on German achievements in the area of social science appear in his "Der Socialismus in Deutschland," 517-520.

Riehl's major work, his popular multivolume *Natural History of the Folk,*
which was the fruit of hundreds of newspaper articles written during the
1840's and early 1850's, will concern us at greater length in another
chapter. Here, we shall consider his sense of what he and other writers
had been doing in the past and ought to be doing in the future.

Riehl was impressed both by the depth of concern with social life
during the whole of the modern period and by the special importance of
social issues in recent history. Since the end of the Middle Ages, he
observed, artistic works had increasingly portrayed the folk as a whole,
not just individuals. Riehl pointed more specifically to a variety of writers
in the nineteenth century (all of them Germans or Englishmen) who had
further enhanced the comprehension of popular life. The period of historical investigation following the years of philosophical greatness at the
century's start had, he noted, been marked by great triumphs in many
areas of empirical research which dealt with social phenomena. Germans
had shown themselves to be far less "doctrinaire" in the area of social
study than the "more impractical and idealistic French." Together with
like-minded Englishmen, such as Henry Mayhew, they had made many
solid contributions to real social knowledge. The new tendency had borne
fruit in the achievements of economists, ethnographers, linguists, and
historical jurists, as well as in modern fiction, painting, and opera. Then
in the 1830's and 1840's the writers of the Young Germany school and
the Young Hegelians had begun to deal with society too. Riehl's remarks
on the "literary proletariat" make plain his distaste for these writers, but
he did feel that their writings had helped to indicate the general development of the German people's interests. He believed that social issues –
related to work, corporate associations, local communities, the family,
and morality – were what really mattered, especially to the lower bourgeoisie, the peasantry, and the laborers. In his view, the revolution of
1848 had shown decisively that purely constitutional questions, having
to do with the state rather than with society, were of much less pervasive
or lasting relevance to the German people.[60]

There still remained the task of drawing together the vast number of
specific observations and suggestions which pointed toward a greater
awareness of social experience. It was time to create a new discipline,
which would stand independently next to the disciplines of public law
and administrative science and serve as essential preparation for them.
"The study of the folk," Riehl wrote, "should be the beginning of all

[60] Riehl, *Die bürgerliche Gesellschaft,* 4, 16, and *Land und Leute,* 3, 9, 13-16,
19-22.

political wisdom, not the study of systems of public law." A new "science of the folk" would have to be invented. What Riehl had in mind, however, was not anything patterned after the natural sciences but rather a more intuitive study of varying customs. The approach was to differ radically from the statistical methods of those scholars whose primary interest lay in economic life. The folk was to be regarded not as an object for quantitative analysis but as a "harmonious work of art." One point of these methodological prescriptions was to make social science more readily serviceable as a tool in the field of social policy. Pursued in the way Riehl recommended, it would serve as a shield against "one-sided doctrines of political parties," presumably by showing the inapplicability of their generalizations to specific social situations. Moreover, it would reveal the particular needs of distinct social groups, for each of which such terms as "freedom" and "welfare" would be seen as having radically different meanings. Although Riehl wrote toward the end of the decade that the new science would have to reveal the "laws of popular life," he was still largely concerned with moral issues and with justifying the diversity of social norms. Social science was not to deal in generalizations but rather to explain and in a sense to ratify social differences.[61]

Stein, Mohl, and Riehl were not alone in pleading for the development of a new social science. Heinrich Ahrens seconded Stein with his contention that "a more comprehensive science of society" was imperative in view of the erroneous ideas propounded by the socialists. He resembled Mohl when he went on to state that the new knowledge would develop "the practical life principles for all areas of human life and their social organization and . . . the true relations of the state to these social life spheres." Constantin Frantz, whose explicit insistence that too much attention had been devoted to purely political matters reminds one of Riehl, and Immanuel Hermann Fichte also paid tribute to the idea of a new discipline. What they both had in mind seems to have been indistinguishable from a socially oriented ethical philosophy, but they did participate in the effort to draw men's attention to social experience.[62]

These would-be scientists of society differed on many points. They disagreed not only over the specific social measures which ought to be undertaken, but also over methodological matters. Most thought of social science as the study of primarily static relationships, but Stein hoped it

---

[61] *Ibid.*, ix, 16-17, 22-23; Riehl, *Die bürgerliche Gesellschaft*, 30-35, and "Zur Volkskunde der Gegenwart," 220, 224.

[62] Ahrens, *Die Rechtsphilosophie*, 149; Frantz, *Die Erneuerung der Gesellschaft*, v, 21; Fichte, *System der Ethik*, I, xiv.

would deal with the dynamics of change over time. These men differed over the relative importance of empirical observation and of generalization about supposed "laws." Finally, they disagreed over their very definitions of society, some of which included the state as one part of society though most did not. All of this variety indicates that there was still no common view of what the "science of society" really ought to mean in specific intellectual practice. Nevertheless, one is struck when considering these men by the similarities which pervade so many of their writings on this subject. Social upheaval and political failure proved to them that traditional intellectual orientations would no longer suffice. In the same way that Roscher, Hildebrand, and Knies criticized the narrowness of classical economics, they all felt that the events surrounding 1848 had greatly intensified the need for disciplined ways of studying and thinking about a range of experience which had at best been only very poorly covered by the older *Staatswissenschaft*. They all wanted both to supplement the older discipline and to introduce coherence into the treatment of some of the subjects which came within its purview. They also hoped that the new science would provide alternatives to a more recent intellectual tradition, nurtured by the dangerously erroneous doctrines of the socialists and communists. In line with this expectation, they generally assumed that it was possible to answer the fundamental social questions of their time objectively – that "science" could indeed resolve even those disputes which concerned differing interests and values.

The relations between these pleas for a more disciplined approach to the study of society and the development of substantive work in this field are not so readily discernible as the connections between theory and practice in the area of historical thinking. Some parallels can be noted nonetheless. A sign of vigor in the field of *Staatswissenschaft* as a whole was apparent at Bonn in the sharply increased numbers of students after the revolutions who designated the discipline as their primary academic specialty. Another sign of vigor can be seen in the establishment of the first *Staatswissenschaft* seminars, starting at Jena in 1849, where Gustav Fischer sensed a greater need for familiarity with a broad range of public affairs.[63] At other universities – for what seems to have been the first time – courses were given which explicitly dealt with "social" matters. Outside the universities, government statistical and census bureaus began to undertake quantitative social research. Particularly noteworthy were the first regional surveys of the rural classes and of the workers, which ap-

---

[63] Gustav Fischer, *Über die Errichtung staatswissenschaftlicher Seminarien auf den deutschen Universitäten* (Jena, 1857), 105-106.

peared in Prussia and Saxony in 1849. An increasing interest in social and economic matters was also indicated by the rising percentage of articles devoted to them in the prominent *German Quarterly Journal.*[64] Finally, there were the extended treatises on society by several notable individuals – especially those by Stein and Riehl, to which we shall turn at some length in the concluding chapter.

[64] Anthony Oberschall, *Empirical Social Research in Germany, 1848-1914* (Paris and The Hague, 1965), 18. On the *Deutsche Vierteljahrs Schrift,* see above, note 39. I grouped together a number of specific headings in order to arrive at a general "social and economic" category. The percentage rose from 40 per cent in the period 1838-47 to 49 per cent in the period 1850-59.

III

DEBATES ABOUT THE RECENT PAST

Early in 1849 numerous authors began to reflect on the revolution which they had just witnessed. Events of the magnitude which Germany had experienced demanded to be recounted and explained. Since Germany was well endowed with historians, many of whom had participated directly in political life, the challenge to make sense out of the recent past was quickly taken up. In scrutinizing contemporary history, the intellectuals hoped to prepare themselves and their countrymen for the struggles of the future. A consideration of their historical thoughts on the revolution is therefore essential to an understanding of their analyses of and programs for the political and social world which they inhabited in the 1850's. Most authors focused on the history of liberalism, especially on events which had occurred in the Frankfurt Parliament; and when men discussed the failure of the revolution they almost always meant the defeat suffered by the moderates. They usually saw no way that the radical revolutionaries, disruptive and threatening (or brave and hopeful) though their efforts had been, could possibly have surmounted the obstacles which faced them. Still, the presence of these other malcontents – men such as the followers of Gustav von Struve and Friedrich Hecker in Baden or the streetfighters of Berlin, whose aims and methods had been far more radical than those of the largely moderate parliamentarians who sat at Frankfurt – had to be dealt with too. The ways in which the major groups of intellectuals portrayed the relations between liberals and radicals varied greatly, but they all revealed the imprint of ideology on history.

LIBERAL SELF-PRAISE

The liberal interpretation of 1848-49 was largely a matter of tracing the prehistory, the deliberations, and the disappointments of the Frankfurt

Parliament. Shortly after the remnants of the Frankfurt Parliament were dispersed in June of 1849, several men who had been moderately liberal delegates rendered their accounts of what had led up to and happened at the meetings of that assembly. Even though men from the parties of the right and left center were not alone in reflecting on the history of the Frankfurt Parliament, their versions considerably outweighed the literary efforts of their opponents. In part this was because so many of the liberals were historians, but the most impressive of these works was Rudolf Haym's *The German National Assembly: A Report from the Right Center,*[1] and Haym was a philosopher. The crucial fact was that those who felt the fondest attachments to the Frankfurt Parliament as a creator and a prototype of Germany's political future were the ones who considered its story particularly worth telling. They believed in parliamentarism, as a means both of attaining national unity and of modifying monarchical power. They affirmed this belief by recounting the history of the first national parliament that Germany had ever had.

These men did not address themselves to anything as comprehensive as "The Revolution of 1848." They made no real effort to view the multiplicity of movements which had affected Germany, much less to comprehend the events which had taken place elsewhere in Europe, within a single context. They sought primarily to explicate the political events in the *Paulskirche.* This emphasis can in part be explained simply as the result of a division of intellectual labor. If, however, we survey the total body of writing that touches on German history in 1848-49 by men who identified themselves with the liberal cause, it becomes clear that they considered the core of that history to have been almost wholly political. Socially and economically inspired movements remained at the peripheries. Indeed, even the more extreme movements of the masses were generally felt to have been politically motivated, or at least to have been caused by political determinants. The liberals' interest in the Frankfurt Parliament, which had been the focal point of political activity for the country as a whole, grew out of their general sense that politics were what had really mattered. It must of course be admitted that there are no works by *any* of the men treated in this study which deal with the years 1848-49 as a whole, even in Germany. None of them seems to have arrived at a detailed comprehension of the whole scene. But not everyone had as narrowly compartmentalized a perspective as did the historians who supported political liberalism. The reasons for the difference between the

---

[1] Haym, *Die deutsche Nationalversammlung.*

liberals and these other writers, whom we shall encounter later, lay not only in divergent views concerning the relative importance of politics and society but also in the emphatic liberal rejection of revolutionary radicalism. It will become abundantly clear that the liberals despised what they regarded as the reckless extremism of the democrats and the socialists. To have treated the activities of these groups in the same context with their own efforts would have been to become contaminated. Extreme conservatives charged that liberalism and radicalism were only slightly varying manifestations of the same revolutionary impulse, and the democratic radicals themselves were wont to portray their own cause as a further elaboration of the liberal heritage. But the liberals – who regarded their own efforts as a "movement" rather than a "revolution" – insisted on maintaining a separate identity.

Understanding how the liberals interpreted 1848 necessitates some discussion of their version of the way in which the reform movement emerged in the *Vormärz*. Karl Biedermann spoke for many liberals in a series of articles on the history of German parliamentary life and of efforts to achieve national unity. He saw a growing desire in Germany after 1814 for constitutional arrangements which would give the "*Stände*," or the "estates," the power to control legislation. During the years from around 1814 up until the late 1830's, which formed "the more ideal youthful period of German constitutionalism," liberals had felt not only that unity might not be *necessary for* parliamentarism, but also that these two objectives might actually be *incompatible*. In the aftermath of the July Revolution, Biedermann pointed out, the south German Karl von Rotteck, Karl Theodor Welcker's senior partner in the task of editing the *Political Lexicon*, had seen France as "the natural ally of all free lands and of all lands striving after freedom." The thrust of his thought had been to remind men of the Confederation of the Rhine, rather than to point them toward closer ties with Prussia or Austria. The only German unity which he and many of the other liberals had wanted was to have been an "inner," or "ideal," unity, based on cultural and intellectual affinities, not the political unity of a national state. But the following years had proved that his conception of unity was thoroughly insufficient, not only for Germany's standing with respect to the rest of the world but also for the support of internal freedom and constitutionalism. Events such as the revocation of the Hanoverian constitution in 1837 and the dismissal of the seven Göttingen professors who protested such arbitrary princely action had shown Rotteck's approach to be a dead end. Effective parliamentarism required a larger stage, unfettered by "the absolutist great powers of the existing states." It therefore came about, wrote Biedermann, "that the attempt was made in 1848 from the opposing standpoint: to pursue freedom through unity or in any case only in close connection with it." [2]

Biedermann identified other impulses as having played a part in the rise of nationalism. He felt that German economic development, starting in the mid-thirties, had been especially favorable to the national cause. The increase of nationwide commerce brought about by the *Zollverein* had contributed to "the consciousness of national solidarity through a still more effective means than political affinity: through the community and intertwining of material interests." The desire for still closer economic integration had of course further contributed to the national movement. Additional impulses came from the French threats to German security which had earlier been posed by Napoleon and more recently by the government of Louis Philippe. All of these pressures meant that the striving for unity had not been simply a "national giddiness," as its cosmopolitan opponents had charged. It had corresponded to real needs which were expressed during the 1840's in nationwide meetings not simply of scholars, artists, and writers but also of farmers, foresters, and lawyers. In summary, the implication was that the German national assembly at Frankfurt grew out of efforts which had dominated a considerable portion of German history during the first half of the nineteenth century. These efforts were seen as having stemmed not from momentary caprice but rather from deeply felt and basically valid convictions.[3]

Other authors similarly celebrated the history of the liberal movement. Welcker's preface to a revised edition of the *Political Lexicon* proclaimed that the main goal of "the general national consciousness" since the wars of liberation from the French had been "a unified and free national citizenry ... or unity and freedom of the fatherland, with personal equality and the right of participation on the part of everyone in a free community, directed by a constitutional government which belonged to and corresponded to this community." Freedom and unity had thus constituted inseparable aspects of a single liberal program, which bore the clear stamp of historical necessity. According to Haym, "the movement of the March days" owed its sudden and spectacular success in

[2] Biedermann, "Die Entwickelung des parlamentarischen Lebens," 128-129, 458-459, 471, and "Die Versuche zur Einigung Deutschlands," part II, 261, 263-264.

[3] *Ibid.*, part I, 353-354, and part II, 265-266, 270-272. For Biedermann's views on the importance of Napoleonic domination, as well as of the examples set by the national movements in South America, Belgium, and eastern Europe, see his *Frauen-Brevier*, 312-316.

large part to the laudable objectives of the men who participated in that
movement and to the rottenness of the system they opposed. The liberals
had succeeded at the start because their cause was just and their behavior was moderate. The movement had stopped respectfully before
the thrones and "purified its impetuosity" by adhering to noble ideals:
"for the great thought that went through the German fatherland was to
develop freedom in national forms and to enlarge it in national unity."
Referring to the situation at the opening of the Frankfurt Parliament in
May, Max Duncker also spoke of the desire to establish both unity and
freedom. In the opinion of Duncker's associates at the time, the proper
sort of freedom had been achieved only in Belgium and England. France's
revolutionary practices were not to be imitated. The constitution the
liberals had wanted was to have been "democratic," but only in the sense
that representation would not have been limited strictly to the economic
bourgeoisie: it was not to have been republican. Duncker emphasized
that at the top of the state, a monarchy rooted in the past would have
stood over the parties to guarantee political stability.[4]

The goals these men remembered having striven for had clearly not, in
their view, been French-inspired. The February Revolution had served
as a trigger, but it had not been the real cause of what they celebrated
in recent German history. As they saw matters, the efforts to achieve unity
were obviously of native origin; they might point to the role played by
French diplomatic and military threats well before 1848, but this in no
way suggested imitation. Nor had French influence been crucial for the
liberals' efforts to bring about a greater degree of political freedom. One
writer was especially insistent that these efforts ought to be viewed as the
nation's own achievement, not simply as "a reflection of foreign enthusiasm." He regarded the contention that the latter had been the case as a
ploy of extremists on both sides – those who were afraid to oppose the
latest events openly and those who felt that Germany had indeed been
summoned to follow the French example of democratic and socialist
revolution, an example which made most liberals shudder. He insisted
that various impulses leading toward a German parliament had been
clearly apparent before anything in Paris had happened at all. The kind
of assembly which had met at Heidelberg early in March, he asserted,
was really nothing new, having followed numerous meetings of the south
German liberal opposition during the preceding decade. Moreover, he
stressed that the assembly sought unity and security for the fatherland.

[4] Welcker, "Vorwort," xix; Haym, I, 4-5; Duncker, *Zur Geschichte der deutschen
Reichsversammlung in Frankfurt*, 3-5.

In short, it had been motivated not by imitativeness but by "independent and patriotic attitudes." [5]

The movement toward constitutional government in which these men had participated was thus felt to have been national in two senses: it had been native and it had been closely linked with the goal of national unification. The liberals also asserted that their movement had been national in the sense that it was truly widespread. Ernst Moritz Arndt emphasized that three quarters of the Frankfurt Parliament's delegates had wanted law, order, and firmer national unity, while only about half a dozen had really wanted a democratic republic. And when Heinrich Laube remembered the general mood of the country during the summer of 1848 he stressed the desire for "lawful freedom, to the extent that order and the capacity for development could co-exist with it. . . . Many a moderate confounded equality before the law with absolute equality, which seeks to exclude enlivening articulation of parts from political life, therefore flattening it out and thus abandoning it to every storm and flood." But "true public opinion" never wavered between the republican and the monarchical forms, always pursuing a constitutional monarchy.[6]

The men who supported revolutionary as opposed to reformist measures, sometimes resorting to violence in order to attain their ends, did not greatly interest most of the liberals, but the efforts of the radicals could not be passed over completely just because the liberals did not wish to be associated with them. Early in 1848 many of the radical slogans had enjoyed great popularity. Laube himself stated that during the March days freedom had been more popular than unity, revolution more popular than reform. During the course of the year the radicals had disrupted political life in a number of states. As we shall see, they also were blamed by the liberals for having vitiated the moderate program of reform. Some consideration of what lay behind their appearance on the German public scene was obviously essential to an understanding of what had happened in 1848-49.

The modern student of this period, having been exposed to the perspectives of Marxist historical interpretation, is inevitably struck by the general failure of liberal writers to explain radicalism as an outgrowth of social and economic conditions. Perhaps the liberals were right, but that is another matter. The important thing to note here is that their explanatory emphases distinguished most of them from a substantial number

---

[5] "Das deutsche Vorparlament" (anon.), in *Gegenwart,* II (1849), 682, 685-686.
[6] Arndt, *Pro populo germanico,* 131-135; Laube, *Das erste deutsche Parlament,* II, 310-311.

of other writers at the time, to be encountered later, who did *not* fail to consider the relevance of social and economic structure.

Even the few liberals who did deal with social and economic factors illustrate characteristic limitations in the liberal outlook. Ludwig Häusser, the leading liberal authority on the recent history of Baden, where the radical left had attempted several coups in 1848-49, serves as a good example. He labelled the radical leaders as "mostly representatives of that sterile, pompous, and unproductive radicalism of lawyers . . . or . . . that half-educated and presumptuous group of schoolmasters . . . or that reckless group of literary men." Häusser singled out the schoolteachers in particular:

The modern schoolteacher is . . . the real representative of that half-education which is infected by the ideas of the time, without having the moderation and the strength within himself to ward off the dangers of such unsettling elements. In this *half*-education can be found for the most part the source of the contradictions between men and the situations in which they find themselves. It is a constant cause of dissatisfaction, especially with social circumstances, and our proletariat has only developed into a political force owing to the fact that inequality and oppression – as they have always existed – have been made known to all through the spread of culture; moreover, this knowledge has become mixed among the oppressed classes of society with the unclear ideas of the modern periods of reform and revolution.

Häusser berated these demagogues for their complete lack of "abstract idealism." Portraying the republic as a form of government without burdens or responsibilities, they appealed to men's baser instincts, their desires for economic gain and sensual pleasure. One reason they indulged themselves so successfully in this "materialism" doubtless lay for Häusser in the social characteristics of the men who followed them. The rank and file of the radical party comprised "every element that was dissatisfied, eager for innovation and adventurous . . . from a stirred up and confused society." They were "the shipwrecked elements of any political society . . . the bankrupt innkeepers and artisans, the ruined merchants, the candidates from all classes who had failed or been afraid to take their examinations, the fresh and undisciplined lads." In short, these men were "the dross from all the estates," who no longer enjoyed a definite social status and therefore hoped to find Eldorado by overthrowing the existing society.[7] It is interesting to note, however, that Häusser's emphasis fell much more heavily on the role played by changes of consciousness in creating dissatisfaction with social status than it did on any changes which

[7] Häusser, *Denkwürdigkeiten zur Geschichte der badischen Revolution,* 103-108, and "Baden im Frühjahre 1848," 467.

might have taken place in social structure. He was far more concerned in his remarks on social background with the thoughts of the radicals – even though he found these ideas relatively uninteresting compared to the more sublime and selfless ones of the moderates – than he was with the objective circumstances of popular life. Like many another liberal, he was quicker to spot unworthy economic demands than legitimate economic or social grievances.

Liberal writers frequently branded the radicals' ideas, whether democratic or socialist, as alien imports from France, and they often pointed an accusing finger at the French in other ways as well. Arndt made a typically strong attack on thinkers from across the Rhine in his defense of such German philosophers as Fichte, Schelling, and Hegel against the charge of having stimulated the recent rise of atheism, socialism, and communism. He traced these insidious developments instead to the influence of foreigners, naming Saint-Simon, Fourier, and Baboeuf as the chief culprits. Harking back to the spirit of the wars of liberation, he urged his countrymen to resist as one man the "desires and . . . poisons" of the French, who were "the most unstable, most impulsive, and vainest people in the world." Biedermann linked German radicalism to France in another way, stressing the German democrats' imitativeness. Attempts in Germany during 1848 and 1849 to impose what Biedermann felt would have been a despotic form of democracy – that is, democracy in its "whole, raw immediacy" – had clearly been "mere copies of French models." The problems posed by both the intrusion of foreign ideology and the imitation of foreign practice were thought to have been especially severe in Baden, but they were identified as major factors in Prussia's disturbances too.[8]

Despite their fulminations against the French, the liberals did not feel that outside agitation had been the root cause of revolutionary activity. In fact, just as frequently as they pointed to foreign influence as a clearly identifiable factor in the recent radical outbreaks they insisted that it had been far from the most important one. Several motives lay behind this ultimate de-emphasis of foreign influences, especially those which might have been exerted by foreign ideas. One was unwillingness to dignify the radicals by admitting that they *had* ideas. As we have already seen, Häusser strongly implied that the concern shown by many of the radicals

[8] Arndt, 192-193; Biedermann, "Demokratie," 345-346; Häusser, "Das Ministerium Bekk in Baden," 309, 326; Gneist, *Berliner Zustände*, 57. On the growth of anti-French feeling in Germany after 1848, see Heinz-Otto Sieburg, *Deutschland und Frankreich in der Geschichtsschreibung des neunzehnten Jahrhunderts, 1848-1871* (Wiesbaden, 1958).

with life's material circumstances precluded true intellectuality. Another
motive lay in the liberals' desire to explain radicalism in such a way as to
reinforce their criticisms of their other enemies, namely the forces of political stagnation. This desire emerges quite clearly both from Häusser's
writings about Baden and from Rudolf von Gneist's account of the events
he had witnessed in Berlin.

Häusser believed that demagogues who sought to imitate the French
had abounded in Baden, but he also insisted that they had been cultivated
by the policies of the government. Officials had undermined popular
respect for law and, by preventing a natural development toward either
free political institutions or national unity, caused popular energies to
become violent and destructive. Although the events of 1848-49 had
painfully demonstrated the moral failings of the German people, in whom
"all the demonic passions of revolution" had revealed themselves, the
Jacobinism of the masses had been furthered by Jacobinism from above.
Häusser admitted that there had been conspiracies from below during
the revolution, but he also asserted that a conspiratorial example had
already been set by Germany's rulers at the Congress of Vienna in 1815.
During the next thirty years, the bureaucratic governments – throughout
Germany as well as in Baden – had themselves flouted the law. "Let us
demand," he wrote, "faithfulness, truth, piety, and a feeling for law from
the people, but let us not forget that our public circumstances in Germany were no school where the people could have learned these virtues."
Häusser thus invoked the traditional liberal norm of the *Rechtsstaat* and
pointed to the government's failure to live up to that norm as a way of
explaining a good deal of the lawlessness among the people.[9]

Häusser also stressed the debilitating effect of the lack of free political
institutions into which men could channel their energies. He emphasized
that even Baden had lacked a parliamentary body which measured up
to the examples of England and Belgium. Instead, royal prerogatives had
been cloaked by parliamentary forms. The effects of this situation had
been two-fold. Since Baden was supposed to have effective representation,
the persistence of absolutism in practice only intensified the general dis-
respect for law. In addition, the lack of representative government meant
that political opposition was forced to take the form of "a brooding
literary activity," which ultimately led to destructive nihilism. To remedy
this defect, there would have to be some concessions to the power of

---

[9] Häusser, *Denkwürdigkeiten*, 3-5, 677.

democratic ideas, which in turn would hopefully be modified and "purified." [10]

Finally, Häusser insisted on the importance of Germany's disunity. Although he considered the evils of particularism to be especially harmful in small states such as Baden, where governments were limited in what they could do for their citizens and relatively easy to overthrow, he stressed that there was frustration everywhere at having been cut off from political greatness. Again, energies which did not have free play had been turned destructively inward. The only remedy was unification.[11]

Even more than Häusser, Gneist attributed the emergence of radicalism to the conditions of public life fostered by the pre-1848 system of government. In his account of events in Berlin, where Germany had experienced both its most serious violence during the March days and the proceedings of the most democratically inclined among its major representative assemblies, he admitted that the left had studied and imitated the speeches made in France during her periods of revolution. But he traced this tendency back to a more general "juristic formalism," which in turn stemmed from lack of contact with practical affairs. This mental habit and a good deal else which characterized the radical forces resulted especially from the role played in Prussian life by its famed bureaucracy. Those "coarser" elements which any revolution stirred up had filled the streets because "the state seemed to exist not for the sake of the people, but for the sake of the bureaucracy." [12] In fact, the bureaucracy was "the actual privileged nobility in Prussia," even though the qualities of culture and honesty for which it was praised abroad belonged not to it alone (and perhaps, Gneist seemed to imply, not to it at all), but to the nation as a whole. Possessing no real constitution, but only "an artificial administrative structure," composed of men whose own lack of independence caused them to be despised by those over whom they stood, the Prussian state became increasingly isolated from its citizens. The bureaucracy had premonitions of the dangers it faced, but no clear understanding – only enough suspicion to generate a futile hunt for demagogues, which in turn simply heightened its estrangement from the people. As a result, in March of 1848 a people from whom the state had separated itself in turn declared its independence from the state.

In the following weeks, a multitude of demands had arisen for special

[10] Häusser: "Baden vor den Ereignissen von 1848," 331; *Denkwürdigkeiten,* 9-10, 675; "Baden im Frühjahre 1848," 443-444.
[11] Häusser, "Das Ministerium Bekk in Baden," 310, and *Denkwürdigkeiten,* 6.
[12] Gneist, 57, 85. What follows is a summary of 85-94.

privileges, tending toward corporate forms which would have become new states within the state. "If community spirit formerly was lacking in the bureaucracy, now it was lacking in the people." This tendency was strongest in the "proletariat." The proletarians (whom Gneist did not really define) [13] had been excluded from participation in all forms of communal, or "corporate," life – not only from political life but also from the activities of private associations. Moreover, they were separated from the educated classes, who had no knowledge of the life they lived. Only the "doctrinaire literati," themselves excluded both from privileged society and from the affairs of state, felt a common bond with the lower classes, whom they hoped to use in order to realize their own fantastic schemes. Such deficiencies prevented these thinkers from realizing what the state could and could not do in the arena of economic affairs. Again, the lack of political experience appeared to have been instrumental in fostering radicalism. According to this view, men rightly criticized the evils of bureaucratic government, but having lived beneath its sway they did not possess the maturity to pursue sensible alternatives.

Häusser, Gneist, and many other liberals thus formulated an analysis of the left which served as a weapon in their own pursuit of political reform.[14] The major thrust of their interpretation was to place the blame for revolutionary radicalism squarely on the shoulders of the established governments, which were said to have fostered popular extremism by setting an example of illegality and by preventing their subjects from acquiring a political education. The liberal intellectuals' criticisms fell with particular severity on the bureaucracies, even though many bureaucrats, especially in the Southwest, had participated in the liberal movement. Several considerations help explain this apparent anomaly. The liberal objectives which the bureaucracies had pursued as institutions had a great deal more to do with social and economic issues than with the political issues which concerned men like Häusser and Gneist.[15] These men approved attacks on internal tariff barriers and on the powers of guilds, but they did not give such matters the highest priority. On the other hand, bureaucratic support for liberal political goals was rendered by the bureaucrats not as functionaries in the state administrative

---

[13] On the use of the term during this period, see Werner Conze, "Vom 'Pöbel' zum 'Proletariat': Sozialgeschichtliche Voraussetzungen für den Sozialismus in Deutschland," *Vierteljahrsschrift für Sozial- und Wirtschaftsgeschichte*, XLI (1954), 333-364.

[14] See Duncker, 6, 107-109, for another expression of this view.

[15] See Mack Walker, *German Home Towns: Community, State, and General Estate, 1648-1871* (Ithaca and London, 1971), 283 ff.

machinery but as members of representative assemblies or as private citizens. Bureaucratic institutions themselves were one of the liberals' main targets for attack.

When the liberals turned from the sources of discontent to the reasons for their own humiliation, the most obvious factor to emphasize was of course the enormous difficulty of the enterprise in which they had been engaged. As Haym put it, "No task which any other nation has ever solved was more extensive and complicated, and no glory would have equalled that which would have accrued to our people in the case of success. . . ." The sheer magnitude of what had been attempted, as Germans sought to overcome in a single year political problems which their western neighbors had taken centuries to solve, appeared to have been the central stumbling block. Moreover, it was pointed out that Germans had lacked the practical political experience required to deal with these problems, inasmuch as one of the many objectives to be attained was the very opportunity to participate in political life, and that the issues to be decided had not been subjected to detailed discussion beforehand.[16]

A more specific difficulty – which had manifested itself most directly in Frederick William IV's crucial decision to refuse the crown of the new empire – was seen as having arisen from Germany's history of princely particularism. As Haym put it, this tradition was inimical both to unity and to freedom, having reinforced regional differences among the various branches of the German people and hindered the development of constitutional liberty. The limitation of princely power was "either recent and artificial, or long lost and forgotten." Liberals frequently charged the dynasties with blind selfishness. Laube, explicitly absolving the Frankfurt Parliament from blame for the liberal failure, reminded his readers in the summer of 1849 of "the large and small steps, the large and small thoughts of the leaders in the individual states," adding that with everything in the hands of the crowns, Germany was farther than ever from its goal. The difficulty, he continued, lay "in the historical conditions of Germany," as a result of which those who had outlived their usefulness refused to admit the fact. The problem, Laube said in effect, was that certain forces in German political life (presumably the lesser princes and the Junkers, since Laube remained a monarchist) had unfortunately lacked the sense to climb into the ash-can of history for which any reasonable man could see they were destined! He added that any attempt to negotiate with these

[16] Haym, III, 191-192; Duncker, 1-3; Rochau, "Die verfassunggebende deutsche Reichsversammlung," 198-199.

men as a way of getting them to go along with unification would clearly have been impossible, since they were even more divided than the men of the *Paulskirche*. Friedrich von Raumer was more sharply critical of Frederick William IV himself, condemning the "juridical-ethical-philo-sophical-Christian" sentimentalism which prevented Prussia from real-izing its "world-historical mission." [17]

Rather than simply pointing to princely stubbornness, the liberals also emphasized the contribution made to their failure by conflicts within the movement for change itself. The liberals regarded these splits almost exclusively as the product of unrestrained agitation by the far left. Indeed, one of the most consistently reiterated themes in the writings of men from the center was that the reaction had been aided and abetted by revolutionary radicalism – that the revolution had derailed the liberal movement. The note was sounded in a variety of ways, but the essential import was always the same: by agitating in the streets, whether in Baden during the spring and summer of 1848 or in Frankfurt itself during September of the same year, the radicals had created a situation in which large numbers of Germans inevitably desired a return to political stability. Welcker's remarks on the subject were typical. Having castigated the Junkers for their blind stupidity, he had this to say of the radicals:

Precisely the same thing is true of those opponents who, to the dismay of all friends of freedom, wish to establish freedom only through revolution, with arbitrary force and cunning and without regard for the unity of their people; who, as in the well-known proclamations of the refugees, wish to terrorize the majority of the burghers and to fertilize freedom and the estate of workers with the blood and money of the "bourgeoisie, the rich, or the aristocrats." They thereby work to such an extent against freedom, that reactionary governments have their proclamations printed and distributed, in order to awaken the anxiety of the property-owners and of the friends of culture and peace and thus to attract them to despotism.

Scorn was also directed at the pressure which radicals had exerted within the Frankfurt Parliament to introduce universal suffrage and a merely suspensive royal veto into the constitution in return for their support of Frederick William IV's election as emperor. This pressure was felt to have brought about a constitution which the reigning princes were clearly bound to reject. In the liberal view, here too the left had worked for the right against the center – just as the right had earlier given unwitting support to the forces of radicalism.[18]

[17] Haym, III, 192; Laube, II, 316-317, 403; Raumer, *Briefe aus Frankfurt und Paris*, II, 408, 418, 420-421.
[18] Welcker, "Abc, politisches," 2. See also: Biedermann, *Erinnerungen*, 144-147; Haym, II, 301, 349; Duncker, vii, 17, 129-130; Laube, II, 307-309, and III, 410-411.

There were two additional ways of explaining the Frankfurt Parliament's failure which liberals invoked from time to time, but they played a distinctly subordinate role. Since later historians have asserted that the feelings implicit in one of these explanations prevailed quite generally at the time and since the other explanation has enjoyed considerable popularity in our own century, the uses made of them by the liberals are worthy of some note.

Several of the liberals pointed to what they saw as a peculiarly professorial incapacity for politics. Biedermann criticized the right-center *Casino* party, which had the heaviest concentration of professors, both for its overattachment to the principle of authority and for the ways in which its members' distinctive excellence in the realm of theory was rendered useless by the absence of practical experience and of the ability to carry through on good intentions. Stressing the influence which the professors had exercised in the assembly as a whole, as well as in the *Casino*, he went on to write the following about the academic politicians:

... Their influence was decisive and beneficial primarily in the area of doctrine, less in questions of immediate practical affairs. They attempted, from a broad view of history, law, and politics, to derive what was necessary, what had to happen. But of course, this did not always happen, since the factual circumstances did not conform to these theoretical views, and then they could not think of any way to set aside these hindrances and carry through what had been recognized as correct, except to appeal to the future and to the good will and rationality of the leading powers.

August Ludwig von Rochau asserted that the failure to achieve either freedom or unity was attributable not only to the resistance of the royal governments but also to the Frankfurt Parliament's own helplessness and lack of direction. He particularly criticized the eagerness displayed by so many members to have their full say on every matter, charging that because of the time wasted in long debates "every creative activity was threatened." The discussions of the basic rights to be secured in the constitution had been especially costly in this respect. Together with the rest of the debates about the constitution, they had taken valuable time just at the point where speed was most essential. If the constitution had been completed six months earlier, he argued, it probably would have been accepted. Although Rochau did not make the connections directly, all of these strictures could of course be understood as falling on those men whose life work was the detailed analysis and discussion of basic principles, namely the professors.[19]

[19] Biedermann, *Erinnerungen,* 260-261; Rochau, 129, 134-135, 139, 160-161.

Nevertheless, only a small minority of the liberals expressed such anti-professorial and anti-intellectual sentiments, and a number of others specifically rejected them. Laube asserted that such influential members of the constitutional committee as Dahlmann, Beseler, and Droysen had in fact possessed a high degree of political character and capability. Men who denied this – using "the current reproach against doctrinaire limitedness" – did so simply because they disagreed with or did not understand their actual policies. He also defended the professors by pointing to the continued lack of success on the part of those who most scorned the "professorial parliament." Haym expressed the same attitudes even more forcefully. His extensive criticisms of the parties of reaction and revolution were joined with effusive praise of the political scholars. The parliament was "the most brilliant and powerful which had ever met in Germany," distinguished alike by its progressive patriotism and by "the wealth of manifold insight and knowledge" which appeared among its members. He found no reason substantially to modify his original expectation that "the insight of the men who devoted themselves to Germany by following the lonely paths of scholarship, especially in the fields of law and history . . . was to contribute to the building of the fatherland just as much as the experience of practical men of affairs. . . ." [20]

The liberals also tended to de-emphasize relations between Germany and non-German states and peoples, which in various ways have been stressed quite strongly in twentieth-century writing about the revolution's failure. Foreign interference has received special prominence in works by German nationalists. According to their accounts, England, Russia, and France helped derail the movement toward German unity because they feared the emergence of a strong new state in Central Europe.[21] But the intellectuals of the 1850's, except to the extent that they considered the Prussian-Austrian dualism, all seem to have been far more concerned with internal than with foreign affairs. Johann Gustav Droysen's remarks on Prussia and the system of great powers did seem to direct attention to the international scene. "It is not," he wrote in the summer of 1849, "as if questions of inner political development and of social order are irrelevant. They are relevant, with as much significance and force as ever. But in order to become soluble, they require decisions of a totally different

---

[20] Laube, II, 37, and III, 458; Haym, III, 193, 191, and "Die Literatur des ersten deutschen Parlaments," 133; see also Mohl, "Die erste deutsche Reichsversammlung und die Schriften darüber," 13.

[21] Criticism of this thesis, as well as discussion of its origins and its political significance, can be found in W. E. Mosse, *The Great Powers and the German Question, 1848-1871* (Cambridge, Eng., 1958), esp. 375-381.

sort. It is international problems which must be solved." During the struggles of the past year, there had been "a need for a power against the other powers, in order to break their opposition and to protect us from their selfish interests." His comments on the international situation, however, dealt more with the relations between Prussia and Austria than with those between Germany and any of the non-German states. Moreover, his oblique references to France, England, and Russia found few echoes in the literature under discussion here or – for that matter – in any of the other writings which we shall encounter. Duncker explicitly stated that the foreign situation in the spring of 1849 had in fact been quite favorable to unification, a judgment which in turn supported his charges of fecklessness against Frederick William IV. Moreover, there was no sense of the ways in which the old powers might have been strengthened by international conflicts of another sort, as they were called out by the liberals to suppress non-German national movements in Posen and Bohemia. Historians who favor this line of argument today are on more solid ground than those who stress anti-German hostility, but for obvious reasons the liberals would have found such an analysis uncongenial, inasmuch as it would have necessitated pointing to an inner contradiction between liberal goals and national ones.[22]

THE DEMOCRATIC MILLENNIUM

The political democrats shared certain points in common with the liberals, but on the whole their version of recent history differed markedly. This difference hardly comes as a surprise, inasmuch as the democrats were among those forces which the liberals pejoratively labelled "radical." Arnold Ruge, a leading democratic intellectual during the revolution, revealed both of these aspects of democratic thought in a brief postrevolutionary pamphlet which treated recent efforts to establish democracy in Germany. He indicated his agreement with the familiar liberal belief that men revolted for primarily political reasons when he stated that revolutions had always been undertaken for or against the self-determination of peoples and individuals, for or against freedom and democracy. As for the European revolutions of 1848-49, he admitted that there had been a social aspect to these upheavals, but he went on to insist that they

---

[22] Droysen, "Preussen und das System der Grossmächte," 212-213; Duncker, 88. For emphasis on aggressive German nationalism as a contributing factor in the liberal failure, see A. J. P. Taylor, *The Course of German History* (rev. ed., New York, 1962), 77-83.

had arisen mainly from widespread opposition to despotism. A violent collapse of the old *"Bedientenstaat,"* the state based on the principles of command and obedience, had become inevitable as soon as "European humanity" achieved self-confidence and understood its humiliating situation vis-à-vis its rulers. These remarks indicate that Ruge also shared the liberal belief that revolutionary radicalism had been closely intertwined with resentment against bureaucratic absolutism. But Ruge differed from the liberals in according the revolutionaries qualities of dignity and purposefulness, rather than portraying them simply as malcontents who had lashed out in blind opposition. Moreover, in his view the men who sought to introduce political equality as well as political and civil liberty were participants in a long European-wide struggle which they would certainly win.[23]

Georg Gottfried Gervinus and Karl Hagen provided long-range historical background to support this view of the movement toward democracy as the indefeasible tendency of the times, each of them reading modern European history as the emergence and progressive realization of the democratic idea. They believed that its champions, particularly during the single "great revolution" which characterized the period since 1789, had wrested more and more territory from their opponents and would continue to do so until the battle was won.[24] The more interesting and certainly the more notorious of these historians was Gervinus, whose introduction to the history of the nineteenth century cost him his professorship and very nearly his personal freedom. Gervinus, who wrote his book "in order to reinforce many men's shattered confidence in our future . . . and to provide for many who had collapsed a place of refuge in the shipwreck of these years," located contemporary history within a much larger epoch, which stretched back three or four centuries. Historical development during this epoch had proceeded "according to an inherent spirit and law in a single direction, despite all hindrances and deflections," furthering "the transition from the rule of the few to that of the many." The whole era since the end of the Middle Ages had been dominated by "a single struggle of the democratic ideas" against their opponents. Gervinus traced the democratic impulse ultimately to "German-Protestant individualism," which he sharply contrasted with the oppressive universalism, centralization, and despotism which infected the peoples of the "Romance nations." The great democratic milestones from

[23] Ruge, *Die Gründung der Demokratie in Deutschland*, 4, 6, and *Briefwechsel*, II, 108.
[24] Hagen, *Geschichte der neuesten Zeit*, II, viii-x.

his perspective were the Reformation, England's Civil War and her Glorious Revolution of 1688, and the establishment of a democratic republic in the United States. On the other hand, he was ambiguous about the French Revolution. It had given early evidence that the progressive Germanic spirit of individual freedom was not confined to the Germanic peoples themselves. But in the end this evidence was outweighed by the traditional French affinity for centralization, which culminated in the rule of Napoleon. And yet even Napoleon continued to develop one aspect of democracy, by consolidating many gains for the principle of legal equality.[25]

Gervinus discerned two great political movements in the period since 1815 and several reasons for expecting both of them to succeed. One continued an important part of the French Revolution, the other carried forward the spirit of the Wars of Liberation. Intertwined with one another, they pointed toward a freer political order within the state and the distribution of peoples among states according to nationality and language. These movements had suffered sharp reverses recently, and it seemed that all of western Europe was threatened by the despotic universalism of the Slavic East. But, argued Gervinus, universal rule flourished only after political decay and popular exhaustion, and Europe had by no means begun to degenerate. "Up to now," he wrote, "the fruit of development in Europe (its political and intellectual enlightenment, its commercial activity, and the wealth that these procure), has still been a source of power and of national self-confidence, not of enervating luxury and human venality." Europe still possessed youthful vigor and would not succumb to despotism. The fact that these movements were supported by great masses of men held especial promise. In contrast to the eighteenth century and the revolutionary-Napoleonic period, the mid-nineteenth century did not possess great individuals, but "the number of middling talents" far surpassed what could be found in earlier times. "Not the quality, not the height of the development of individuals distinguishes this period," he observed, "but rather the quantity, the broad spread of development among the many; nothing great and sublime has happened in particular, but on the whole this is a great and sublime change in the form of public life, that the history of this age does not comprise merely biographies and stories of princes, but also the story

---

[25] Gervinus, *Einleitung in die Geschichte des neunzehnten Jahrhunderts,* 6, 12, 18-20, 41-42, 45-47, 78-81, 84-88, 93-95, 98, 136-137, 141-142. The *Geschichte des neunzehnten Jahrhunderts* itself only went up to 1830. For discussion of the larger work, see G. P. Gooch, *History and Historians in the Nineteenth Century* (2nd ed., Boston, 1959), 104-105.

of peoples." This popular vitality in the area of private life had inevitably led to and would continue to support the demand "that the state should finally make the well-being of the many its concern, and not that of a few individuals." Gervinus did not elaborate upon what he meant by "the well-being of the many," but he clearly felt that due regard for its realization would be ensured only by democratic government. Other factors which pointed to democracy's ultimate victory were the following: the loss of prestige and moral standing suffered by the monarchs; the inability of the middle class (which lacked both the corporate ambition and the leisure that were required) to assert itself as an independent political force, and the publicistic activities of a numerous literary proletariat. These aspects of the contemporary scene, along with the widespread efforts being made to raise the living conditions of the poor through education and the elimination of feudal servitude, all pointed to the victory of democratic principles.[26]

Gervinus admitted that he could not prophesy the future in detail, but he made several specific predictions nevertheless. He felt that America, whose institutions he had studied through a close reading of Tocqueville, rather than England revealed the shape of things to come. He also foresaw that the future would witness "the rule of the popular will according to the decisions of the majority." He sensed the possibility that the struggle might continue after political equality had been achieved, in the form of social conflict between the third and fourth estates, or the middle classes and the proletariat. But he insisted that "a general idea" (the democratic one) rather than oppression and misery had produced the great movements of the age, and basically he expected that the achievement of democratic government would mark the end of the long revolution.[27]

Gervinus thus portrayed democracy and the democratic revolutions not as sharp antitheses of liberalism but rather as logical and historical extensions of the liberals' preparatory efforts. According to this view, Germany's liberals had pointed to something beyond their own limited aims without really sensing that they were only part of a much wider process of historical development, the fulfillment of which lay in the attainment of political equality. What the liberals had begun the democrats would finish. Needless to say, Gervinus' democratic interpretation of history failed to elicit any enthusiasm from the liberals, some of whom

[26] Gervinus, *Einleitung*, 152-153, 157-161, 165-168, 171-174.
[27] *Ibid.*, 176-181.

had been his close friends in earlier years but most of whom were at best willing to tolerate his radical heresy.[28]

Although the radicals consoled themselves with assertions that the long democratic revolution bore the imprint of historical inevitability, they still had to account for the failure of the revolution in 1848. Their analysis of this problem set them clearly apart from the moderates – much more so than their remarks on the revolution's origins. Rather than lamenting an excess of revolutionary zeal, they contended that the real problem had been too much caution. Some of their strictures fell quite generally on the progressive movement as a whole. The radicals thus seemed by implication to hold themselves at least partially accountable for the revolution's failure, but they confessed to a very different sin from the one of which they stood accused. According to Ruge, the revolutionary forces had met disaster because of their reluctance to replace the old state with a popular one of their own. The first step should have been to remove all civil servants and military officers. Beyond that, reactionary professors, teachers, and clergy should have been dismissed, reformed municipalities should have been given increased administrative powers, and all the armies should have been turned into popular militias. This last step would have eliminated the standing armies, which had been so instrumental in carrying out the counterrevolution. Failure to do these things added up to a series of disastrous omissions by "the party of the people," although Ruge did not explain how the measures might have been accomplished. Wilhelm Schulz-Bodmer criticized the men who had headed the movement toward a "people's state" in 1848 for their failure to go beyond mere criticism of what existed and found a new *order,* an order based on the people themselves. To forestall both anarchy and reaction, the single most important measure would have been to dissolve the large standing armies and to replace them with civil guards, a point which Schulz-Bodmer stressed even more heavily than Ruge. The people would have been less willing to rebel against such a force, and this in turn would have prevented the resurgence of sympathy for the old powers. Moreover, those very powers would have been deprived of their single most effective retaliatory instrument. Thus, Schulz-Bodmer also traced failure to halfheartedness. The revolution had failed not because it went too far but because it did not go far enough.[29]

These men directed heavier fire at the groups which had made cautious moderation one of their very principles. Ruge, for instance, placed much

---

[28] Droysen, *Briefwechsel,* II, 145-147, 151, 157.
[29] Ruge, *Die Gründung der Demokratie,* 6-9; Schulz-Bodmer, "Anarchie," 499-501.

of the blame for the failure of the progressive forces at the door of those who had formed the liberal opposition during the *Vormärz*. In his view, they had only wanted a milder form of despotism, such as the system of Louis Philippe. One could not, however, overthrow the relations of command and servitude and yet retain them at the same time. The attempt to get by with such contradictory half-measures was a deception, to which the people had rightly responded with basic mistrust of all the representative assemblies. Dominated as they were by pre-1848 liberal leaders who had given up on "popular sovereignty and the true spirit of revolution, sincerely radical democracy," they could scarcely succeed in any of their tasks.[30]

The moderates' behavior during the spring of 1848 came under sharp attack from two unnamed contributors to a popular political encyclopedia. One of them focused on the Committee of Fifty, which had met at Heidelberg in March to organize a parliament, pointing out the inconsistency between its mode of operation and the sources of its authority. Having been given their power by a tumultuous popular movement, the men who formed the committee sought nevertheless to strengthen the existing legal order, so that they could later reform it in a purely legal fashion. "Thus, the unlawful delegates of the people acted highly lawfully; they acted more cautiously and conscientiously than history shows us to have been the case on the part of the legitimate advisors to the kings." The author added, "Perhaps this recognition which we must give to the committee at the same time contains the strongest reproach against the political insight of its members." Another author wrote that in order to unify Germany a highly developed revolution would have been necessary, either from above or from below. He chided the liberals for dulling the only weapons with which the unity they said they desired could possibly have been won:

The intention was to subordinate eminent princes, whose early ancestors had already been accustomed to self-government, beneath the power of a single ruler, and yet all the means of resistance had been left to them, without considering that neither the compliant fear of the princely courts nor the enthusiasm of the people could be of long duration. It was wished that the German princes would obey a parliament whose power and right rested on the strength of revolution, and yet there was great concern to weaken the revolution before the achievement of victory... Such self-deception, such miscalculation of the moment in time and of the possibilities, has seldom revenged itself so thoroughly as it did on the German national assembly which sat at Frankfurt a. M.

[30] Ruge, *Die Gründung der Demokratie,* 16-17.

The prospects of winning significant concessions had thus been clouded at the very start.[31]

The democrats similarly castigated the liberals for their unwillingness to participate in the spring uprisings of 1849, which they felt ought to have been a common venture. Ludwig Bamberger attacked the moderates for having withdrawn from the parliament in May, precisely at the height of the popular struggle for the constitution. He went on to lament the absence of a clear signal from the parliament which might have unified the whole country beneath the revolutionary banner. Another writer said much the same thing when he asserted that "the stupidity and inaction on the part of the Frankfurt Parliament removed from these [popular] movements the basic requirement for their further development." He also denied liberal charges that the democrats had hindered the attainment of unification, contending that ". . . only the united strivings of all progressive parties can lead to unity and freedom." For both of these writers and for other democrats too, the moderates' precipitate reaction against their radical allies had helped defeat not only radicalism but also liberalism.[32]

THE CONSERVATIVE CRITIQUE OF THE FORCES OF REVOLUTION

The political conservatives took far fewer pains than either the liberals or the democrats to distinguish between moderate and radical opposition to the old order. Although they sensed some variety within the progressive forces, they basically grouped them all together as the party of revolution. Leopold Ranke's general view of Europe's recent past typified conservative thinking. He located the present in "the constitutional period," which he portrayed both as the successor to the Napoleonic period and as part of a larger epoch, "the age of revolution." During the last phase of this epoch, all of Europe had experienced an intense conflict between the principles of monarchical and popular sovereignty. This struggle was the most noteworthy aspect of the recent period as a whole: all kinds of other conflicts depended on and coincided with the contests between the people and their rulers. "Our age," Ranke wrote, "is marked both by

---

[31] "Der Fünfzigerausschuss" (anon.), in *Gegenwart*, IV (1850), 442; "Die deutsche Nationalversammlung, I: Vom Zusammentritt der Versammlung bis zur Erwählung des Reichsverwesers" (anon.), in *Gegenwart*, V (1850), 169.

[32] Bamberger, *Erlebnisse aus der pfälzischen Erhebung im Mai und Juni 1849*, 3-6; "Preussen seit Ende 1849 bis Ende 1850" (anon.), in *Gegenwart*, VII (1852), 488, 517; see also Oppenheim, "Zur Kritik der Demokratie," 9-12.

the development of material energies and by the growth of the natural sciences, but it receives its character from the impulses of revolution and from the resistance offered to them." [33]

Friedrich Julius Stahl expressed the same idea with more specific reference to 1848 and also at a higher philosophical level. In his view, the Frankfurt Parliament was a revolutionary assembly, its actions having gone well beyond its limited mandate. "Whether one overthrows the existing order and authority," he wrote, "by storming the Tuileries or by an attack of armed bands, or whether one does this through unauthorized legislative acts and decrees, reckoning on the power of the revolutionary mood in the people, it is all the same in fact and in principle." Stahl summarized his position in more theoretical terms:

There is no middle way between popular sovereignty and authority from God, between revolution and legitimacy, between the sacredness of the existing order and popular power over the existing order. Therefore, whoever is not a legitimist is necessarily a revolutionary, even though by temperament or moral characteristics he may strive against every measure of exterior violence and seek reform instead of revolution.[34]

This viewpoint was obviously anathema to men like Haym and Biedermann.

Conservative reluctance to make the distinctions employed by the liberals, like the similar disinclination on the part of the democrats (at least when the democrats were discussing the revolution's origins), poses problems for the historian who seeks to establish a basis for comparability. But at the same time, even more than in the case of the democrats, it serves to point up a basic substantive difference in the outlooks of the two groups: the liberals saw themselves as occupying quite a different position on the political map from that held by the radicals, whereas the conservatives felt that the liberals were nearly indistinguishable from the radicals and that in any case they had greatly helped to prepare the way for them.

Much of what the conservatives wrote about the sources of revolution centered on the dire effects of diminished religious faith, the rise of modern rationalism, and French examples as well as French thought. Stahl pointed implicitly to the decline of piety in order to explain revolutionary activity when he described revolutions as "the basing of the

[33] Ranke, *Über die Epochen der neueren Geschichte*, 229-234. The last quotation is taken from the introduction to an unpublished lecture which Ranke gave sometime after 1852. The whole introduction is reprinted in Rudolf Vierhaus, *Ranke und die soziale Welt* (Münster, 1957), 237.
[34] Stahl, *Die Revolution und die constitutionelle Monarchie*, 15-16, 19-20.

whole public state of affairs on the will of man, instead of on God's order and decree." The revolutionaries believed that the basis for temporal authority lay in the popular will, not in the dictates of divine providence. They also thought that the purpose of the social and political order was not to fulfill God's plan for the world but rather to satisfy the arbitrary whims of mortal men. In short, they were sinners. A Catholic publicist saw the revolutionaries' belief that constitutions could be created through debates and their refusal to recognize that sovereign power was "a gift by a higher decree" as proof that revolutions were "the culmination of all false doctrines and religions" and "the complete denial of God." Another Catholic, Franz Joseph Buss, insisted that the revolutionary volcano had been seething in Germany not just for the past few years but rather for the past three centuries. "Deviation from the principles of justice, from the laws," he wrote, "is only the outer form; the essence of our sickness is the abandonment of God and his sacred Church. The revolution is apostasy, the disunity of the nation is schism, the anarchy is atheism." [35]

What lay behind the decline of religious faith was of course, as Stahl put it, "that mode of thinking which one designates by the expression rationalism," or the whole set of beliefs and attitudes which had found classic expression in the enlightenment. It is important to note in this regard that just as Stahl's definition of revolutionary activity was a much broader one than that employed by the liberals, so too the roster of thinkers whom he indicted for having nourished the revolutionary mentality was a good deal more inclusive than the list of democrats and socialists drawn up by the men of the center. Grotius, Kant, and Fichte as well as Rousseau were all seen as having played a part.[36]

Nevertheless, the greater part of the ideas which the conservatives felt had helped precipitate the recent revolutions did seem to have come from France. As Ranke put it, during the *Vormärz* Germany had experienced "an invasion by foreign ideas," which had helped prepare the way for the events of the March days far in advance. Several authors who wrote for the *Historical-Political Journal* were particularly insistent on drawing their readers' attention to the role of the French. The critical ideas that had spread eastward from France in the eighteenth and nineteenth centuries had, they complained, undermined the whole existing order of

[35] Stahl, *Was ist die Revolution?*, 4-5, 10; Phillips, "Kirche oder Revolution?," 421, 430; Buss, *Die Aufgabe des katholischen Theils teutscher Nation in der Gegenwart*, vi.
[36] Stahl, *Was ist die Revolution?*, 11-13, and *Die Philosophie des Rechts*, II, part I, vii-xii.

things. And in 1848, the "French spirit" had found a haven not only among the German socialists, but also in the Frankfurt Parliament. One author wrote, "The foreign, un-German spirit of an unlimited sovereignty, standing individually and alone over everything, recognizing no existing right . . . considering none of the inequalities that are found in nature and in every organic life, but instead decreeing everything by majority – *a priori, souverainement,* in the name of popular sovereignty – already predominated in the Pre-Parliament, in the Committee of Fifty, and in the parliamentary elections themselves." Universal manhood suffrage seemed to afford especially striking evidence of influence from across the Rhine. The forty-eighters, according to this author, had preferred to imitate foreigners rather than adhere to political ideas based on "the history and the spirit of the German nation." It bears noting that much of what these passages identified as being of foreign derivation was far from either the political or the social extremities. Even moderate liberalism appeared as an invading force. According to this perspective, radicalism and liberalism stood together, both having received a large part of their momentum from abroad.[37]

The conservatives did not always place the liberals and radicals under the same heading, but when they bothered to separate out the more extreme revolutionaries for special consideration they still found a way to condemn the moderates. They did this by insisting that the radicals had in large part been stimulated precisely by the men who took the greatest pains to proclaim that these obstreperous troublemakers were an altogether distinct breed. Just as the liberals made the conservatives take the brunt of the blame for revolutionary extremism, so too the conservatives insisted that one set of their enemies had been encouraged by the other. Although they might admit occasionally that some of the liberal demands for greater national unity and other political reforms had been at least partially valid and not revolutionary per se, they sought nevertheless in any way they could to discredit the men who were trying to achieve them. One of the best ways to do this was to declare that the liberals had in fact opened the gates through which others tried to pass.

Stahl employed this strategy with his customary skill. In his view, one did not have to leave the extent of monarchical power limitless, but one could not challenge the basis of that power without transforming kingship

---

[37] Ranke, "Politische Denkschriften," 587-588, 591, 601-602; "Das Wesen und das Wirken der Fortschrittspartei" (anon.), *HPB*, XL (1857), 641; "Frankfurt und Deutschland, die Grundrechte und der bayerische Adressensturm" (anon.), *HPB*, XXIII (1849), 400-402.

into a "hollow mechanism" toward which nobody would feel any loyalty at all. Was it not inevitable, he asked, that the momentum generated by the liberal middle class's successful onslaught against royal power should give rise to attacks on personal property too? In the summer of 1848, Stahl wrote the following: "Exactly corresponding to this *constitutional kingship* which liberalism and the bourgeoisie have invented there will be a *constitutional property*, which socialism and the working class will invent." Property rights would exist, but public officials would control the ways in which they were exercised. These officials, seeking to provide for the workers, would leave little or no more income in the hands of the owners than in those of the propertyless. The liberal middle classes would be hoist by their own petard. Stahl indicted the liberals in another way when he directly linked attacks on property even to the movement for national unification:

Its [revolution's] last step is necessarily the *overthrow of property, communism*. For what else is property, but that man recognizes the priority in possession which God's decree has assigned and allotted to one before the other, through birth and inheritance, through earlier appropriation, through more successful work, through more fortunate utilization; and what else is the sacredness of property, but the fear of and submission to God's decree? If now man nowhere recognizes God's decree as binding, not accepting the authority and the constitution and the vocation which God has decreed, why should he therefore recognize the rights of property? And if man undertakes to make everything anew – the state, the municipality, the divisions among peoples and states in Europe – why not also a new division of goods?

This passage reveals with especial clarity Stahl's conviction that a breach in the dike of the old order at almost any point would lead to the ultimate calamity.[38]

Many of the same attitudes appear in writings by Ranke and some of the Catholic publicists from Bavaria. Ranke admitted that the reforming ministers in Prussia were constitutionalists rather than radicals, but he insisted that the electoral law they introduced in the spring of 1848 had opened the way to political radicalism and the redistribution of property. After reproaching the Frankfurt Parliament for having needed protection by the Prussian army during popular disturbances in September of 1848, he wrote the following: "The great lesson of the year 1848 is that the constitutional system needs an independent monarch, equipped with his own power, for its own survival. ... When destructive parliamentary majorities control the army, then the revolution in Germany will acquire

[38] Stahl: *Die Revolution*, 110-111; *Parlamentarische Reden*, 134-135; *Was ist die Revolution?*, 7-8.

full control. . . . But there will then probably be neither kingship nor a constitutional system." [39]

The Catholics made several causal links between liberalism and radicalism, reformers and revolutionaries. They maintained that the liberals had hoped to exploit lower-class dissatisfactions for their own ends but that they had deceived themselves concerning their ability to bring the revolution to a standstill after achieving their own relatively limited objectives. The liberals did not realize "that every violent upheaval overshoots its goal, and that the prize goes to the boldest." Furthermore, the rapid succession of new laws only undermined the citizens' respect for law in general. The connection could be illustrated most clearly by reference to the rise of radicalism in the south German constitutional states:

It was the opposition leaders from all these German legislatures . . . who made any government in their native land impossible and above all brought Baden to a state of complete disintegration . . . These same men wanted to attempt an identical experiment with the whole fatherland, and if the same process of decomposition had taken place in all of Germany, then only one thing could have been foreseen: that it [Germany] would have lost all its steadiness and become a prey to its neighbors. This sort of constitutionalism had been part of the scene in the smaller states for less than thirty years, and already they were so completely corrupt that they produced nothing except masses who were alienated from the throne and from the legal order and revolutionary leaders.

In concert with Prussians such as Stahl and Ranke, many of the south German Catholic publicists thus placed the greatest responsibility for left-wing extremism at the feet of the very men who saw their own moderate program not as a forerunner of but as the only alternative to revolution.[40]

The political conservatives had much less to say than either the liberals or the democrats about the reasons for the defeat which the forces of movement had suffered. Their lack of interest in explanations for the dismal end of the Frankfurt Parliament and of Germany's other attempts at representative government was hardly fortuitous. From their standpoint the liberals' failures were matters which men like Haym and Biedermann could ponder for themselves. It sufficed for the conservatives to have castigated all opposition to the old order in the way that they did, since their condemnations implied that the setbacks experienced by the dissi-

---

[39] Ranke, "Politische Denkschriften," 588-589, 603, 610, 604-605.
[40] "Das Wesen und das Wirken der Fortschrittspartei," 738, 848-849; "Das deutsche Verfassungswerk" (anon.), *HPB*, XXVI (1850), 245.

dents could be interpreted as a sort of divine judgment. Because failure was felt to be deserved, it seemed inevitable.

When the conservatives did analyze the forty-eighters' disappointments, they consistently attempted to reinforce their central thesis that defeat was all that their opponents had a right to expect. The use of this tactic can be observed clearly in a series of articles on the Frankfurt Parliament by a Catholic publicist writing for the *Historical-Political Journal*. In his view, the parliamentarians had not realized "that existing relationships which have been rooted in the nature of peoples for centuries may be forgotten and overlooked in moments of upheaval but not permanently misunderstood and misjudged." The men at Frankfurt had displayed "the parliamentary absolutism of our time," a heretofore peculiarly French phenomenon which quickly proved just as fragile as any princely despotism, calling down upon itself the inevitable reaction of "offended nature and disregarded divine laws." Discussing the parliament's all-important constitutional committee, the author continued in the same vein. He pointed out that the members were largely professors, literary men, and other intellectuals: "north German authors of books and inflammatory south German writers." The committee had been domi-nated by the former, with their "north German academic wisdom, their pedantic obstinacy, their impractical theories" (these phrases revealing an anti-Prussian side of the Catholic mentality which of course was far from universal in the conservative camp). What had begun with "French arrogance" was continued with "German pedantry, learning and thor-oughness. . . . That German ideology, for which Napoleon, in his practical spirit, had so little regard . . . asserted itself far and wide. They [the committee members] acted as if nothing had existed previously and as if no one but themselves were there." Sitting in the *Paulskirche*, they had been isolated both from the past and from the contemporary world which existed outside the seat of their deliberations – a point which the author made implicitly in the very title of his article, beginning as he did with the distinction between "Frankfurt and Germany." Real success could have been achieved only by working with, not against, the existing govern-ments. But German impracticality and parliamentary absolutism had prevented even the moderates at Frankfurt from perceiving this essential truth.[41]

Particularly noteworthy in these writings and in others like them is

---

[41] "Frankfurt und Deutschland," 386-387, 397-407, 652-655.

the repeated charge that the liberals had failed because they were too "doctrinaire," that they had suffered from too much reliance on the power of their ideas. This charge was implicit in the contention by men on the left that the men of the center had refused to do what was necessary to put their principles into practice, but it had quite a different ring when it came from the right. The basic import of the conservative analysis was not that the liberals ought to have fought harder in order to win but rather that they had grossly overestimated their prospects in the first place. Such over-weening confidence had inevitably been punished.[42]

FROM POLITICAL NARRATIVE TO SOCIAL ANALYSIS

The men whose primary interests lay in social questions developed an interpretation of recent history which resembled the one offered by the politically oriented conservatives in a number of respects, and yet the two groups differed profoundly. Indeed, the differences already begin to emerge from a closer look at the similarities. Like the conservatives, the social thinkers applied terms such as "radicalism" to a broader range of phenomena than did the liberals. But whereas the conservatives lumped together German liberalism and German radicalism, many social thinkers fused German radicalism with similar currents in France. Instead of confounding liberals and revolutionaries, they tended to talk about popular upheaval on both sides of the Rhine without always making clear just which country they were discussing. The social thinkers also echoed the conservatives in saddling the liberals with most of the blame for the acts committed by the avowed radicals. But they arrived at this judgment in a very different way, stressing the putative effects on the masses not so much of liberal attacks against authority as of liberally supported social and economic exploitation.[43]

[42] See also Huber, *Suum cuique in der deutschen Frage*, 7-8, and Erdmann, *Philosophische Vorlesungen über den Staat*, 40. Bruno Bauer, whose conservatism was less evident when he wrote about the Frankfurt Parliament than it was to become during the next few years, did seem to echo the democrats when he pointed out that the liberals had thrown away the one chance they had by turning against their most determined supporters almost from the very start. The liberals were content to be "heroes of the idea" when only a real revolution would have succeeded. But even though Bauer felt that ruthless determination would have been required for success, he seemed to doubt that it would have sufficed (see his *Untergang des Frankfurter Parlaments*, 261-269, 272-273, 291, 300).

[43] In several cases, most notably the writings by Lorenz von Stein and Wilhelm Heinrich Riehl, the reflections by these men on the recent revolutions are nearly inseparable from their more general theories about and programs for society. Since the latter are dealt with in Chapter V, more extensive discussion of their ideas about the sources of revolutionary upheaval will be found in that chapter.

The habitual reference by many social thinkers to the events of 1848-49 in France and Germany under vague general headings – "recent history," "what we have seen," or the like – which failed to distinguish between the two countries did not arise simply out of confusion. Instead, it afforded a way of bringing to bear on German history a wider analytic perspective than that employed by the writers whose foremost concerns were political. The social thinkers might well admit that on the whole Germans who participated in the recent revolutions had been primarily motivated by political impulses. Lorenz von Stein, for instance, stated explicitly that the overriding objective among the forces of opposition in Germany had been the achievement of political unity, "the first precondition of ... progressive development," and he left no doubt that the political question retained the utmost importance. Robert von Mohl similarly admitted that the greatest struggles of the day centered on the organization of political power. But Stein, Mohl, and most of the other social thinkers did not believe that social and economic questions – which even in Germany had in their view been a good deal more pressing than most men realized – would remain in the background. Since French history suggested to many writers that political revolutions prepared the way for social ones, it seemed inevitable that new issues would command increasing attention in the near future. Germany, it was felt, would certainly have to endure more of the same social struggle which it had just begun to experience of late – the kind of conflict which had been present in all of recent French history and had come to a head so spectacularly in Paris during the June days of 1848. As Wilhelm Heinrich Riehl put it, "The social struggles are going to be fought out among us very bitterly. France may provide the point of departure for the coming social revolutions; nevertheless, Germany will become the central arena, the battlefield where the decision will be made." The habit of referring to both countries in the same breath thus betrayed a widely-held belief that historical trends in France and Germany bore striking resemblances, despite their differing stages of development at mid-century.[44]

Even though these men occasionally discussed the liberal movement which culminated in the Frankfurt Parliament (analyzing it of course to a far greater extent than other writers in terms of the social needs as well as the political ideals of the middle classes), they were much more concerned with popular radicalism. They discerned the causes of the radical

[44] Stein, *Geschichte der sozialen Bewegung in Frankreich*, I, cxxxiii-cxxxix; Mohl, "Das Repräsentativsystem, seine Mängel und die Heilmittel," 196; Riehl, *Die bürgerliche Gesellschaft*, 27.

movements which had recently dominated public affairs in France and threatened to do the same in Germany primarily in social concerns, not in purely political ones. They were convinced that the men who had sought a democratic republic had not wanted a redistribution of political power for its own sake – that political democracy was in fact only a means to the end of redistributing social and economic power. Social discontent itself could be explained in several ways. The activities of literary men frequently appeared as a prime source of disruption: socialist and communist theorizing took on great significance as an active force in the process of revolutionary upheaval. According to Immanuel Hermann Fichte, socialism and communism had exercised enormous power over French public opinion and "driven the tempestuous masses to action." Surveying the German scene, Riehl traced a large part of the reason for violent attacks against the prevailing social and economic order to destructive agitation by "the proletarians of intellectual work," among whom the leading elements were unsuccessful and bitter journalists and academics. But there was also an awareness that tangible conditions of life had contributed to the movements of which these ideas were a part and that they could not be understood simply as links in a chain of intellectual history. As Heinrich Ahrens put it, the social theories which had arisen in France and made their way to Germany via the "intellectual proletarians" were not simply causes of but also evidence of "a deep and wide *wound* in the social body." However one might feel about the motives of the men who developed and spread these critiques of contemporary society, it was difficult to deny that their widespread success in finding followers indicated the presence of real problems which had not been created by intellectuals alone.[45]

In seeking to account for these "wounds" from which European society suffered, the social thinkers singled out economic liberalism. Regardless of considerable disagreements with one another about the appropriate cures for a sick society, they almost all felt that belief in the desirability of free competition among profit-seeking industrial capitalists lay at the root of the malady. Since most of Germany's political liberals subscribed to some version of this creed, the social thinkers were in effect blaming the forces represented by men such as Haym and Droysen for a good part of the disturbances perpetrated by the radicals. In so doing they joined hands with the political conservatives. But their criticism of the liberals was a far more searching one. They did not present the liberals as men who had

---

[45] Huber, *Berlin, Erfurt, Paris,* 20; Fichte, *System der Ethik,* I, 663; Riehl, 304 ff.; Ahrens, *Die Rechtsphilosophie,* 145-147.

unwittingly set an example of revolutionary opposition to the established governments which the masses went on to supersede in degree rather than kind; nor did they make their case by arguing that the liberals had breached the dike of authority for their own purposes only to find that others were all too eager to enlarge the initial cavity. Instead, the crux of their indictment was that the liberals had helped directly to create the very conditions which social revolutionaries wished to eliminate. They insisted that the most disruptive of the liberals' revolutionary activities had consisted not in their sporadic attacks on the powers of princes and bureaucrats but rather in their long and steady assault on the fabric of society.

Karl Marlo, a democratic socialist, made the case with particular cogency from the left, developing one of the period's most extensive interpretations of nineteenth-century European social history. He denied that the period since 1789 had witnessed two revolutions, one seeking civil freedom and the other seeking material welfare. There had been only one long revolution. The people had always wanted general well-being, which they had expected the liberal order to provide. But liberalism had disappointed them, bringing misery rather than happiness. All countries which had experienced unrestrained competition had undergone – and were still undergoing – an indirect revolution, as big businessmen expropriated small ones. This process, along with the other sufferings brought about by the rise of industry, had in turn led to the outbreak of a communist counterrevolution. The events of 1848 throughout Europe were thus to be regarded as the opening barrage of an inevitable attack against a new moneyed nobility, which had been the sole beneficiary of the liberal order. Proletarian workers and the lower bourgeoisie had risen up together against the higher bourgeoisie, which had enriched itself with goods produced by the rest of the population. The members of this higher bourgeoisie called themselves constitutionalists and claimed to represent the people as a whole, but they were selfish, heartless, deceptive, and cowardly. They richly deserved the retribution which they were beginning to receive from those who had been their victims.[46]

Robert von Mohl, one of the few political liberals who showed a deep concern with social problems, laid great stress on the part played in the recent growth of "general dissatisfaction" by the sufferings to which "the major parts of our whole society" had been subjected, and he too traced these grievances to the application of liberal ideas about the proper organi-

---

[46] Marlo, *Untersuchungen über die Organisation der Arbeit*, I, part I, 476, 229-230, 389-390, 395-397.

zation of social and economic life. These essentially nonpolitical complaints had resulted "partly from wrongheaded measures, partly from the admittedly natural but also fully unhindered process of a new economic development." Unrestrained economic freedom ("mere dissolution") had had – and continued to have – a disastrous impact on artisans, factory workers, and farmers alike. As a consequence, both welfare and morality were under attack.[47]

Constantin Frantz, a staunch conservative both politically and socially, developed much the same sort of attack on social and economic liberalism as that made by Marlo and Mohl. The disappearance of governmental authority in 1848 stemmed in his view largely from the governments' failures to further the welfare of their citizens. During the preceding decades they had increasingly followed the liberal principle according to which their activities should be limited to tax collection, military recruitment, and administrative and judicial matters. At the same time that the proponents of liberal doctrine distracted the governments from their obligation to deal with problems in the social and economic realm, they also exacerbated the problems which demanded attention. Liberalism for Frantz was essentially an antisocial principle. Its extreme emphasis on the rights and interests of the individual did not serve as a basis for organizing communal life but rather as a means for destroying the very substance of community. Believing as they did that social relations should be based on the pursuit of private gain, the liberals in effect glorified the exploitation of one man by another. In so doing they also glorified what Frantz called "the system of permanent revolution ... the very worst kind of revolution, which not only overthrows states but also dooms nations both physically and morally." The import of Frantz's critique was that men who explicitly invoked the principle of self-interest as the highest good and thus set a revolutionary example could hardly protest their innocence when faced with the unintended but still inevitable consequences of their beliefs. General violence and destruction of the sort which Europe had witnessed in 1848 were the predictable outcome.[48]

Another notable element in the attempts to explain revolution made by many of the more conservative social thinkers concerned the harmful effects of overdeveloped bureaucratic power. Sometimes they pointed to this development as a stimulus to liberal constitutionalism. Viktor Aimé Huber, for instance, felt that the concentration of authority in the

---

[47] Mohl, "Das Repräsentativsystem," 196-197.
[48] Frantz, *Die Erneuerung der Gesellschaft und die Mission der Wissenschaft*, 24, and *Vorschule zur Physiologie der Staaten*, 295-300.

Prussian bureaucracy had helped to engender the desire for parliamentary institutions which would serve as a counterweight. But the central thesis of the social thinkers regarding the revolutionary effects of bureaucratic centralization was not at all identical with the liberal and democratic belief that bureaucratization had stimulated countervailing impulses toward self-government or that popular unruliness was the inevitable concomitant of exclusion from the political process. The real cutting edge of their argument was typically displayed by several Catholic publicists who argued that royal officials had been instruments of liberalism, not its opponents. In any case, they argued, the liberals heartily approved much of what the bureaucrats had undertaken. The liberals and the bureaucrats had mounted a joint attack against the powers of all corporate bodies, with devastating results for political and social tranquility. By accepting the liberal demand that education should be taken out of the hands of the Church, the bureaucratic state had prevented the younger generation from being raised in piety and loyalty toward their rulers. More generally, the governments had set their own example of revolutionary encroachment on a whole host of historically legitimated rights besides those of the Church. By attacking the privileges of such institutions as the Church, local communities, and craft guilds and seeking to take over their traditional functions, they had undermined the "organic" articulation of a highly differentiated social structure, heretofore one of the best sources of resistance to the "intemperate desire for change." Men whose sense of special group identity had been destroyed by the bureaucrats – and who had lost the protection which membership in a privileged group afforded – were far more likely to revolt than men who still enjoyed a well-defined place in the social order. Finally, these Catholic writers argued that by involving themselves in all the affairs of their subjects the bureaucrats had accustomed them to demand from the state what they would otherwise have been content to provide for themselves. Despite the governments' refusal to assist positively the individuals who lived beneath their authority, the extent of their administrative activity made men feel that they had a right to such assistance and encouraged them to support socialist and communist extremism. In sum, the princes and their servants had contributed to the growth of the radical movements in a whole host of ways, none of which had anything to do with refusing the citizen an opportunity to participate in the affairs of state. Once again the final emphasis fell on matters which lay beyond politics.[49]

[49] Huber, *Bruch mit der Revolution*, 14-15, 32-33; "Das Wesen und das Wirken

The social thinkers saw the liberal defeat from much the same perspective, demonstrating an awareness of factors which other men barely glimpsed or more likely failed to see at all. Depending on their politics, they might invoke one or another of the explanations employed by the liberals, the radicals, or the conservatives. But a large number of them from across the whole political spectrum went beyond the analyses which we have encountered up to this point, locating the basic difficulty in the area of social conflict. They could agree with the liberals and the radicals that splits among the opposition's own ranks had weakened their effectiveness from within. But they did not stop with assertions that the radicals had pressed too far and too fast with their revolutionary demands for a democratic republic or charges that the liberals had dropped out of a movement they once had led. They also identified the liberals' stance toward newly emerging social problems as one of the fundamental reasons for their ultimate debacle. The liberals' fear that under a republic they would have to accept solutions which frightened them seemed to lie at the heart of their unwillingness to push the political revolution through to a successful conclusion. At the same time, their neglect of social in favor of purely political reform at the Frankfurt Parliament appeared to have cost them a good deal of the popular support on which they thought they could rely in their pursuit of moderate objectives.

Social conflict appeared as a prime reason for the demise of political reform in writings by social thinkers of all political persuasions. On the left, Marlo stated the case as follows. The events of 1848 in Germany had brought about a brief victory over the aristocrats for the constitutionalists, who had then split into plutocratic and democratic factions. The former, comprising the new nobility of money, had thought that the revolution was liberal, but they now saw its socialist tendencies too. In order to suppress the people, they formed an alliance with the aristocrats. If the plutocrats had really wanted the Frankfurt Parliament's constitution to be accepted, the Prussian king would have been forced to relent. But even though the constitution had been written by "diminutive pedants, educated in half-liberal principles and used by the far more perspicacious moneyed nobility as unconscious tools, [men who] succeeded in extending their limited understanding neither to the idea of the democratic state nor to that of social reform," the plutocrats feared the degree of influence it

der Fortschrittspartei," 847-860; "Frankfurt und Deutschland," 676-677; see also the review of Alexis de Tocqueville's *Ancien régime et la Révolution* (Paris, 1856), "Die Centralisirung des öffentlichen Lebens und die Allmacht der Staatsgewalt als Grundursachen der Revolution" (anon.), *HPB,* XLIII (1859), 442-501, 573-599, 682-715; see also Buss, 5-6.

granted to the people. At the same time, they saw that blocking the fulfillment of even the limited desires for unity and political freedom for which the constitution provided would ensure the failure of social reform. Marlo seemed to regard achievement of the first two objectives – despite his assertions elsewhere that social reform could take place under any form of government – as preconditions for an effective attack on the ills of society. His belief that a powerful group of plutocrats shared that view lay at the heart of his explanation for German liberalism's failure.[50]

Ferdinand Lassalle, who was also on the left, remarked on the ways in which the limitedness of the liberals' avowed objectives had inevitably undermined their appeal to the great mass of the population. He regarded political reform alone as insufficient to arouse popular enthusiasm. Lassalle did not spell out his argument in a lengthy analysis, but judgments such as these were implied clearly enough in his statement of what he had learned as a result of the events of 1848-49: "that no future struggle can succeed in Europe that is not from the start ... *purely socialist*; that no future struggle will succeed if it carries the social questions merely as an obscure element, as background, within itself and emerges externally in the form of a national rising or of bourgeois republicanism." [51]

Robert von Mohl, who had earlier praised the work of Rudolf Haym and defended his liberal political allies against the accusations directed at them by their conservative enemies, developed some second thoughts later in the decade. The thrust of his argument now took a different direction. Mohl criticized Welcker and the other "old liberals" for their "purely political standpoint" and strongly suggested that their failure had in large measure been self-inflicted. "If the old liberals," wrote Mohl concerning the future, "persist in their predominantly negative tendencies and demands, if they maintain their superstitious faith in the mechanism of the constitutional form and in the power of the spoken word; if they still underestimate the power relationships of the monarchical and aristocratic interests [and] *disregard the demands of the lowest and most numerous classes* ... they will have little prospect of a future victory." Again, the historical lesson was that in 1848-49 the liberals had fatally damaged their own cause because they obstinately refused to consider the needs of their erstwhile allies.[52]

---

[50] Marlo, 390 ff., 464, 466-469.
[51] Lassalle, *Nachgelassene Briefe,* III, 14.
[52] See above, note 20; Mohl, "Drei deutsche Staatswörterbücher," 252-254 (my italics).

Two of the conservative social thinkers, Stein and Riehl, developed particularly trenchant variations on this theme. Stein summarized his views in the following passage, which is matched only by the work of Friedrich Engels for its contemporary grasp of the situation:

Germany was penetrated by two movements *at the same time*. Consequently, in the individual violent breakthroughs of the progressive elements a mixture of the two elements arose . . . which necessarily weakened the movement as a whole. . . . The national movement, which wants Germany's unity, considered the social movement that was at hand as the subordinate one and spent a good part of its energy in warding it off. The social movement in part scorned and in part mistook the political one and split off from it. Thereby, the best energies of both were broken; and in this relationship lies the true core of the history of the German parliament in Frankfurt. For the national, political movement was – precisely through its aversion to the social one – first weakened, then split, and then overcome. That is the history of that remarkable time.

Stein asserted that the social movements had contributed heavily to the failure of political reform, and in so doing he criticized them. But he also blamed the liberals for having responded negatively to those movements, which he regarded as basically justified in their aims.[53]

Riehl adduced the liberals' failure as prime evidence to support his contention that social issues were the foremost concern of the day. Hopes for a new German constitution had been dashed in 1848-49 because the political parties were "beginning to abandon the field of battle," while the social ones were "holding the flaming torch under the ashes." In other words, the defeat of constitutionalism stemmed in large part from the emergence of the social question. Riehl did not indicate precisely how interest in the social question had worked to the detriment of political liberalism. He seems to have felt in part that threats of social revolution had had a dampening effect on all progressive impulses, just as in France the fear of a social upheaval explained the general acceptance of Louis Napoleon's coup. Riehl brought a social perspective to bear on the failure of liberalism in another way when he asserted that social differences had provided the real basis for the fatal conflict between Austria's supporters and Prussia's. Austria's social structure, he argued, had been too diverse and traditional for those who favored the end of a corporate society. Austria could not have been assimilated into the kind of liberal society that Prussia had started to become as a result of the reforms undertaken

---

[53] Stein, cxxxvi. Engels' analysis of 1848-49, originally published in the *New York Daily Tribune* in 1851-52, appeared in book form as *Germany: Revolution and Counter-revolution* (New York, 1933).

by Stein and Hardenberg at the beginning of century. In any case, Riehl predicted quite emphatically that real opportunities for constitutional politics would not return until after men had made substantial progress in the area of social reform. Recent events showed that a political truce was possible in Germany's political struggles. ". . . In the social ones," Riehl wrote, "there will be no truce, let alone a peace, until long after the grass has grown over our graves and those of our grandchildren." Until such time, the efforts of the constitutionalists would be pointless.[54]

In conclusion, the question inevitably arises, which of these interpretations of recent revolutionary history was the most perceptive and telling, the most adequate as a rendering of historical reality? Some evaluations have been suggested along the way, but the problem of the quality of thought needs to be confronted more directly at this point. There is no question but that the writings of the liberals provided the most detailed account both of the events which had led up to the revolution and of the revolutionary year itself. Moreover, the liberal version of the objectives which had been pursued by the majority of Germans who participated in the revolution is difficult to challenge. The desire to replace bureaucratic police states with a nation state in which administrative and executive power would be more effectively limited by a constitution and a parliament had almost certainly been uppermost in the minds of those who acted out their discontent with the status quo in 1848-49. But that version of the revolution was still rather narrow and one-sided, failing as it did to take any account of the economic hardship which provided much of the impetus behind lower-class dissatisfaction with Germany's prerevolutionary political institutions. At the same time, the liberals consistently underestimated the vital role which men motivated by social and economic grievances had played through their disruptive agitation in forcing Germany's established rulers to turn to the moderates during the March days for support. As for the matter of the revolution's failure, it seems to me that although much of what the liberals had to say was unexceptionable — especially insofar as they pointed to the enormous difficulties which confronted them and the even greater difficulties which stood in the way of establishing a democratic republic — they failed almost wholly to perceive other, perhaps equally important factors. Writers such as Mohl and Stein showed far more insight than Haym, Duncker, and Biedermann in focusing on the vitiating effects of the deep cleavages which separated the liberals from the social movements and caused them to lose the support of ordinary Germans and those who were motivated by the desire to improve their lot.

[54] Riehl, 4-14.

IV

POLITICAL HOPES AND FEARS

Analyses of recent history set the stage for more explicit discussion of the still unsolved political and social problems which confronted Germany in the 1850's. We turn first to the continuing debates in the area of politics, which had already agitated large numbers of intellectuals for two decades before 1848 and still claimed a greater share of most men's attentions during the later period than the emerging social questions. Partly because of external controls, these debates did not include much in the way of a contribution by the radical democrats, but there was considerable argument between liberals and conservatives, who found much ammunition for renewed attacks against one another in the events of 1848-49.

The liberals supported their programs both by pointing to what had happened recently in German public life and by arguing that despite it all very little had really changed. Their feelings that significant political reform had failed to take place were rooted in a number of obviously compelling circumstances. Germany was still divided into more than three dozen separate states. In none of the more important ones did elected representative bodies stand on the same footing with the hereditary princes and their bureaucratic servants, who still played far and away the leading role in public affairs. Repressive bureaucratic controls still remained in force in many areas; for instance, the right of association was quite generally subjected to severe limitation from above. Landed nobles exercised great power within the upper houses of state legislatures, and in many rural regions they still dominated the institutions of local government and controlled the only police forces.

Much of what had happened in recent German history only strengthened the liberals in their belief that basic changes in these institutions and practices had to be brought about. Even though the princely powers had finally regained the upper hand, they had been badly shaken during both the opening and the closing months of the year of revolution. Consequently, as one observer put it, men could now see "how brittle an organism the old administration had become." The outbreaks of radicalism in such places as Berlin and Baden suggested to some liberals that Germany was standing at the edge of a chaotic abyss; they demonstrated to almost all liberals the glaring inadequacies of the old political order. Despite the ultimate suppression of these outbreaks, the mere fact of their occurrence, let alone the fact that they had come as close as they did to success, proved that reform was essential. The liberals wanted to exorcise the radical threat through the establishment of constitutional government at the national level. The cyclical pattern of revolution and reaction would be halted, asserted Karl Biedermann, only after "the victory of the parliamentary system in the individual states and [of] a *parliamentary collective constitution*" for Germany as a whole. Moderate liberal thinking, on both the constitutional and the national issues, had established a clear set of goals which were still to be pursued despite the Frankfurt Parliament's defeat.[1]

The conservatives, although they took pleasure in the failure of the Frankfurt Parliament, often expressed the feeling that all too much had changed. And indeed, political institutions had changed in some cases. Despite the general pattern of reaction, many reforms survived even in Prussia. Although it turned out to be a good deal less liberal after a year of revision than it had appeared it was going to be when first announced in December of 1848, a constitution did remain in force. This document provided for an elected legislature which at least in theory was to exercise control over the state budget and also to limit the Prussian king's power of promulgating general laws by simple decree. Certain kinds of censorship had been eased, and trial by jury had been introduced. In the countryside, the Junkers had lost patrimonial jurisdiction over the peasants on their estates. The conservatives' sense that their positions had been subjected to an at least partially successful attack and that the assault had threatened to be far more devastating fed their hostility toward the forces not only of the left but also of the center. As we have already seen, the moderate liberals were considered to have opened the gates for the extreme radicals. Many conservatives were therefore all the more de-

---

[1] Duncker, *Zur Geschichte der deutschen Reichsversammlung in Frankfurt,* 107-109; Häusser, *Denkwürdigkeiten zur Geschichte der badischen Revolution,* 1-2, 8-10; Fallmerayer, "Gegenwart und Zukunft," 199-207; Biedermann, "Die Entwickelung des parlamentarischen Lebens in Deutschland," 473.

termined to guard their remaining territory, around which they erected new intellectual defenses.[2]

Several difficulties stand in the way of presenting post-1849 German political thought in an essay of this kind. One stems from the fact that many basic political positions had already been spelled out in the *Vormärz*. Men therefore could frequently indicate their general orientations by referring to arguments which were so familiar that they did not require explicit restatement or by bringing out new editions of earlier works, without engaging in fresh literary creation. Perhaps the clearest example of such a phenomenon was the third edition of Rotteck and Welcker's liberal *Political Lexicon,* which appeared in fifteen volumes starting in 1856. Welcker explicitly proclaimed his firm loyalty to past positions in the preface and the introduction to the first volume.[3] Allegiance to the ideals of the past was expressed even more forcefully by the content of the work as a whole, which consisted largely of articles reprinted from earlier editions.

Another difficulty arises from the growing preference referred to earlier on the part of many men, especially liberals, for a more specifically empirical and less generally theoretical mode of discourse. This tendency poses a real problem for the historian who seeks to extract a coherent body of intelligible doctrine from the multitude of individual statements on specific issues. The problem confronts us in typical fashion in the work which most nearly performed during the two postrevolutionary decades the functions which the *Political Lexicon* had performed during the two prerevolutionary ones. Johann Caspar Bluntschli's *German Political Dictionary*, which overtook its predecessor in popularity, resembled the work of Rotteck and Welcker in its scope and in its subject matter, but it was much less explicitly argumentative. It was a compilation, much more reportorial in nature than the *Political Lexicon*. Although its articles contained political opinions, the work did not offer itself in any obvious way as a political tract. This was hardly surprising, inasmuch as Bluntschli avowedly preferred a mode of reasoning standing midway between "abstract-ideological" and "merely empirical" thought, an historical rather than a speculative approach to politics. Nevertheless, general political persuasions were already implicit in historical judgments about the revolution and they could be discerned as well amidst the welter of comments about matters of detail during the decade of the 1850's.[4]

[2] See Stahl, *Die Philosophie des Rechts,* II, part I, v-xxx.
[3] Welcker, "Vorwort zur dritten Auflage des Staats-Lexikons," and "Abc, politisches."
[4] Bluntschli, *Allgemeines Staatsrecht,* 15-19, and *Denkwürdiges aus meinem Leben,*

ARGUMENTS OVER THE DISTRIBUTION OF
POWER WITHIN THE STATE

Even though the national issue, as we shall see later, continued in this period to assume increased importance, questions concerning the internal structure of the state remained very much alive. The proper distribution of political power between princely sovereigns and their subjects, among bureaucrats, noblemen, ordinary citizens endowed with education or property, and the common masses was still a subject of great concern. It figured just as prominently in political writing as did the national question.

One senses in the political writings of several liberals a real fascination with power, a heightened respect for success which had doubtless been stimulated by the liberals' own lack of success and has often been strongly emphasized by later historians. This sentiment, which we shall encounter again when discussing the national issue, sometimes seemed in discussions of internal politics to imply that the assertion of right against might was meaningless. It appeared in turn to militate against the advocacy of any political change at all. But two points need to be added: the liberals who displayed this fascination, while often quite vocal, were relatively few in number; and even these men set forth the familiar liberal demands that greater political power should be given to the educated and propertied middle classes.

The most extended and notorious paean to power appeared in August Ludwig von Rochau's *Principles of Realpolitik*. Modern political theorists, he wrote, had not understood that power was essential in order to rule, and this error had contributed heavily to the failures of constitutionalism throughout Europe in recent years. Who *ought* to rule was a question for speculative philosophy. Rochau's concern was to demonstrate that only those who had power *could* rule. "To rule," he wrote, "is to exercise power, and he alone can exercise power who possesses it." Furthermore, it was irrational to demand that power should be subject to law. Power could only submit to greater power; it could not be ruled by weakness, even if it wished to be. Scorning the "castles in the air" of the political system-builders, he reminded his readers that existing po-

II, 109, 219; see also his article on "Doktrinarismus." Robert von Mohl compared Bluntschli's and Welcker's encyclopedias in his "Drei deutsche Staatswörterbücher." See Hans Zehntner, *Das Staatslexikon von Rotteck und Welcker* (Jena, 1929), 97-98, on the relative popularity of the two works. See Droysen, *Briefwechsel*, I, 774, for advocacy of a "practical" instead of a "transcendental" approach to politics.

litical power had only tolerated "defenseless right" at its own convenience. In his view, the constitution of the state was determined by the changing relationships of the various forces within it. "Each social force," he wrote, "has a claim to a political position which corresponds to its extent, and the strength of the state consists simply of the social forces which the state has incorporated into itself." The correct constitution for any state would have to accord each social force a degree of political influence commensurate with the strength it already possessed. To suppress politically a rising social group – or try prematurely to drive out of power a declining one – would only do harm to the state itself. Some of Rochau's remarks strongly suggested that he viewed success as its own justification – or at least that he viewed failure as sufficient cause for contempt. This sentiment was always implicit in his assumption that "real life" would inevitably win out over a false constitution. It was also implicit in the way he lapsed into using the word "*Macht*" at times when one expects him to have used the work "*Kraft.*" Rochau wanted to distinguish between political "power" and social "strength," the second being the prerequisite for the first, but in practice he seemed to be saying that power was the prerequisite for power – an apparent tautology but a significant turn of phrase nevertheless. To put it another way, political success often seemed to be the very criterion according to which social strength itself was evaluated. Moreover, the most important standard by which to judge the worth of a revolution was whether or not it succeeded.[5] But Rochau did not display the quietist acceptance of the world as it existed which his rhetoric seemed to imply. He in fact made some of the most forceful statements of the liberal case for a restructuring of the state's internal organization.

The liberals had no desire to do away entirely with monarchical prerogatives, but they did seek to limit them. Rochau asserted that the maintenance of absolute royal power in Germany would necessarily cripple all the capacities which made for a people's greatness: patriotism, pride, and self-confidence all suffered under absolutism. For a nation such as Germany, he asserted, a share in the exercise of political power was as necessary as water to a fish and air to a bird. Karl Welcker regarded the generally laudable performance of the Frankfurt Parliament as proof that the German people could accept the responsibilities entailed by representative government, and he implicitly supported the notion that

[5] Rochau, *Grundsätze der Realpolitik*, 2-7, 19, 21, 35 (see also his remarks about the coup by Louis Napoleon, on 208) ; see also Droysen, "Preussen und das System der Grossmächte," 222, and Rössler, *System der Staatslehre*, 408, 538-540.

ministers should be responsible to an elected assembly. Proposals for ministerial responsibility to parliament were seldom spelled out in detail. Often one cannot be sure whether a man who advocated such responsibility meant that royally appointed ministers would be accountable to parliament for the constitutional legality of their conduct or whether he really wanted the government to be dependent on a parliamentary majority for its existence. But when men like Rudolf Haym spoke in glowing terms of the constitution written by the Frankfurt Parliament, holding it up as an example for later political reformers to follow, in effect they supported the latter notion: although the constitution had not been entirely clear on this whole matter, it had envisioned a close working relationship between ministers and parliamentary representatives.[6]

A rather conservative liberal, Johann Caspar Bluntschli, while insisting that historical conditions militated against the lasting displacement of royal power and that the bulwark of kingship was needed in order to maintain public security, nevertheless sharply criticized the existing realities of monarchical and bureaucratic government. He demanded that the monarchy should be constitutional, acting only according to the law, which it could not proclaim alone. He had a sense of real uneasiness about the Prussian constitution which had been granted in 1849, and he strongly opposed the conception of governmental absolutism, which failed to do justice to any highly developed people's sense of dignity. The perfection of civilization in the future would necessitate the elimination of force as a primary instrument of rule. The ultimate goal, he suggested, might well resemble England's representative constitution, "the noblest . . . form of political organization." Bluntschli also supported traditional liberal positions by criticizing administrative centralization, and by asserting that the present danger of succumbing to mere bureaucratic routine was far more ominous than any threat of overly liberal "doctrinairism."[7]

The liberals did not simply advocate restrictions on monarchical and bureaucratic power. They were also anxious to limit the political power of the landed nobility and the great "masses" of the German people. This

[6] Rochau, "Absolutismus," 85; Welcker, "Vorwort," xxv-xxvi. See Ernst Rudolf Huber, *Deutsche Verfassungsgeschichte*, II (2nd ed., Stuttgart, 1968), 827-829, on the provisions of the Frankfurt Parliament's constitution which bore on this problem. See Otto Pflanze, "Juridical and Political Responsibility in Nineteenth-Century Germany," in Leonard Krieger and Fritz Stern, eds., *The Responsibility of Power* (New York, 1967), for general analysis of the issue.

[7] Bluntschli: "Demokratie," 711-712; *Allgemeines Staatsrecht*, 232-242, 256; "Absolute Gewalt," 8-12; "Civilisation," 515; "Bürgerstand," 306-307; "Doktrinarismus," 161.

desire appeared in a variety of contexts: occasionally in social analysis but more often in discussions of the criteria for promotion to high office within the state bureaucracy, of the proper ways to organize the representative bodies which were to limit royal and ministerial autonomy, of the suffrage which ought to obtain in electing these bodies, and of government at the local as well as at the national level. In all of these writings one can detect basic liberal criticisms both of those who stood above them and of those who stood below them in the social hierarchy.

The nobility was viewed as a useless holdover from an earlier age. Rochau contended that as their economic fortunes declined the Junkers had lost everything which might formerly have given them a claim to political power. As a result, he believed, the conservative political principles to which they adhered could now be maintained only through force. They were unable to rely on a belief among the people that their authority deserved to be obeyed, and this in turn meant that their position was untenable. Gustav Freytag's widely read novel, *Debit and Credit,* portrayed the aristocrats as members of an estate that was culturally as well as economically bankrupt. Treitschke referred to the Junkers as a "morally outmoded estate" and then went on to denigrate their capabilities for managing the business of government.[8]

Opposition to noble power at the highest level of the state was evident in attacks by men like Karl Arnd and Theodor von Bernhardi on the estatist principle of representation, according to which social groups rather than geographical districts formed the basic constituencies. Such criticisms were of course motivated by considerations which went well beyond the status of the nobility. At their center lay the liberal view of the legislator as the disinterested advocate of the general welfare rather than the special pleader for a particular interest. But these strictures militated particularly against the preponderant noble power which so often resulted when the estatist principle was applied.[9]

An even more pervasive line of attack against the political position of the nobility grew out of liberal polemics concerning government at the local level. Heinrich von Sybel strongly condemned the German nobility's insistence on claiming nearly absolute power in this area. Its members had failed in his view to assume anything like the broad civic responsibility demonstrated by the English aristocracy in state affairs, opting

---

[8] Rochau, *Grundsätze der Realpolitik*, 47-52, 127-130; Freytag, *Soll und Haben,* trans. by L. C. C. as *Debit and Credit* (New York, 1858); Treitschke, *Briefe*, I, 348.
[9] Arnd, *Die Staatsverfassung nach dem Bedürfniss der Gegenwart*, 308-315; Bernhardi, "Unsere Verfassung im Sinn der extremen und im Sinn der gemässigten Parteien," 192.

instead for an indefensible assertion of unlimited prerogatives within the counties where they lived and on the estates which they owned. The most famous attack of the period against noble power at the local level appeared in Rudolf Gneist's lengthy study of contemporary administrative practice in England, with its many favorable remarks on the justices of the peace, which was generally regarded as a mirror held up to the Prussian administrative system. What the writings of Sybel and Gneist, and many other men as well, all maintained was that the attempt "to institute a small caricature of the whole state" on one's own land was unjust and anachronistic. The remnants of patrimonial jurisdiction and hereditary noble control over local branches of the state administration would have to go.[10]

At the same time that they mounted their offensive against the powers of the hereditary landed nobility, the liberals were equally and perhaps even more anxious to deny the incipient political claims of other social groups as well. Liberals were becoming consciously antidemocratic in a way that they had not been before the revolution. Then, they had simply assumed that the suffrage would be limited. Now they were much more explicit in arguing that it had to be.

The liberals' arguments against political power for the "masses," or the "fourth estate (two of the terms they frequently used to denote those below them on the social ladder) sometimes centered on the dangers of incompetence in government if the lower classes were permitted either to hold political offices or to choose others for such positions. Bluntschli felt that manual laborers clearly lacked the capacity to administer state offices; at best, some of them might be capable of service at the local level. He argued that they needed someone to protect their interests in a legislature, but that they should certainly not play a prominent part in the electoral process whereby popular representatives were chosen. Bluntschli, like many others, wanted to make sure that "those with the best attributes and insight" would be chosen. For this purpose, mere numbers alone could not be allowed to decide the issue: wealth, education, and professional standing had to be given their due in the electoral process too. Placing ultimate power in the hands of the lower classes, he warned, "gives to the feet the position of the head and to the latter the position of the feet." Such an arrangement was obviously unthinkable.

---

[10] Sybel, "Die christlich-germanische Staatslehre," 20-22; Gneist, *Das heutige englische Verfassungs- und Verwaltungsrecht*. Gneist's work is discussed in Heinrich Heffter, *Die deutsche Selbstverwaltung im 19. Jahrhundert* (Stuttgart, 1950), 372-403 and in Charles E. McClelland, *The German Historians and England* (Cambridge, Eng., 1971), 135-144.

Similarly, Rochau chastised the democrats for their naive belief that the proletariat could participate fully in the normal management of the state: it might sometimes overthrow a despotic regime (and the events or 1848-49 had shown that it could do even that only temporarily), but it could not build and conduct a working government of its own.[11]

Other sentiments also lay behind the liberal rejection of democracy. Bluntschli dreaded "the bad qualities in the mass ... arrogance, flightiness, immoderation, the seeking after continued and vain innovation, arbitrariness, rawness." Haym rejected the notion of "rule by those without insight or interests, by the corruptible and revolutionary masses." What Bluntschli's and Haym's remarks reveal is the pervasive fear that the realization of democratic principles in politics would lead to a form of tyranny exercised over the better elements by their inferiors, which would in turn lead to confiscatory economic measures directed against the well-to-do by the poor.[12]

Liberals had yet another reason for opposing universal suffrage. They genuinely feared not only that the lower classes might be seduced by radical agitators, but also, paradoxically, that they might fall prey to authoritarian conservatives. Waitz expressed this feeling when he spoke the following words in the Frankfurt Parliament: "These people [the masses] are exposed to all influences, now perhaps more to those of the demagogues in the popular sense, so that elections could bring very liberal results. But soon the time of calm and relaxation will come, and then these people will elect those who are the most servile." The traditional subservience of the peasantry to its Junker landlords – which seemed highly likely to continue under conditions of public balloting – provided an obvious danger at home. In France, as Biedermann pointed out, the "combination of universal suffrage with the most absolute despotism" had already emerged as a result of the election in 1848 of Louis Napoleon.[13]

Liberal criticism of royal absolutism, noble privilege, and popular democracy was accompanied by strong advocacy of greater political power for the middle levels of society – variously referred to as the "middle classes," the "middle estate," the "third estate," or the *"Bürgerstand."* Possessing property and education, the groups denoted by these

[11] Bluntschli, *Allgemeines Staatsrecht,* 94-97, 182-183, 337; Rochau, *Grundsätze der Realpolitik,* 162, 212-213.

[12] Bluntschli, *Allgemeines Staatsrecht,* 175; Haym, *Die deutsche Nationalversammlung,* II, 295; see also Arnd, 293-299.

[13] Waitz is quoted in Walter Gagel, *Die Wahlrechtsfrage in der Geschichte der deutschen liberalen Parteien, 1848-1918* (Düsseldorf, 1958), 9; Biedermann, "Demokratie," 346; see also Rochau, *Grundsätze der Realpolitik,* 84.

terms were seen by the liberals as deserving a far greater say in political affairs than they then possessed. Again, Bluntschli represents the conservative end of the liberal spectrum. He argued that as a result of their education the members of the third estate were prone to "doctrinairism," that they were easily led away from realities by abstract ideas, and that this tendency disqualified them from exercising the primary responsibility in matters of state. But he also praised the third estate as the bearer of national culture and stressed its capacity for criticizing legislation and fulfilling certain administrative offices. Other intellectuals were much less ambiguous in their praise. Freytag joined his denigration of "nobles and mere bondsmen" with a view of the urban middle class as the essential prerequisite for the development of culture, civilization, and progress. Treitschke, who recognized education as a primary element of political power, specifically defended the political capabilities of professors. Finally, Welcker found his faith in the middle classes confirmed by the course of the radical revolution. He argued that the revolution's failure had resulted from their unwillingness to support it and had thus proved once again that they were "the core and strength of the nation." [14]

To conclude this discussion of the liberals' high esteem for the middle classes, let us return to Rochau's treatise on *Realpolitik*. The real point of Rochau's political advocacy was to make an aggressive claim on behalf of the "middle estate," a group which in his view could no longer be denied the right to participate in a system of representative government. In the same breath that he pointed to the economic decline of the Junkers, he heralded such new forces as "the civic consciousness, the idea of freedom, the national spirit, the idea of equal human rights," all of which had to receive their due. In his opinion, these ideas demanded recognition not because they were ethically superior but because they were widely supported and because the men who believed in them possessed the most vital elements of social strength: wealth, intelligence, and education, which counted for far more in Rochau's eyes than either hereditary titles or mere numbers. The middle estate was an inevitable bearer of and key to political power, its abundant possession of those attributes which made for influence in society dictating that it must enjoy a commensurate role in the process of government.[15]

It bears emphasis that although Rochau sometimes appeared (as in his comments on the fortunes of the Junkers) to regard economic superiority

[14] Bluntschli, "Dritter Stand," 178-181; Freytag, *Debit and Credit*, 125, 173; Treitschke, *Die Gesellschaftswissenschaft*, 33-34, and *Briefe*, I, 103, 105; Welcker, "Vorwort," xxiii.
[15] Rochau, *Grundsätze der Realpolitik*, 10-12, 24, 211-213.

as the crucial element of social and hence political strength this was by no means the whole story. The middle estate's self-assertiveness was based in his view on its "ideal" as well as on its material accomplishments: its intelligence and its education. He fully recognized that this group was distinguished just as much by *Bildung* (education) as by *Besitz* (property), and he insisted that the former as well as the latter underlay its growing political claims. Just as he stressed that widely held ideas (as opposed to the concoctions of isolated theorists) would inevitably exercise an enormous political influence whether they were correct or not, so too he felt that men who possessed the ability to comprehend and express ideas could not be denied an important share of political power.[16]

One is frequently struck in liberal political writings of this period not only by criticisms of the established powers but also – as in Bluntschli's case – by willingness to leave considerable prerogatives in royal hands. Many liberals were quite adamant that although they wished to limit royal power they by no means wished to eliminate it. Such sentiments might appear to represent a reaction against the events of 1848-49. But it is important to note that these feelings did not really vary in substance from the assumptions of most pre-1848 liberal thinking. The liberals had seldom disputed the monarch's right to veto legislation, to appoint his own ministers, and to conduct foreign affairs. Similarly, the revolutions appear to have stimulated the liberals' aversions to sharing political power with the common man, but one ought to remember that the liberals had never been real democrats in the first place.

By way of conclusion, two changes among the liberals need to be mentioned. One aspect of the pre-1848 situation which does not seem to have persisted into the later period was the separation of the liberals into a primarily constitutional group of northerners who admired the English and a more parliamentary group of sympathizers with France who were located in the South. Such a distinction can only be made in qualified fashion for the *Vormärz*, but it does have some utility. It becomes much more difficult for the period after 1848-49 to draw neat lines of this sort. One reason for this change lay in the fact the French had been pretty thoroughly discredited everywhere in liberal circles. The sequence of bloody social revolution and then another Bonapartist dictatorship suggested to many liberals that Frenchmen were incorrigibly corrupt and

[16] *Ibid.*, 28-29. Leonard Krieger's discussion of Rochau in *The German Idea of Freedom* (Boston, 1957), 356, underestimates Rochau's arguments for the middle class on the basis of its education, making the argument out to be largely a matter of economics.

hopelessly incapable of sound political action.[17] Moreover, German political realities were much less variegated than formerly. Prussia had
officially joined the ranks of the constitutional states, even if her rulers
did not always act constitutionally. As the bastions which the liberals
attacked became less dissimilar, so too their own programs for political
reform varied less from one region of the country to another.

One other change is particularly worthy of note. Owing not only to
the granting of a constitution in Prussia but also to the introduction there
of public judicial procedure and of jury trials and to the easing of censorship everywhere, liberals seem to have become less concerned with the
protection of civil rights.[18] Of course, the rights of the individual were
still far from secure in most German states, and some men did feel
compelled to defend them. Bluntschli advocated the individual's right to
freedom from bodily attack and to freedom of movement, of speech, and
of assembly, while Karl Arnd argued that open political discussion was
essential for progress in every area of human existence.[19] The reaction
notwithstanding, however, there had been enough improvement with
regard to civil rights so that the pursuit of these rights seemed less urgent
than before. In any case, other matters had come to the fore. When
talking about constitutional issues, men therefore turned increasingly to
the subject of government in the stricter sense of the term. As protection
of individual freedom from government assumed decreased importance,
the major constitutional questions concerned the right to participate in
the political process.

One current of opposition to these liberal arguments for a *juste milieu*
came from the radical democrats, who criticized both the liberals' willingness to compromise with the established political powers and their eagerness to restrict the political influence wielded by the common man. In
his private correspondence, Georg Gottfried Gervinus repeatedly proclaimed his radical republicanism and his bitter disdain for liberal moderation. He expressed his radicalism most forcefully late in 1850 in a letter
to Rudolf Haym. The letter asserted that the correct path to tread in
Germany was the one leading toward a republic. Only in this way could
all the energies of the country – including its "physical" ones (i.e., the
masses) – be united in a common effort. These forces, he believed, could

[17] See Duncker, "Die neuere Geschichte Frankreichs," a warmly favorable review
of Rochau, *Geschichte Frankreichs*. More generally, see Heinz-Otto Sieburg, *Deutschland und Frankreich in der Geschichtsschreibung des neunzehnten Jahrhunderts, 1848-
1871* (Wiesbaden, 1958).
[18] See above, Chapter I, note 25, on censorship; see Huber, III (Stuttgart, 1963),
101-112, 121-126, on basic rights and on the courts in post-1850 Prussia.
[19] Bluntschli, *Allgemeines Staatsrecht*, 667-671; Arnd, 42.

not be appealed to by the monarchy or by constitutionalism, but three quarters of them could be won over by the call for a republic, and the rest could be frightened into going along. In his opinion even those men who supported the constitutional monarchy as an article of faith would find it possible to join in, since they could view the republic as a means to an end. "For it has not yet been shown," he argued, "that an absolutist dynasty has ever made a sincere transition to constitutionalism ... without having gone through the purgatory of a republic and revolution." The question for the present was "whether those who until now have been constitutionalists insist on being so principled, so conscientious, so doctrinaire, so loyal, so moral, [and] on remaining true to themselves and the tendencies they have championed up till now, or whether they [will] let themselves be led by the *summa lex* of political sense, whether they will be political enough to seize the only opportunity still remaining." The greatest service Haym could render would be to abandon moderation and tell the nation that its rulers were beyond redemption.[20] Although in this particular letter Gervinus seemed to argue for republicanism primarily as a means to an end rather than as an end in itself, it is important to remember that he was writing to a liberal. As we saw earlier, he firmly believed in political democracy as the welcome destiny toward which all Europe was moving.

Other writers proclaimed democratic principles more elaborately, defending the pursuit of popular sovereignty in philosophical as well as tactical terms. In 1849, just before his departure for England, Arnold Ruge set forth his democratic credo. "Now," he wrote, "we want to be free; there should be no more masters and no more servants." In a despotism, the people did what the government willed, acting as the unwilling subject. But under a democratic constitution, the only one worthy of free men, the people would do what they themselves willed, serving no one. The men who handled their affairs would be regarded as managers, subject to recall, not as masters. "The principle of the world that is coming to an end," he wrote, "is the *service* of subjected and violently suppressed men, [but] the principle of the new one [is] *the free community* and the working together of *self-determining men, who are equal comrades in everything*." Heinrich Bernhard Oppenheim clearly echoed Ruge, his former editorial colleague, when he summarized the basic principle for which he stood in the following terms. "The *essence*

[20] Eduard Ippel, ed., *Briefwechsel zwischen Jakob und Wilhelm Grimm, Dahlmann und Gervinus*, II (Berlin, 1886), 101-102, 327-328, 415; Haym, *Ausgewählter Briefwechsel*, 121-123.

of democracy is that there should be as little rule *from on high* as possible, that the will of each individual should be subjected to the will of others as seldom as possible and [then] only as a result of the most basic common needs." The rule of law was not to be eliminated, but political inequality would have to go.[21]

Despite their avowed radicalism, men like Gervinus, Ruge, and Oppenheim hardly offered a real alternative to liberal doctrine. Gervinus, who had been a moderate in the *Vormärz,* arrived at and the others reiterated certain general political ideas which diverged sharply enough from the tenets of liberalism. But they had little to say about the details of government and certainly wrote nothing comparable to the liberals' reflections on the relative political capabilities of society's various component groups. Moreover, very few other intellectuals supported them.

Given the weakness of the democrats, the major alternative to liberalism lay in the political thinking of the conservatives. Like the liberals, the spokesmen for the forces of postrevolutionary reaction reiterated many of their earlier ideas. For instance, in the preface to the third edition of his influential *Philosophy of Law* Friedrich Julius Stahl boasted that the course of recent history had not led him to deny anything he had written earlier. Nevertheless, the work did contain extensive revisions, by means of which Stahl sought to relate his broadly theoretical ideas to the experience of revolution. Contemporary upheaval not only forced conservatives to reaffirm those political arrangements and attitudes which stood in sharp contrast to their revolutionary opposites, but also enabled them to supply old arguments with a renewed and more specific thrust.[22]

The basic political principle which the conservatives set against the demands of both the liberals and the democrats was that of legitimacy. In Stahl's words, this principle implied "respect for the existing legal order and authority," which were a "dispensation from God." The existing element in the political order which men had to cherish above all others was kingship, which putatively deserved respect both because it was part of a divinely ordained status quo and for other reasons too. The state had to have a center of political activity to co-ordinate its various organs, and for Stahl this function could best be performed by a monarch.

---

[21] Ruge, *Die Gründung der Demokratie in Deutschland,* 3-5; Oppenheim, "Zur Kritik der Demokratie," 24-27.

[22] Stahl, *Die Philosophie des Rechts,* II, part I, v. See Sigmund Neumann, *Die Stufen des preussischen Conservatismus* (Berlin, 1930), 105-106, on Stahl in relation to other conservatives. Although some of them criticized him for being too liberal, he was certainly the leading spokesman for the reaction in Prussia. See William O. Shanahan, *German Protestants Face the Social Question* (Notre Dame, 1954), 241-254, for a summary of his ideas.

Stahl stated that strong monarchical power was especially needful during
a time of "chaotic movements" by the people, such as the mid-nineteenth
century: at such times, only a "strong center" could maintain order and
save society from utter destruction. Arthur Schopenhauer asserted that
because the great majority of men were "egoistic, unjust, inconsiderate,
deceitful, even malicious, and in addition equipped with very little intelligence," the need arose for "a fully nonresponsible power concentrated
in one man, itself standing over the law and justice, before which everyone bows down, and which is regarded as a being of a higher kind, a
ruler by the grace of God." Whereas the liberals usually admitted
monarchy's utility, the conservatives proclaimed it. Kings, it was felt,
stood above narrow partisan interests and could therefore be expected to
mediate conflicts among them. They were seen as being ideally suited for
maintaining the domestic tranquillity which Germany so badly needed.[23]
    A number of Catholic publicists upheld royal prerogatives from an-
other perspective when they argued that strong monarchical power was
not incompatible with individual freedom but instead consistent with and
even conducive to such freedom. Sometimes they simply denied that the
basis and distribution of governmental authority in any way affected the
individual citizen's personal liberty, in which case they opted for the
system of rule which seemed to promise the greatest efficiency, namely
a government directed by a hereditary king. But some men went farther,
contending that a strong monarchy helped to foster freedom: although it
might limit the scope of free activity quite narrowly, it protected individual liberty within the sphere of private life. Conversely, popular sovereignty was decidedly harmful to such freedom. Popular rule was always
tyrannical, asserting itself far and wide. Moreover, it could take shape
only through party government, and as a result every citizen would either
belong to the ruling party or face the prospect of being persecuted by that
party.[24]
    General apologias for royal power of the sort made by Stahl, Schopen-
hauer, and many of the Catholic publicists led to substantial claims on
behalf of monarchical government. Some conservatives, like Viktor Aimé

---

[23] Stahl, *Die Revolution und die constitutionelle Monarchie,* 18-19, 26, 108;
Schopenhauer, *Parerga und Paralipomena,* II, 269; see also Erdmann, *Philosophische
Vorlesungen über den Staat,* 168.
    [24] "Scheinfreiheit und wahre Freiheit, rechte und falsche Souverainetät" (anon.),
HPB, XXVII (1851), 305-310; "Frankfurt und Deutschland, die Grundrechte und
der bayerische Adressensturm" (anon.), *HPB,* XXIII (1849), 495; "Beiträge zur
Anatomie und Physiologie des doctrinären Liberalismus" (anon.), *HPB,* XXIII
(1849), 104; "Die Volkssouverainetät" (anon.), *HPB,* XXIII (1849), 806-807;
"Republik und Freiheit" (anon.), *HPB,* XXVII, (1851), 67.

Huber, adamantly rejected all legal constraints on the king's freedom of action in matters of state, even the self-imposed ones contained in the Prussian constitution of 1850.[25] Others, like Stahl, admitted that monarchical discretion should be clearly circumscribed both by representative "estates" and by written law,[26] but they went on nevertheless to mark out quite a broad area within which the king would continue to exercise ultimate authority. Stahl, for instance, demanded that the king retain an absolute veto over any laws passed by the legislature and complete power to appoint his ministers, who would in no way depend on a parliamentary majority for their continuation in office. Moreover, the king's government was not to be denied budgetary appropriations unless the reasons for the denial were purely financial: parliament would not be permitted to withhold money as a way of punishing executives of whom it disapproved. The distinction between the two kinds of motivation was of course so difficult to apply in practice that Stahl's requirement in effect vitiated any real parliamentary control over the budget. Johann Eduard Erdmann, who shared most of Stahl's ideas, repeated all of these prescriptions. In addition, he pointed to the need for monarchical control in the whole area of military and foreign affairs.[27]

Although conservatives were united in defending the king's prerogatives in matters of state, they frequently sought to restrict the scope of state activity as a whole. Lorenz von Stein's praise of the bureaucratic monarchy, which was strongly reminiscent of what Hegel had written on the subject over thirty years earlier, found few echoes among other conservative intellectuals.[28] They might urge that within certain legally defined boundaries royal power should be absolute or even that it should not be limited by any constitutional restraints whatsoever at the top of the body politic, but they wished to preserve substantial spheres of autonomy at the bottom. Constantin Frantz summarized his typically conservative views on the matter as follows:

Decentralization is thus the generally felt need, which cannot, however, be satisfied by a hierarchy of officials but instead only by a refusal of the state power to interfere inappropriately in communal and corporate affairs. Only in this way can an effective guarantee of freedom be attained, which men seek in vain in the mechanism of the state power. It is instead a matter of

---

[25] Huber, *Bruch mit der Revolution und Ritterschaft,* 12-13.
[26] Stahl, *Die Revolution und die constitutionelle Monarchie,* 20, 76, 93, and *Die Philosophie des Rechts,* II, part II, 137.
[27] Stahl, *Die Revolution und die constitutionelle Monarchie,* 67, 89, 94, 101; Erdman, 171-187.
[28] Stein, *Geschichte der sozialen Bewegung in Frankreich,* III, 16 ff.

ensuring that there are many vital areas of life into which the state power does not reach.[29]

Arguments against bureaucratization appeared most strikingly in the writings of those conservatives who, like Frantz, took a particular interest in social questions. As the quotation from Frantz suggests and as we shall see in more detail later, they were often joined in the thinking of such men with pleas for the retention or the refounding of a corporate social and economic order. But from a political perspective they also formed an integral part of conservative efforts to defend the governmental prerogatives of the hereditary nobility.

The hereditary nobles were the other element in the political status quo besides the monarchs which merited the special solicitude of conservatives. More particularly, one encounters frequent praise of the landed nobility. One author lauded their political virtues in typically conservative fashion when he wrote the following:

The estate of the great [hereditary] landowners is the only one ... which without work or speculation and without being concerned to increase its acquisitions can maintain its wealth. It alone is therefore free from profit-seeking and pointed toward the higher concerns of its own refinement and of the public interests. ... The continuity of possession in the same families is the precondition ... for effecting solidarity of the estate and a corporate spirit, without which it [the estate] has no political significance. ... It also contains an ethical impulse: an elevation of attitudes through inherited political virtue and also, in the case of a highly developed public life, through an inherited political tendency.

One particular trait which this author felt the German nobles had cultivated was support for the princes of the states in which they lived. Stahl shared this view. He contended that the Prussian monarchy could always count on the allegiance of the East Elbian landed aristocracy, whose attitudes toward royalty he sharply differentiated from those of the French nobility in the eighteenth century. The French nobles, he pointed out, had opposed the kings, but the Prussian ones had remained essentially loyal. Both in return for their support and in order to help them render it again in the future, the Junkers were to retain a strategic share of the places in the national representative bodies and a preponderant share of local administrative power in the areas where they lived. Stahl insisted that in the upper and lower chambers of the Prussian Diet and in the countryside the rural nobility should enjoy a political position which was fully commensurate with its great social prestige. More specifically, he advocated various efforts to revise the constitution in a reactionary sense

[29] Frantz, *Vorschule zur Physiologie der Staaten,* 309.

during the first half of the 1850's. These efforts led in 1853 to new legislation concerning local government, which returned many of the powers the nobles had lost several years earlier, and to the reorganization of the upper chamber of the Prussian Diet in 1854, as a result of which it became largely a hereditary and royally appointed house of peers.[30]

While they upheld the political prerogatives of the traditional landed elites, the conservatives resisted the claims made by the liberals on behalf of the middle classes. The political capacities demonstrated by two important segments of this broad middle part of society drew particular criticism from the conservatives. One of these comprised intellectuals, especially scholars. In Erdmann's view, even though men needed education and insight in order to help select legislative representatives, professors did not make good statesmen. German professors, he charged, had shown in 1848-49 that they were not politicians and that they did not understand how to direct the affairs of the state. He compared the relationship between the politician and the academic student of politics to the relationship between the artist and the connoisseur and to that between the builder of machines and the physicist who understood the basic principle according to which the machine worked. Many professors seemed to be suited for *Politik* if the term meant political knowledge, but not if it meant the art of governing. Similarly, Frantz asserted that the scholar always seemed alien to the common man in a way which rendered him far less effective politically than a great soldier. The other segment of the middle classes which aroused conservative ire comprised the rising economic bourgeoisie, whose social position rested on liquid wealth derived from commerce and industry. One conservative hinted strongly that its members lacked true insight even into their own political interests: they had undermined the old political order in 1848 in such a way as to encourage the very forces which posed the greatest threat to their own wealth. In any case, their insistence on treating the monarchy merely as a "pompous decoration," combined with their selfish insistence on using political power in order to promote purely material interests, clearly made them ineligible for an elevated role in directing the affairs of the state.[31]

The conservatives shared the liberal aversion to universal suffrage. Stahl, for instance, asserted in the upper house of the Prussian Diet that it was unreasonable and unjust to demand elections based on mere

---

[30] "Adels-Theorie und Adels-Reform" (anon.), in *NCL*, I, 383-384; Stahl: *Die Philosophie des Rechts*, II, part II, xix ff., 119; *Die Revolution und die constitutionelle Monarchie*, 38, 44, 54-59; *Parlamentarische Reden*, 172-183, 364-380.

[31] Erdmann, 1-2; Frantz, 261-262; "Bourgeoisie" (anon.), in *NCL*, IV (1860), 364-366.

numbers, since such elections would result in "an intolerable tyranny . . . [of] the propertyless majority." [32] But conservatives did not feel the same degree of compulsion as did the liberals to declaim against the common man. Perhaps they sensed the possibilities of using the masses as a counter-weight against the liberals – a possibility of which the liberals themselves were well aware. In any case, they felt that the greatest threat to their bastions came from men with education and nonlanded property.

Conservatives sought to ensure the proper distribution of political power in a number of ways, some of which have already been referred to. One further constitutional provision which they were likely to recommend deserves separate emphasis: corporate rather than strictly geographical constituencies for elections to the state legislature. Stahl, as in so many cases, made the clearest case for this arrangement. He contended both that there should be an upper house heavily weighted with hereditary and royally appointed notables and that the lower house should be organized so as to represent "real interests." He rejected what he took to be the liberal view that the deputies who sat in such a body should be chosen by undifferentiated agglomerations of individual citizens, lumped together only because they lived in physical proximity to one another and possessed a certain amount of wealth. Elected constituencies ideally coin-cided with identifiable social groups. Moreover, special consideration should be given not only to wealth as such but also to the various forms of wealth, both urban and rural. In the cities and in the countryside, the members of each vocational group should assemble in political guilds in order to determine their collective interests and to select local officials, who in turn would appoint the representatives to the diet. In Stahl's view, one advantage of this procedure was that it would eliminate the agitation which surrounded regular national elections.[33] Stahl did not make the point explicitly, but he might also have argued that this arrangement would help to preserve the political power of the nobles. As the dominant element in a corporately defined group of large landowners, they would exercise far more influence than if they were pitted as individuals against their competitors for political power.

Even though he felt that his electoral proposals would help maintain the political order he supported, Stahl did not feel that they were suf-

---

[32] Stahl, *Parlamentarische Reden,* 166; see also Stahl, *Die Revolution und die con-stitutionelle Monarchie,* 50-56.
[33] *Ibid.,* 56-66; see also Erdmann, 119-123. These proposals did not represent a defense of the status quo in Prussia, where the electorate was subdivided into three economic classes, membership in which depended simply on the amount of taxes paid by the individual.

ficient. No electoral law by itself would assure the preservation of traditional authority. A return to religious piety was also required. "There is," he wrote, "a power, but only *one* power, with which to suppress revolution. *This is Christianity.*" Only Christianity would divert the revolutionary impulse and protect the status quo. "The Christian spirit," he continued, "does not long for an authority which it establishes for itself, for a constitution which it has made itself, for a law which it has discovered with its own reason. It prefers to receive all this from divine governance and is satisfied to contribute its modest share to world history as God has ordained." Catholic conservatives fully shared such views. They felt that in order to avoid a recurrence of the misfortunes that Germany had just experienced it would above all be necessary to make full use of the resources afforded by the Catholic Church. The Church was seen as offering the princes and their governments an essential instrument in their attempts to resist challenges to their authority.[34]

The articulation of conservative political views with reference to the dictates of revealed religion suggests a certain continuity with an older, romantic and mystical, mode of discourse. A strong thread of anti-rationalism can certainly be found among conservative writers during the period – among men who invoked the authority of Christianity and among those who resisted all forms of constitutionalism. And yet Stahl's prominence during these years does indicate an important change which had occurred in much conservative thought since the *Vormärz*. Despite his religiosity, he also sought a coherent institutional basis for government. His influence shows that the center of gravity in conservative thinking had shifted away from purely emotional traditionalism. The liberal challenge had rendered that kind of response alone hopelessly inadequate.

In concluding our discussion of domestic politics, we turn briefly to the men whom I have chosen to call the "social thinkers." To repeat, these men were united not by a shared political ideology but instead by the feeling that problems of an essentially nonpolitical sort had failed to receive proper attention, and they came from a wide variety of political camps. Nevertheless, one idea about the structure of government did recur in the writings of many social thinkers from across quite a broad political spectrum. This was the proposal for corporate representation of social interests rather than of theoretically undifferentiated individuals, a suggestion which quite clearly reflected their dominant social concerns. The idea of corporate representation, as our discussion of Stahl has

[34] Stahl, *Die Revolution und die constitutionelle Monarchie*, 66, and *Was ist die Revolution?*, 15; Phillips, "Kirche oder Revolution?," 420.

indicated, was basic to political conservatism, and it is hardly surprising
to encounter it in the thought of a socially oriented conservative such as
Frantz.[35] But it did not appear simply in conservative literature. It was
also developed by social critics from the center and the left.

One of the most notable exponents of corporatism was Robert von
Mohl, whose demand that governing ministers should be politically responsible to parliamentary majorities marked him unmistakably as a
liberal. Although Mohl advocated parliamentary government, he also
insisted that the members of a representative body which was organized
around purely geographic constituencies would never understand the
particular needs of the state's various social groups. Geographic areas
seldom coincided with the "organic circles of popular life." As a result,
the discussions in parliaments based on such constituencies dealt more
often with the protection of individual rights than with social questions.
The "inorganic assemblies of the present, composed without any regard
to the conditions and needs of society" had played an essential part in
permitting the process of "mere dissolution" which Mohl so greatly
feared, and they would have to be reorganized, so that the "organic
circles" would be truly represented. Mohl sorted out the entities which
were to receive representation under three main headings, depending
upon the particular interests which concerned each of them. There were
groups united by material interests (large and small landholders, industrialists, men of commerce, wage laborers), by intellectual interests
(churches, educational institutions, artists, civil servants), and by interests
arising from geographical proximity (the local communities). All of these
groups were to be represented at every level throughout the state. To use
more modern terminology, Mohl wanted to supplement geographic representation with representation of classes and status groups. Not only the
conservative Frantz but also two other liberals, Immanuel Hermann
Fichte and Heinrich Ahrens, and a democrat, Carl Ludwig Michelet,
echoed Mohl's pleas. The first three proposed the corporate principle as a
substitute for electoral individualism, and the last of these men suggested
it as a supplement. Of course, the specific proposals which men from the
center and the left developed did not favor the traditional social groups
which took pride of place in Stahl's designs. The aim of men like Mohl
(who recognized the danger that his views would falsely be interpreted
as constituting approval of the plans offered by the reactionaries) was
not to preserve ancient hierarchies as a way of bolstering royalty but

[35] See the quotations from Frantz's *Unsere Verfassung* in Eugen Stamm, *Konstantin Frantz' Schriften und Leben, 1817-1856* (Heidelberg, 1907), 210-219.

rather to lay the groundwork for meeting the social needs of a whole host of groups. They hoped that corporate representation would force the public authorities to help secure the well-being of every segment of society, thus facilitating solutions for a wide range of social and economic problems.[36] We shall turn at greater length to Mohl's and other men's analyses of and solutions for these problems in the next chapter. First, however, we must consider the answers men gave to the national questions.

THE NATIONAL QUESTIONS

Debates about the internal structure of the state, while still important, dominated political discourse less after the revolution than they had in the *Vormärz*. The fact that a parliament representing all of Germany had deliberated at Frankfurt for almost a year, only to see the introduction of constitutional government at the national level frustrated by the reigning princes, forced men to devote more attention to the problem of political unity. How desirable was such unity and for what reasons? How should greater national unity be achieved and how far should it extend? These questions could no longer remain subordinate to the so-called "constitutional" ones. Still, the broad positions men took on most of these issues were largely predictable from the positions they took on matters of internal politics. Liberals provided one set of answers, while conservatives offered another.

Many liberals were coming to feel that unification was the foremost need in German public life. Their desire for unity often seemed to represent an alternative to the pursuit of parliamentary or even constitutional government, and thus it might lead them away from liberalism itself. But they still managed – at least in their own minds – to harmonize their growing nationalism with their traditional quest for constitutional reform.

Adherence to the national cause revealed itself most strikingly in the writings of men who were fascinated with power. Even though such fascination by no means precluded a desire for domestic reform (from which liberals expected additional power for the middle classes), it often led to the conclusion that German unity should be pursued before other political objectives at almost any cost. Rochau, Dahlmann, and Treitschke frankly stated their willingness to subordinate the search for freedom to

[36] Mohl, "Das Repräsentativsystem," 181-183, 186-203, 217-218; Fichte, *System der Ethik*, II, part II, xi, 310-313; Ahrens, *Juristische Encyclopädie*, 773-780; Michelet, *Die Lösung der gesellschaftlichen Frage*, 86-88. On the whole question, see Erich Angermann, *Robert von Mohl, 1799-1875* (Neuwied, 1962), 418 ff.

the pursuit of national power. Rochau condemned the far left at the Frankfurt Parliament for its lack of national feeling. He wrote that the left had "failed to understand that nationality is the first and most sacred principle which a people has to defend. It was always ready to sacrifice the unity, the power, and even the honor of Germany . . . to a freedom which – without unity, power, and honor – would at best have a beggarly existence. . . ." Dahlmann had declared in the Frankfurt Parliament during the summer of 1848 that "the path of power" was the only one which would satisfy "the fermenting impulse toward freedom," his belief being that Germans really wanted more of the former than the latter. He reiterated this sentiment in a letter to Gervinus during the 1850's, asserting "that for the Germans power is especially necessary, far more than freedom." He added that he could see no way to attain this power except in concert with the monarchs. National power and republicanism were mutually exclusive. Treitschke was writing in a similar vein when he proclaimed his "radical" attachment to unity. "I consider freedom . . . to be a pure phrase," he wrote, "so long as there is no unified people, the only foundation of any political development. The path which leads the most quickly to this national unity is the one I prefer, even if it should be a despotism." [37]

Whether or not a liberal considered unity more desirable than freedom, he was quite likely to argue that for one or more reasons it was urgently needed. Part of the stimulus for the national movement among liberal intellectuals is suggested in the remarks by Rochau quoted above: liberals continued to maintain, as they had done increasingly in the *Vormärz,* that unity was required in order to make freedom itself secure. They felt that to seek freedom without unity would be self-defeating, since the entrenched rulers of the individual states presented the greatest obstacles to constitutional reform. But there were other motives too, which were less directly related to political liberalism.

For many liberals, nationality and the national state possessed high inherent value in their own right. These sentiments were not all novel in German political discourse, dating back as they did to the early part of the century. But the importance they now assumed relative to the argument according to which national unity served as the underpinning for political freedom indicates a change from the pre-1848 period. "Nationality for a people," Biedermann wrote, "is approximately the

[37] Rochau, "Die verfassunggebende deutsche Reichsversammlung," 177-178; Dahlmann is quoted in S. A. Kaehler, "Realpolitik zur Zeit des Krimkrieges: Eine Säkulärbetrachtung," *HZ,* Vol. 174 (1952), 418; Ippel, II, 412; Treitschke, *Briefe,* I, 260.

same as the family tie is for the individual man." Freytag said much the same thing when he celebrated the accelerating effort during the nineteenth century to create a German national state, praising the folk as the true source of the individual's intellectual and cultural capacities. Droysen's comments on historical method and Constantin Rössler's elaboration of Hegelian political philosophy affirmed at a more highly theoretical level that the national state provided the focal point for all that was best in human existence. "Man," wrote Droysen, "first develops in the ethical collectivities; the ethical forces form him." The highest of these "ethical forces" was the state. For Rössler the essence of the state was "to give men freedom, since freedom is power, the development and unfolding of great energies, not powerless and unproductive independence." Rössler thus sustained the liberal argument that freedom required national power, but he was operating with a different definition of freedom than most other liberals employed. With his Hegelian conception of a "positive" freedom, he asserted not simply that national power, or unity, was necessary for freedom, but also that freedom and power in a very real sense were indistinguishable.[38]

These rhapsodies implied of course that national unity was a good thing in part because it had a beneficial effect on individual character. Rochau made this point explicitly in his discussion of particularism. One of the major disadvantages which he discerned in Germany's multiplicity of sovereign states was the demoralizing effect both of having to bow and scrape before so many "diminutive majesties" and of being confined within the small political units over which these princes ruled. The narrowness of vision and outlook which the small state enforced upon its citizens had, he complained, produced whole generations of small and deformed men. Conversely, a united fatherland would expand men's horizons and accustom them to new and invigorating ideas.[39]

Germans gave several other reasons for nationalism which were independent of political liberalism. Many strongly emphasized a benefit to be derived from unification which had obviously been impressed upon them by their experiences during 1848-49: averting the danger of revolution. The threat from below made a solution of the national question all the more imperative. Rochau's work again provides one of the most convenient ways of getting at the general run of liberal thinking:

---

[38] Biedermann, *Frauen-Brevier,* 306; Freytag, *Bilder aus der deutschen Vergangenheit,* II, 405-408; Droysen, "Grundriss der Historik," 346, 353; Rössler, 376 (also, 1, 201, 206, 210-211).
[39] Rochau, "Die deutsche Kleinstaaterei und ihre Folgen," 119-120.

The reconciliation of two conflicting opinions is furthered by nothing so much as the discovery and cultivation of an interest which they have in common with each other, a third more comprehensive thought in which they are joined. . . . Thus, love of fatherland and national spirit are the natural and indispensable mediators in politically partisan struggles, struggles which the state requires for its higher development but which – without that mediation – regularly end with its decline. When the political bonds which tie the public energies of society together slacken, when all political views, wishes, and strivings proceed in opposing directions, when wild party passion tears the community into bloody fragments, then for those peoples which have not fallen irrevocably into decay there remains as the last force of mediation, of reconciliation, and of agreement the awareness of the obligation to save the national existence.

With more explicit reference to Germany, Rochau argued that the armed forces of the individual German states, which were pursuing a policy at odds with the popular desires of the nation in their effort to uphold particularism, nowhere provided sufficient protection against popular upheaval. A unified country, however, would certainly be able to resist any threats from this quarter.[40]

Other men vigorously supported this line of argument. Karl Friedrich Nebenius pointed out that the conditions of life in small states such as Baden would prove a continual source of discontent and thus serve to facilitate the work of radical agitators. Paul Pfizer also believed that failure to achieve unification would only increase the ranks of the democrats. Their point was essentially that the institutions of a large national state could meet popular desires in a way that those of a small one could not. It was also argued that the large state's institutions would provide greater security in cases where popular dissatisfaction did arise. For instance, one writer emphasized the strict discipline which prevailed in large armies. A long chain of command greatly impressed the common soldier with the need for obedience, which was all the easier for him to render inasmuch as it was also required of his superiors. In other ways too, the large state seemed to possess a degree of stability which made it a far less inviting target for revolutionaries.[41]

The intellectuals could also point to the obvious material benefits that would accrue from the introduction of a common currency, common weights and measures, and all the other economic concomitants of political unity. When they did so, their nationalism was based on economic

---

[40] Rochau, *Grundsätze der Realpolitik,* 14-15, 219, 223-224.
[41] Nebenius, *Baden in seiner Stellung zur deutschen Frage,* 48-49; Pfizer, "Preussen und Oestreich in ihrem Verhältniss zu Deutschland," 16; Eiselen, *Preussen und die Einheitsbestrebungen in Deutschland,* 13-14.

liberalism. Nevertheless, most of them failed to place much emphasis on the possibilities for material progress as a reason for seeking national unity. This line of reasoning appeared in statements made by men who were actively engaged in commerce or industry, but it formed a distinctly subordinate part of the case made by the scholars and publicists. Indeed, even men who did use this argument might feel some embarrassment, as the following quotation indicates:

To be sure, in emphasizing the above-mentioned subjects [the economic benefits of political unity] we are dealing with little more than subordinate interests; nevertheless, these interests cannot be neglected; moreover, the cultivation of these interests is especially suited for binding Germans more closely together. Even if, therefore, one did not feel that these interests were important in their own right, one would still have to recognize them as means toward the unification of Germany, which is required out of other considerations.

The author hoped that economic developments would lay the foundations for political ones, but he ultimately shied away from portraying economic growth as an end in itself.[42]

Another argument had of course to do with the danger of attacks from without. Rochau was especially fearful that Louis Napoleon would be unable to maintain his newly acquired empire unless he continued the traditional French policy of expansion toward the East. Other writers expressed similar anxiety concerning Germany's diplomatic and military position vis-à-vis its more powerful neighbors. And yet – like the thesis that foreign interference had been responsible for the revolution's failure in 1848-49 – pleas for unity based on considerations of national security were voiced a good deal less emphatically than arguments which focused on various aspects of the domestic situation.[43]

When it came to proposing designs for the shape of a unified Germany, there were a few liberals who refused to admit that German Austria could not be included within the new state, but the great majority came out strongly for a *Kleindeutschland* under Prussian leadership.[44] Droysen was especially insistent on this point. Emphasizing the historical oppo-

---

[42] *Ibid.*, 15. Theodore S. Hamerow's works, *Restoration, Revolution, Reaction* (Princeton, 1958) and *The Social Foundations of German Unification, 1858-1871* (2 vols., Princeton, 1969-72), seem to me to place more emphasis than is warranted on economic interests as a source of nationalism.

[43] Rochau, *Grundsätze der Realpolitik*, 216-217; Eiselen, 15-18; Duncker, *Vier Wochen auswärtiger Politik*, 18-19.

[44] For *grossdeutsch* sentiments on the part of liberals, see Fritz Fleiner, ed., *Ein politischer Briefwechsel zwischen Johann Caspar Bluntschli und Wilhelm Wackernagel* (Basel, n. d.), 50-51; see also Wuttke, *Der Stand der deutschen Verfassungsfrage*, 1-26.

sition by multinational Austria to specifically German greatness, he
asserted that the conflicts between Austria and Prussia which had plagued
the attempt to achieve unity in 1848 could only be overcome in one way.
They could not be solved by trying to effect an accommodation between
the two powers, but only by turning decisively to the one German power
which possessed both the interest in and the capabilities for the task of
unification. That power was Prussia, which Droysen saw as having been
entrusted with an historic mission to bind the other German states together
– a mission which arose out of its exemplary achievements in the fields of
education and administration and out of its own needs. Prussia had
supposedly indicated its willingness to undertake this mission for centuries
by pursuing a national policy from the very start, although of course there
had been occasional lapses. In Droysen's view, Prussia's worthiness for
the task had grown during the eighteenth and early nineteenth centuries,
as enlightened reformers put its universities, its armed forces, its finances,
and its bureaucratic apparatus as a whole in good working order. Then
in 1815 the territorial settlements of the Congress of Vienna had defined
the Prussian mission still more sharply. Prussia's various parts were now
spread out across the whole breadth of Germany, from East to West.
As a result, the line of Prussian fortifications was nearly contiguous with
the points where Germany was bordered by France and Russia. Prussia
was thus ideally situated for the purposes of defense. Moreover, its need
for greater territorial cohesion and the objective of German unification
in large measure coincided. One result of Droysen's growing insistence on
these facts was a disappearance of his prerevolutionary demand that
Prussia be dissolved into its historic provinces, so that its influence in a
united Germany would not be too preponderant. Instead, Prussia was
now to be seen as "the old and healthy core of power," whose consoli-
dation would serve not only its own interests but Germany's as well. In
any case, if Prussia was to be won for a role outside her own borders, one
could not realistically ask her to submit to being dismembered.[45]

Other liberal analyses of the national issue echoed most of these arguments. In addition, they suggested further points that militated in Prussia's
favor. Recent history had only fortified the traditional antipathy to

---

[45] Droysen, "Preussen," 213-216, 220, 225; on the Prussian mission, see also the
first volume of Droysen's monumental *Geschichte der preussischen Politik*, 3-5 (on
the work as a whole see Günter Birtsch, *Die Nation als sittliche Idee: Der Nationalstaatsbegriff in Geschichtsschreibung und politischer Gedankenwelt Johann Gustav
Droysens* [Cologne, 1964], 242-248); Droysen, "Zur Charakteristik der europäischen
Krisis," 335-336; see Felix Gilbert, *Johann Gustav Droysen und die preussisch-
deutsche Frage* (Munich and Berlin, 1931), 67, 93, 114-117, on Droysen's change of
attitude concerning the position of Prussia in a new German state.

Austria as a center of political reaction, whereas Prussia at least had a constitution. Men also felt that Austria's need to call on Russia for help in maintaining herself as a state against the national uprisings within her borders had revealed decisively disabling internal weaknesses. Another consideration was economic strength. Prussia's dynanism, which contrasted sharply with Austria's backwardness (as indicated, for instance, by her failure to join the *Zollverein*) also militated in favor of a Prussian solution.[46]

Of course, the liberal expectations of Prussia almost always went hand in hand with great despair over the policies of the Prussian government in the present. After the Manteuffel government gave way to Austrian opposition and set the seal on its abandonment of Radowitz's Prussian Union plan in December of 1850, after Prussia again abandoned the German cause in Schleswig-Holstein, and after the tide of reactionary legislation began to set in at home, Prussia had, as Treitschke put it, done everything it could to lower itself in public esteem. It was not easy, Treitschke lamented, to prove that these disasters were the fault of the present government rather than of the state itself. Treitschke, however, and many others too, insisted on making a distinction between the "momentary" Prussia of the reaction and the "true" Prussia, the Prussia of Frederick the Great, of Stein, and of Hardenberg, which would hopefully serve as the instrument for fulfilling the liberal program.[47]

Even though relatively few men expressed such extreme sentiments as those voiced by Rochau, Dahlmann, and Treitschke, there can be no denying the strong desire during this period for national unity and power. And yet the men who manifested such desires had not really made a sudden discovery of power's usefulness and nationality's value. Their statements seemed to betray a newfound recognition that the attainment of national power was necessary for their purposes, and it is true that there appears to have been a greater concern with power after the revolution than before it. One can also argue, however, that "the liberal showed himself to be open and susceptible to power long before Treitschke." [48] The liberal historian Georg Gottfried Gervinus had already

[46] Duncker, "Die Politik der Zukunft," 42; Rochau, *Grundsätze der Realpolitik,* 175-176; Arndt, *Pro populo germanico,* 143-161; Eiselen, 20-23; see Duncker, *Vier Wochen,* 12, 29, for opposition to Schwarzenberg's abortive attempt in 1851 to overpower the other German states by bringing all of Austria's territories into an expanded German Confederation.
[47] Treitschke, *Briefe,* I, 225; see also Droysen, *Briefwechsel,* I, 737, and Duncker, *Vier Wochen,* 1, 43-47.
[48] Walter Bussmann, "Zur Geschichte des deutschen Liberalismus im 19. Jahrhundert," *HZ,* Vol. 186 (1958), 532.

written before 1848 that "freedom without power is impossible," and he was supported in this belief by many others. Liberals were increasingly coming to feel during the 1830's and 1840's that national unity was an indispensable part of their program. And certainly there was no shortage of aggressive nationalism in 1848, when German liberals and even democrats often showed scant regard for the rights of non-German peoples who lived on Germany's borders, such as the Czechs, the Poles, and the Danes. Post-1848 attitudes toward national power represented not so much a sharp departure from previous thinking as an accentuation of trends which had already been operative in the *Vormärz*.[49]

In any case, men who devoted their best energies to pursuit of the national goal often did so both with the feeling that half a loaf was better than none and in the expectation that once unity had been achieved political freedom would inevitably follow. Biedermann supported the Prussian Union plan of 1849-50, which would have brought about greater unity without the more liberal provisions of the Frankfurt Parliament's constitution, but he asserted that the path pursued by the Frankfurt Parliament would have been more direct and fruitful. Other liberals also expressed support for the Prussian Union plan, not only in their writings but also by their attendance at the Gotha assembly in June of 1849, where a declaration in favor of the plan was signed by 130 men, most of whom were former liberal delegates from the Frankfurt Parliament. But their comments as well as Biedermann's usually made it clear that they were following this path only because it seemed to be the one course which offered any promise of leading to even a partial fulfillment of the liberal program.[50]

The liberals could adopt such a policy all the more easily inasmuch as their faith in the ultimate triumph of their basic aims remained unshakable. They could relegate their demands for constitutional and parliamentary government to a somewhat subordinate place for the time being precisely because they continued to believe that the attainment of this end was inevitable. The liberals certainly felt intense disappointment in the months and years following 1849, but their disaffection with the present was tempered by a consoling belief that the future would bring an eventual triumph for their program. Treitschke spoke for many liberals when he coupled his support for the program of the Gothaers with a strong affirmation "that any unnatural constitutional form, after the

[49] *Ibid.*, 530-531; see Lewis Namier, *1848: The Revolution of the Intellectuals* (London, 1947), on expansive nationalism during the revolution; see Birtsch, *passim*, for emphasis on continuity in Droysen's thinking about the national question.

[50] Biedermann, *Erinnerungen aus der Paulskirche*, iv-v; also on Gotha, Haym, *Ausgewählter Briefwechsel*, 81.

achievement of a true national unfication of our people, could only last a short time." The German people, once unified, would presumably be unwilling to accept autocratic government.[51]

The liberal intellectuals who advocated a unified *Kleindeutschland* under Prussian leadership were confronted by other writers who held very different views about the proper solutions to Central Europe's nationality problems. Resistance to the national program supported by the liberals largely coincided with political conservatism and concern about social issues. The proposals advanced by the liberals' opponents were therefore frequently related either to a desire to maintain the existing structure of political authority or to a feeling that the liberal program was incompatible with satisfactory solutions for other problems facing Germany which were even more important than her political ones.

Most of the conservatives and the social thinkers felt far less enthusiasm for national unification than did the liberals. Some of them expressed their coolness toward the national cause simply by failing to assign it any special priority, even though they might admit in passing that a somewhat greater degree of unity was not a bad idea. Others revealed their misgivings about political nationalism and their support for the status quo more directly. Stahl cautioned against substituting a conception of the folk based either on "natural" characteristics (common physical features, language, or customs) or on shared historical experience for a view of the folk as a legal entity:

The legality and the authority of states with regard to their subjects does not depend on the distribution of these subjects according to folkish relationships of a natural or historical sort, and the contrary situation never justifies war or rebellion. . . . In the illegal manufacturing of nationalities there is at the same time a moral frivolity: men resist God's decisions and judgments, wishing to set aside his direction of the peoples in order to take it over themselves.

Ranke urged that Austria and Prussia should continue to maintain their separate identities. Each state was to go its own way, with the smaller German states continuing to exist in the middle. Ranke felt that Prussian military strength was needed as a bulwark against revolution for all the German states and that this strength would remain intact only if Prussia kept substantial autonomy with respect to its neighbors. He and Stahl both had serious reservations about the ill-fated Prussian Union plan, fearing not only that Prussia would lose her autonomy but also that the

[51] Treitschke, *Briefe,* I, 260; see also Droysen, *Briefwechsel,* I, 718 (letter from Beseler), and Pfizer, *Deutschlands Aussichten im Jahre 1851,* 10-13; see Bussmann, 544-547, on liberal optimism during the period.

proposed constitution was actually too radical. A Catholic publicist defended particularism in a way that was typical for many southern conservatives. He denied the validity both of genetic and of linguistic criteria as bases for establishing national differences and then went on to assert that the only legitimate definition of nationality for political purposes had to center on common historical experience. It was not physical similarity or language that united men, but rather the fact that they had lived together within a particular state and adhered to the same customs. Germans did not possess a political fatherland, and whoever wished to force one upon them was seeking to do "equal violence and injustice thereby to nature, to facts, to the whole people, and to the individual states." It was madness to ask the citizens of the existing states "to forget their feeling, their love, their singularity and with complete disregard for the continuation of their own house, which is *real,* to help build the castle in the air of a German political empire which would be unstable if it existed and today can in no way be created." [52]

When they did talk about the need for greater German unity, the conservatives and a good many of the social thinkers were likely to urge both that any new political unit should remain highly decentralized and that it should be a *Grossdeutschland,* not a *Kleindeutschland.* Those among them who could join liberals in advocating political nationalism still preferred a federal rather than a strictly unitary structure and refused to accept the idea that German Austrians might have to be excluded from a German empire. These objectives obviously bore a close relationship to one another, since it would have been impossible to incorporate the Austrians into anything but a federal state. The necessity of federalism was even more obvious in the arguments of men who advocated not simply the inclusion of Cisleithian Austria in a predominantly German empire but beyond that the creation of a vast multinational unit comprising the German states and all of Austria's non-German nationalities. Proposals for such a federation came from a number of political conservatives with strong interests in social questions. The most noteworthy was Constantin Frantz, who vigorously advocated the federal principle and urged that it be extended to encompass not only non-German Central Europe but also other areas which had traditionally not been joined with German-speaking territories in any political union at all. Austria, Prussia, and the other German states would form a series of confederations, in-

[52] Stahl, *Die Philosophie des Rechts,* II, part II, 165-166, and *Parlamentarische Reden,* 9-16, 55-64; Ranke, *Das Briefwerk,* 360-363, and "Politische Denkschriften," 613 ff.; "Die Nationalität" (anon.) *HPB,* XXVI (1850), 689-698.

cluding large numbers of Slavs and other non-German peoples. These confederations would then join together in a larger unit, governed by a directory with an elected president and a diet chosen by the representative assemblies of the individual German states. Frantz hoped that various national groups which were ethnically related to the Germans, such as the Dutch, the Scandinavians, and the English, would also adhere to this federal union. Edmund Jörg, Lorenz von Stein, and Viktor Aimé Huber did not propose anything this far-reaching, but all of them wanted a large multinational unit in Central Europe rather than an overwhelmingly German empire dominated by Prussia. Huber, for instance, supported the Austrian effort in 1851 to gain admission for her non-German territories into the German Confederation.[53]

Several considerations lay behind these varying alternatives to the liberal proposals for a tightly knit *Kleindeutschland*. Not only in arguments that the German empire sought by the liberals would be too small rather than too large but also in attacks against the liberals from a particularist standpoint, one frequently encounters a cosmopolitan affection for diversity. A Catholic author upbraided the representatives to the Frankfurt Parliament for their "national egoism," labelling it an essentially pagan attitude and contrasting it with the ecumenical universality of the Catholic Church. Heinrich Ahrens coupled his defense of the *grossdeutsch* position with a glowing description of "the organism of humanity," mankind being basically one in his view despite its national subdivisions. A large multinational empire in Central Europe would have marked an important step in his eyes toward awareness of this principle, whereas efforts to establish a purely German state cut off from Austria's southern and eastern territories seemed to point in precisely the wrong direction. Johann Eduard Erdmann, echoing sentiments which had already been popular among German intellectuals at the time of the French Revolution, insisted that Germany's "world-historical mission" was to provide a meeting ground for other nations and thus to help forestall international conflict. Germany, he believed, was well equipped for this task, inasmuch as many Germans were subjects of non-German rulers and several German states had absorbed large numbers of non-German citizens. Not only Austria's but also Prussia's greatness had stemmed in large part from successful assimilation of foreign elements. Moreover, Erdmann insisted that widespread art and learning within Germany's

[53] See the quotations from Frantz's *Von der deutschen Föderation* in Stamm, 197-205; on Jörg and Stein as well as on Frantz, see Heinrich Ritter von Srbik, *Deutsche Einheit*, II (Munich, 1935), 307 ff.; Huber, *Berlin, Erfurt, Paris,* 17-18, and *Suum cuique in der deutschen Frage,* 24-25.

boundaries were essential if Germans were to play their proper role in the realm of culture. A multiplicity of competing princely courts obviously went a long way toward ensuring that such cultural activity would persist in a large number of cities, not simply in a national capital.[54]

Attempts to keep alive the prenationalistic tradition of cosmopolitanism were not the only tactic these men used in order to combat the programs offered by writers like Droysen or Pfizer. They reminded their readers frequently of the past glories associated with the Holy Roman Empire, in which the Habsburgs had for so long played the leading role. But beyond these idealistic and emotional considerations there were other motives of a more practical sort. In the first place, there was the conviction that nationalism led to revolution. One Catholic writer asserted that the nationalists had not conceived the idea of a united Germany because they really believed in it, but rather so that they could use it as an instrument for undermining the old order. "It was not thought up at all so that something would arise but so that something would pass away: namely, Austria, and Prussia, and all the others; order and law in the individual German states; and any power which would not place itself completely and absolutely at the disposal of the revolution." [55] Whether one believed that the nationalists were pursuing unification simply as a means of overthrowing the established authorities or felt that they were patriots, there could be no denying that given Europe's territorial arrangements at the time political nationalism would inevitably cause many traditionally legitimate rights to be infringed. Men who sought to defend the existing distribution of political power had every reason to resist a development which clearly pointed toward a loss of power for most of Germany's reigning princes and the bureaucratic and military institutions over which they presided.

Another argument against the national program of the liberals focused on the disadvantageous position in which German Catholics might find themselves if they became citizens of an empire dominated by Protestant Prussia. Franz Joseph Buss voiced a widespread apprehension when he asserted that under Prussian hegemony there could be no guarantees for the Church's vital confessional interests, especially in the area of education. After all, he pointed out, the Prussian government had already severely curtailed the Catholic Church within its own borders. Catholics

[54] "Die Nationalität," 615-619; Ahrens, *Die organische Staatslehre*, x-xiii, 57-64; Erdmann, *Philosophische Vorlesungen über den Staat*, 44-52.
[55] "Die Nationalität," 697-698.

felt that Prussia could only be expected to pursue a similar course else-where if it had the chance.[56]

Intellectuals rejected a *Kleindeutschland* not only for these politically conservative and confessional reasons but also for reasons having to do with social policy. Many men seemed to feel that the German empire designed at the Frankfurt Parliament would take precisely the wrong steps in this whole area. This line of argument was not developed as explicitly as the ones referred to above, but several men hinted at it. What some writers suggested and others probably assumed was that a Prussian-dominated Germany would inevitably move still further in the direction of social and economic liberalism.[57] Prussian administrators had taken the lead early in the nineteenth century in the campaign both for free trade and for an end to the older corporately based society. Their achieve-ments in these areas substantially enhanced Prussia's reputation among some men, but not among those who felt that Germany's social problems required measures of a more positive sort. Writers who rejected the liberal model for social and economic life – whether they were politically conser-vative or not – were unlikely to look with favor on the domination of Germany by a state which had done so much to effectuate this part of the liberal program.

Some social thinkers also appeared to feel that the national movement as a whole – not simply that segment of it which looked to Prussia – represented a diversion from more pressing concerns. This attitude was implicit in the failure by most of them to devote much energy to support-ing the national cause. It also appeared more openly in Frantz's denial that the emergence of larger nation states was the trend of the times. Writing in 1850, he expressed the view that the political developments of the nineteenth century's first half had lost their earlier momentum. There were all sorts of ways in which unity could be achieved other than through the formation of new states: academies and universities, banks and joint stock companies, technical conventions and associations for wandering artisans were only a few of the substitutes for political unity. For the future, he predicted and hoped that political energies would be diverted to the solution of problems connected with society.[58] As the following chapter makes clear, many men agreed with him.

[56] Buss, "Die deutsche Einheit und die Preussenliebe," 176-177; for additional Catholic criticisms of Prussia, focusing specifically on the Prussian Union plan, see "Preussens Politik" (anon.), *HPB*, XXVI (1850), 651-662, 700-720, 783-800.

[57] Buss, 178; Ahrens, *Die organische Staatslehre*, x; Riehl, *Die bürgerliche Gesell-schaft*, 7.

[58] Frantz, *Von der Föderation*, quoted in Stamm, 200.

V

CONFLICTING ANSWERS TO
THE SOCIAL QUESTIONS

The events of 1848-49 forced men not only to rethink their politics but also to confront more systematically a newer set of problems such as pauperism, crime, emigration, and the other consequences of urbanization, industrialization, and population growth. The "social questions," which had already begun to agitate Germans during the 1840's, received closer scrutiny from many writers after the upheavals at mid-century, even though the intellectuals who felt that these problems actually outweighed political ones in importance still remained in a minority.[1]

Much of the impetus behind this concern stemmed from a feeling that the recent revolutions had in large measure been social conflicts. Even if social grievances had not been uppermost in Germany, it was argued, the prominence of such discontent in recent French history clearly indicated the sorts of controversies which Germans would experience in years to come. At the same time, one cannot overlook the evidence of ongoing social and economic change which confronted the intellectuals throughout the 1850's. Although political life seemed up until 1858 or 1859 to be in a protracted state of suspended animation, Germany had entered her first decade of intensive industrialization. Politicians appeared to be marking time during most of these years, but financiers and entrepreneurs were visibly on the move. In the area of the *Zollverein* during the decade from 1848 to 1857, the production of pig iron almost tripled and coal output and the value of mining more than tripled. During the decade of the 1850's the increases in the value of all capital and consumer goods produced by German industry, the size of the German railroad network, and the amount of Germany's foreign trade were approximately two-fold. Much of the capital for this industrial and commercial growth

---

[1] On the history of the phrase *"die soziale Frage,"* a direct translation from the French *"la question sociale,"* see Otto Ladendorf, *Historisches Schlagwörterbuch* (Strassburg and Berlin, 1906), 291.

came from joint-stock banks, fourteen of which were founded in the years leading up to the financial crash of 1857. As industrialization set in, the percentage of the German population dependent on farming for its livelihood began to decline, dropping from 80 per cent to 60 per cent during the period 1830-60. In Prussia, a marked divergence appeared between the growth rates of urban and rural areas, so that by 1864 municipalities numbering more than 10,000 inhabitants accounted for twice as much of the population (about 15 per cent) as they had thirty years earlier, and similar patterns were apparent elsewhere. Factory workers began to move toward numerical parity with artisans: by 1860 the ratio in Germany was about two to three. In Prussia, after an increase in the middle and late 1840's, the artisans began to decline as a percentage of the overall population. Within the ranks of the artisans, the numbers of masters fell quite sharply in a number of trades, as small producers found it more and more difficult to compete against large ones. Real economic hardship probably declined for most people from the peak it had reached during the "hungry forties," but the persistence of substantial discontent was indicated clearly enough by the continuing emigration, over a million persons having left the German Confederation between 1850 and 1861. In any case, the rapid social and economic changes which affected a still largely rural country in the early throes of industrial revolution provided a serious enough array of problems for German writers to ponder and debate.[2]

It is possible to identify four basic attitudes toward these problems. A large number of those political liberals whose main interests centered on the structure of government espoused a classically liberal view of society and the economy as well. They were joined by a few writers who denied that Germany's most troublesome difficulties were political and argued that social and economic reform was the first order of business, but then went on to support programs which pointed precisely in the direction of reducing rather than increasing the scope of governmental activity in this whole area. But most of the men who stressed the primacy of social issues demanded solutions of a more positive sort. They condemned what they regarded as the blind inadequacy of the liberal outlook. Some advocated the maintenance or the establishment of well-defined social groups, which would be encouraged to uphold their separate identities and to ensure their own well-being according to the

[2] Theodore S. Hamerow, *Restoration, Revolution, Reaction* (Princeton, 1958), 207-210, 241-242, and *The Social Foundations of German Unification, 1858-1871: Ideas and Institutions* (Princeton, 1969), 12-13, 20, 25, 27, 29, 41-43, 50, 54, 57, 78-83.

principle of self-help through mutual solidarity – an appeal which was made on behalf both of the traditional estates and of emerging elements such as the factory proletariat. Another alternative to liberalism was offered by men who advocated an active role by the state. In their opinion, group solidarity and self-help alone would not suffice. Central bureaucracies had an important role to play too. Some of these men were content for the most part to argue for the principle of state activity or to make rather limited specific suggestions in the area of policy. Others went much farther, advocating state socialism.

THE SHORT ANSWERS OF THE CLASSICAL LIBERALS

Most intellectuals who identified themselves closely with the constitutional and national causes shared similar attitudes toward social and economic issues. The political liberals were generally loathe to admit that a really pressing "social problem" existed. Even when they conceded that some distress did afflict the lower classes, they were likely to blame it on those who were doing the suffering rather than on structural malfunctioning in society as a whole. In any case, to propose that positive remedies be pursued through vigorous state action was in their view to verge on the acceptance of dangerously erroneous theories, namely socialism and communism, which bore the added stigma of having been imported from France. Even though they might admit that the state could render certain kinds of positive assistance in a few cases, they felt that the only effective solution would be to carry forward the still incomplete task of removing the obstacles to individual initiative and achievement.[3]

One approach to social problems frequently adopted by liberals was simply to deny their existence. Often this denial was implicit, indicated more by what was left unsaid than by any specific pronouncement. But some writers insisted explicitly that those who complained most vociferously about problems such as poverty vastly exaggerated their seriousness. After all, they argued, the condition of the lower classes had improved enormously since earlier times. The following is a fairly typical expression of such sentiment:

We live better than our ancestors – that is indisputable. Even our residences have become roomier and better ventilated and therefore also healthier. The simple artisan now lives just as well as the highest official did a hundred

---

[3] On arguments for free enterprise during the *Vormärz*, see Donald G. Rohr, *The Origins of Social Liberalism in Germany* (Chicago and London, 1963), 78-101; for similar sentiments during the 1860's, see Hamerow, *The Social Foundations of German Unification*, 95-106, 167-172.

years ago. . . . Only the blind man or one who does not wish to see can still believe in a regression; all our conditions have generally improved, and they are still visibly progressing. Anxiety over an ever-increasing proletariat rests on a delusion, on a lack of knowledge about the old conditions.

Karl Biedermann wrote in a similar vein when he stated that although there was much contemporary concern about pauperism, poverty afflicted far less of the population than it had a century earlier. This solicitude was therefore to be regarded not as an indication of increased hardship but as proof of an improvement in men's moral sensibilities. It gave the society as a whole cause for self-congratulation rather than for self-examination.[4]

When men did admit poverty's existence, they often insisted that a large share of the blame lay with the poor. August Ludwig von Rochau suggested such a view when he wrote, "Every healthy creature and every vigorous force *should* and *will* help itself, and in order to retain its health and vigor it *must* help itself." Eduard Baumstark contended that the working class, in placing the blame for its material deprivations on society, had overlooked "its own manifold lack of virtue." Friedrich von Raumer expressed a similar viewpoint when he wrote that even though in some cases the individual was powerless to improve his lot, in many others a man's suffering was clearly his own fault. "Idleness," he warned, "is the beginning of all troubles," and he went on to remind his readers that labor was "no punishment, but rather a joy and a reward, without which neither the individual nor a people can develop." He felt that the lazy poor should start working, cut down on their consumption of liquor and tobacco, and stop breeding so many children. Liberals believed that moral self-improvement of this sort would go a long way toward ameliorating the lot of the lower classes.[5]

German writers who proposed extensive action by the state to alleviate lower-class distress directly were likely to be identified by the liberals as the intellectual stooges of the French. Friedrich Gottlob Schulze expressed this feeling in the very title of one of his works, where he located the new social theories in a long line of alien importations: *The Workers' Question, According to the Principles of German National Economics, with Attention to the Systems of Feudalism, Mercantilism, Physiocratism, Socialism, Communism, and Republicanism, Which Have Been Trans-*

---

[4] G. Landau, "Die materiellen Zustände der untern Classen in Deutschland sonst und jetzt," in *Germania,* II, 625, 627; Biedermann, *Frauen-Brevier,* 347-348.

[5] Rochau, *Grundsätze der Realpolitik,* 168; Baumstark, *Zur Geschichte der arbeitenden Klasse,* 42; Raumer, "Briefe über gesellschaftliche Fragen der Gegenwart," 323, 348.

planted to Germany from France. Even in France, it was contended, socialist thinking had not really arisen in the first place from social hardship. It could be seen instead as the product of essentially political developments. Carl Fortlage regarded socialism and communism as particularly degenerate forms of the democratic ideas which had grown up in protest against absolutism. These doctrines simply represented a logical transference of egalitarianism from politics to society. Liberals also asserted that administrative centralization had greatly furthered the tendency to ask the state for the solution to every sort of difficulty faced by the individual.[6]

Liberals rejected theories according to which the state should actively seek to improve the social well-being of its citizens not only for reasons having to do with the genesis of such ideas but also for other reasons. For some, an ethical commitment to individual freedom was paramount. Johann Caspar Bluntschli repeated a familiar liberal credo in defending man's right to remain free from incursions by the community into his economic affairs. World history, he argued, showed a close connection between the rise of civilization and security of private property. All modern states recognized that property rights and the right of inheritance had to be maintained. To eliminate these rights in the manner proposed by the communists and socialists would not only suppress all individual freedom but also destroy culture, dissolve the family, and "lead to a barbarism such as has never before been seen in history." [7]

For other writers, the decisive point was that the proponents of state-directed efforts to alleviate social and economic hardship, however well-meaning, did not understand the facts of economic life. Two liberal economists, Karl Arnd and Max Wirth, pointed to "natural laws" which they felt invalidated many proposals for social reform. Arnd insisted that workers' wages depended on the relationship between the number of those who sought employment and the level of demand for their services. Their remuneration certainly could not be regulated by public authorities. Echoing Thomas Malthus, he wrote that according to another natural law the number of persons seeking poor relief depended on the amount of alms available for distribution: every part of the population would increase in proportion to the increment in its food supply; moreover, if alms were so readily available that no stigma was associated with accept-

---

[6] Schulze, *Die Arbeiterfrage;* see also his *Nationalökonomie,* 129-130, 139, 201-202; Fortlage, "Ueber den Unterschied von Staat und Gesellschaft," 785; see also Biedermann, "Demokratie," 354, and Arnd, *Die Staatsverfassung nach dem Bedürfniss der Gegenwart,* 220.

[7] Bluntschli, "Eigenthum," 315-322.

ing them, they would only encourage men to cease supporting themselves and their families. Both Arnd and Wirth therefore cautioned against providing public support for the poor except in the most dire circumstances. Similarly, Rochau argued that a socialist state would take the form of a hospital, its institutions directed primarily toward the assistance of weaklings and cripples, and that in such a state both economic energy and the general level of material well-being would diminish. In any case, he asserted, the state simply lacked the power to undertake certain measures whether they were desirable or not. It certainly could not meet the socialists' demand that the "right to work" be guaranteed through the provision of jobs to all who wanted them. The state could no more organize the labor market than an academy could organize a language, although it might seriously disorganize this market by its intervention.[8]

The liberals sought improved living standards not through unworkable attempts to interfere with the natural operation of the labor market or through self-defeating efforts to provide assistance to the indigent but by rewarding initiative and hard work. This meant not only withholding unearned benefits from the undeserving poor and avoiding taxation except in cases where it was absolutely necessary in order to maintain the state, but also eliminating whatever remained in the way of legal barriers to individual enterprise. According to Wirth, the proper policy for the state was "to remove all the obstacles which burden the free activity of human labor, in short, to employ every means in order to increase production, which is the same as solving the 'social question' in so far as it can be solved for this generation." Nature shrewdly made use of human self-interest so as to aid the development of humanity. "The laws of nature," he wrote, "are so ingenious that in general each person increases the well-being of the whole when he pursues his private interests." But in order for men to do this effectively, they could not suffer from legal disabilities. They had to be able to compete freely on an equal basis. In Wirth's view, this sort of competive situation would best be fostered by ending monopolies and protective tariffs, by making it possible for men to move freely in search of employment, and by withdrawing state support totally from the restrictive practices of the declining handicraft guilds. For Rochau, the social question was to be solved through tariff reforms, reductions in state budgets, tax cuts, and abolition of the remaining privileges enjoyed by craft guilds. The true meaning for him of the "right to work" was not that the state should undertake vast public works

[8] Arnd, 58-59, 99-101; Wirth, *Grundzüge der National-Oekonomie*, 1, 136; Rochau, 168-171.

programs but rather that it should remove legal barriers which prevented men from pursuing the vocations of their choice. John Prince-Smith and Victor Böhmert held much the same views. Prince-Smith, one of Germany's leading campaigners in behalf of free trade, summarized his position succinctly when he wrote, "The prerequisite for social well-being – 'abundant' satisfaction for all – can only flow from the heightened productive energy of free labor and secure property. Free trade and the free right of acquisition offer the only guarantee for a just distribution of the goods which will give satisfaction." According to Böhmert, in a polemic against the guilds, "Every state which wishes to further the happiness of its citizens and to combat poverty should . . . recognize as the highest of its duties guaranteeing each citizen the right and the freedom to work, to develop himself, to use his energies, and to enjoy the fruits of his labors." In sum, the liberals placed their hopes not in measures which would redistribute wealth but in ones which would increase the total amount of wealth available to the nation as a whole, by clearing away the legal and institutional detritus which prevented the competitive enterprise so essential to an expanding economy. The correct answer to the social question was not to weaken liberalism but to apply liberal principles to the hilt. Some of them, Wirth and Böhmert for instance, went on to approve of organized self-help by groups of workers, which was entirely compatible with liberal principles. But they channeled most of their enthusiasm into more purely negative reforms. As we shall see later, the foremost proponents of the co-operative association were men who considered the problems which such associations were designed to alleviate a good deal more pressing than did the writers whom we have been considering here.[9]

It should be noted that in several cases the attitudes expressed on this whole subject during the period represented a substantial shift from opinions which men had held earlier. Karl Theodor Welcker and Karl Biedermann had been quite insistent during the 1840's on the need for various measures of social reform but now assumed a very different stance. In Welcker's case, the shift was simply a matter of a change in emphasis: the few articles he wrote during the 1850's no longer had anything to say about the social question. In Biedermann's case, there was not only a reorientation of interests but also a distinct change in tone. When he did address himself to the social question, the general import of his remarks was to assert the undesirability and impracticality of the solutions pro-

---

[9] Wirth, 184-185, 147, 498-499, 520-525; Rochau, 162-165; Prince-Smith, *Gesammelte Schriften*, III, 311; Böhmert, *Freiheit der Arbeit!*, 4, 17-20.

posed by others, rather than to suggest any solutions of his own. These shifts illustrate a general tendency among political liberals during the period to devote less of their attention to social issues than they had in the *Vormärz*. "Social liberalism," in the sense of positive measures designed to ensure economic welfare for the population as a whole, had of course never been central to the liberal program, but there had been a growing current in this direction during the earlier period. Part of the explanation for the changed tone of the liberal writers after 1848 doubtless lies in the lessening of economic hardship which took place during the 1850's. As Germany entered a period of great economic expansion, the issues raised by social reformers during the preceding decade did not seem as urgent as they had before. One must also remember, however, that the liberals placed the emergence of revolutionary social protest in 1848-49 alongside radical efforts to achieve political democracy as a chief cause of their own failure. It seems reasonable to infer that this belief helped push many of these men away from their earlier positions. To call attention to social ills and to advocate social reform might appear to encourage the very forces whose activities had proved so disruptive.[10]

A more general reason for the stance which liberals adopted toward social and economic problems stemmed from their feeling that too much concern with these matters was incompatible with more important considerations. Carl Fortlage regretted that although man was primarily a political animal he was unfortunately an economic creature too. Fortlage continued as follows: "So long as he does not learn to attain in his thought that height of abstraction of which he is capable, to abstract completely from the economic concept and to elevate the political as the highest measure for human affairs, then he cannot arrive at a sound policy which does not injure some individuals." Heinrich von Treitschke displayed a similar outlook when he scorned "social claims" as the product of "politically exhausted times." Like Fortlage, he clearly attached a pejorative connotation to such demands and implicitly denigrated attempts to meet them. It is almost as if they and many other liberals felt that it was a mark of indecent vulgarity to be overly concerned about issues which had to do with the "material" side of life. In any case, social demands and social programs constituted a diversion from what really mattered: the development and strengthening of political institutions.[11]

[10] On Welcker and Biedermann before 1848, see Rohr, 112-116, 147-154; for the 1850's, see Biedermann, *Frauen-Brevier*, 334 ff., 352-354. See Hans Rosenberg, *Grosse Depression und Bismarckzeit* (Berlin, 1967), 81, 127, on the effect of economic improvement on social protest in the 1850's.

[11] Fortlage. 775; Treitschke, *Die Gesellschaftswissenschaft*, 1, 88.

THE VARIETIES OF GROUP SOLIDARITY
AND GROUP SELF-HELP

The classic liberal belief that whatever might be wrong with society could be remedied by additional doses of essentially negative reforms encountered strong opposition from a number of men who rejected liberal individualism and sought to elevate the principle-of group solidarity. They regarded the breakdown of a corporately based social order as the crucial problem facing Germany at mid-century. How, they asked, could the disintegration of the old order under the impact of liberal reforms be either arrested or counterbalanced? These writers looked to a variety of social groups – the estate, the corporation, or the association – whose members would be encouraged to maintain a common identity and to render support and assistance to one another. According to some of them, the state had an important role to play in guaranteeing the rights and privileges of these groups and in additional ways as well, but others specifically rejected action by the state as a means of alleviating social distress. In any case, the foremost advocates of mutual solidarity did not rely on the state for any extensive measures of positive assistance. Their hopes lay with organizations which stood mid-way between the state and the individual.

One version of this theme was quite clearly a defense of a traditional social order characterized by landed aristocrats, small farmers, and artisans. The writers who expounded it, who were conservative politically as well as socially, dwelled incessantly on the problem of social "dissolution." In their view, Germany's social difficulties arose from the fact that men were drifting away from the clearly identifiable "estates" of the past, each of which had possessed its own sense of honor and its own special rights. Society was instead becoming an agglomeration of individual "atoms." The lack of identification with honored and protected groups in turn set the stage for revolutionary discontent with the whole political and social status quo. More specifically, these writers indicted the centralizing bureaucrats who had tried to dissolve particular social identities in favor of an abstract general citizenship, industrial capitalists, and the irresponsible intellectuals who had incited the "estateless" proletariat. They pleaded that the old social estates be retained as much as possible or even reinstated in their unalloyed purity so that their members could protect themselves from the forces of change. This program was to be effected primarily by permitting the component parts of the estates to keep the corporate organizations through which they had always regulated their own affairs, retention of the artisan guilds being the most obvious application of this principle.[12]

Wilhelm Heinrich Riehl emerged early in the decade as the most articulate spokesman for this viewpoint. As we have already seen, Riehl believed that political affairs held only a secondary claim on the attention of both the ordinary citizen and the intellectual: the great issues of the day lay outside the state, in the area of society. Riehl contended that the struggle between political radicals and political conservatives had already given way to a new set of conflicts, in which even the social democrats and the aristocrats held much in common, since they both rejected economic liberalism. The major participants in the new struggles appeared under such headings as the proletariat, the burghers, and the Junkers, groups which he referred to as "estates." Riehl emphasized that estates were by no means identical with the purely economic or vocational groupings which resulted when men were fitted within such categories as basic production, artisanal manufacturing, industry, and intellectual labor. "Estate and vocation," he wrote, "are essentially different." The estates were "the few large groups of society, which differ from one another partly with regard to vocation, but basically with regard to custom, to mode of life, to their whole historical manifestation, and to the principle which they represent in the historical continuation of society." Society consisted for Riehl not of economic classes but of traditional status groups.[13]

In his widely read treatise, *Civil Society*, Riehl delineated the "normal" characteristics of German society's various elements through the centuries and argued that Germany's recent social turmoil resulted from failures by members of each of these groups to maintain the specific social identities which they had been assigned by history. He sought in this way to make good on his promise that the "science of the folk," by elucidating the singular "particularities" of social experience, would reveal the preconditions for well-being which each of society's major component

[12] See the following studies on this current of German social thought: Hamerow, *The Social Foundations of German Unification, 1858-1871: Ideas and Institutions* 117-132, 200-221; William O. Shanahan, *German Protestants Face the Social Question* (Notre Dame, 1954), 239-301; Karl Valerius Herberger, *Die Stellung der preussischen Konservativen zur sozialen Frage, 1848-62* (Meissen, 1914).

[13] Riehl, *Die bürgerliche Gesellschaft*, 5, 273. Many highly appreciative pieces have been written about Riehl, but there is still no satisfactory full-scale treatment. There are interesting analyses of his ideas in Eckart Pankoke, *Sociale Bewegung – Sociale Frage – Sociale Politik: Grundfragen der deutschen "Socialwissenschaft" im 19. Jahrhundert* (Stuttgart, 1970), 61-66, 115-119.

groups required. The following passage, in which he described the book's "ethical tendency," summarized his prejudices and his hopes:

... Only through the return of the individual, as well as of entire estates, to greater *self-limitation* and *self-moderation* can social life be improved. The burgher should again want to be a burgher, the peasant again a peasant, the aristocrat should not deem himself privileged and strive to rule alone. I should like to awaken in everyone pride in recognizing himself with joy as a member of that social circle to which he belongs by birth, upbringing, education, custom, [and] vocation and in rejecting with scorn that dandified manner with which the parvenu plays the genteel man and is ashamed to admit that at the end his father was simply an honest shoemaker or tailor. ... Regret, atonement, and conversion of the individual are what I mean by "reform of society." My book is ... in this sense ascetic, and the sublime tendency toward the self-moderation of the individual and of social groups is at the same time Christian.

It should be added that in Riehl's view the only alternative to the continued existence of separate social estates was socialism. No third possibility existed.[14]

The first half of Riehl's study discussed "the forces of social stability": the peasants and the aristocrats. The peasants, to whom Riehl devoted considerably greater attention than most social thinkers, were the conservative social force *par excellence,* and any conservative policy which was to succeed in Germany had to base itself on them:

There is an unconquerable conservative force in the German nation, a solid core in spite of every change, which consists of our peasants. They are truly unique, and no other nation can offer a counterpart to them. The conservatism of the educated may be theoretically grounded; the conservatism of the peasant is his way of life. In the social crises of our days the peasant has played a more important role than most people suspect, since he has formed the natural barrier against the overflow of revolutionary French doctrines among the lower classes. Only the passivity of the peasant saved the German thrones in March of 1848. ... But this passivity was not accidental: it stemmed instead from the innermost nature of the German peasant.

Riehl took pleasure in noting that most peasants still lived much as they had always lived, speaking traditional dialects, inhabiting their ancestral houses, and feeling sufficient pride in their inherited status so that they had no cause to envy anyone else. But in order for the peasantry to fulfill its conservative role to the utmost, it would have to be purified of its degenerate members, who had increased rapidly during the preceding fifty years, and further assaults upon its integrity would have to cease. Morally corrupt members of the estate, who did not properly maintain

[14] Riehl, *Die bürgerliche Gesellschaft,* 34-36.

what they possessed and instead sought to acquire what was not rightfully theirs, should be encouraged to emigrate. But others had suffered economic decline through no fault of their own. Reforming bureaucrats had forced too many peasants to subdivide their holdings among their heirs to the point where no one could eke out a livelihood. Farms which had become too small in this way had to be built up again, and those which were still adequate had to be protected. In matters having to do with political organization Riehl urged statesmen to heed the peasant's preference for estatist representation. They should also give the peasants greater opportunity to identify themselves with the state through participation in the government of the local community, from which they should be allowed to exclude outsiders whom they did not wish to accept. Riehl argued in addition against giving children in rural areas a "general education" based on "levelling rationalism," which would tend to tear them away from their estate. Finally, he asked the state to stop suppressing traditional rural customs. Drunkenness and the other vices associated with festivals in the countryside were seen as a small price to pay in order for the peasants to gain the satisfaction that made them happy in their estate and content to keep their inherited place in society.[15]

Like the peasants, the aristocrats supported the social and political status quo in a whole host of ways, and their vital interests also had to be protected. But the conservative role of the aristocrats differed from that of the peasantry. In contrast to the instinctively conservative peasants, the aristocrats felt a conscious traditionalism, based on their historical knowledge both of their social estate as a whole and of their particular family connections. Moreover, just as the aristocrats had given classic expression during the Middle Ages to the principle of social exclusiveness by erecting moats and drawbridges, so too they upheld this principle with clear determination in the nineteenth century. "The nobility of our time," wrote Riehl, "has no more fortresses, and it needs no more moats and drawbridges. But inasmuch as the exclusiveness of this estate belongs to its essence, the nobility represents the right of the drawbridge as the basic precondition for social differentiation. It is the nobility's particular vocation in life to express and maintain this differentiation. . . ." In other words, by strongly upholding its own right to exclude outsiders from its ranks the nobility implicitly supported the right of other established social groups to do likewise, a right which Riehl considered essential for the maintenance of the old order. The aristocrats also helped to maintain social differentiation by creating an exemplary

[15] *Ibid.*, 41, 42-57, 65 ff., 108-119.

"microcosm of society," as they formed their own highly articulated network of relationships among themselves. The aristocrats had best fulfilled this microcosmic function during the Middle Ages. Since that time the nobility had begun to decline, owing in large part to the economic impoverishment of its members, but Riehl hoped that they could retain the standing and prestige they still possessed and perhaps regain some of what they had lost. He suggested a number of ways in which the nobility might be strengthened. Since they, like the peasantry, depended for their very existence on the security of their landed holdings, their entailed estates had to remain intact. Moreover, they required social representation in the legislatures. In order to be worthy of their high position, the aristocrats were to render positive assistance to the rest of society. They were to aid the peasants by setting an active example of technical improvement and to assist the artisans by spending generously on domestic manufactures. The aristocrats were to help society as a whole by founding institutions for the general welfare and by encouraging literature and other forms of intellectual culture.[16]

The second half of Riehl's work treated "the forces of social movement." The "estate of burghers," or "third estate" (roughly equivalent to what historians broadly refer to as "the middle classes"), stood in the forefront of these forces. A more heterogeneous group than the peasantry or the nobility, including men as different from one another as the artisan and the scholar, it sought, Riehl emphasized, to bridge the traditional distinctions of historical society and to break down the estatist order in favor of general citizenship. Since the French Revolution, it had predominated in Europe both materially and morally, impressing its values everywhere on the tendencies of the age. Politically, it had provided the main impulses leading toward constitutionalism and national unification. Riehl did not reject either of these objectives completely. He admitted that many of the reforms instituted during the March days were excellent. But he felt that the movement had gotten out of hand: it had led to anarchy and finally to reaction. Riehl thus betrayed little if any real regret over the fate of the liberals and his concluding remarks on the burghers therefore came as no surprise. Even though he saw some advantages in the liberal tendencies supported by the third estate, these lay not so much in the goals which the liberals themselves pursued as in the revival of the more traditional social forces which their efforts had generated inadvertently.[17]

[16] *Ibid.*, 128-132, 156 ff., 183-191.
[17] *Ibid.*, 193 ff., 195, 245-250, 271.

The year 1848, Riehl argued, had witnessed not only enthusiasm for the principle of brotherhood at the level of the nation but also a multitude of attempts to organize more limited forms of association in the areas determined by men's social estates and by their occupations. Through these attempts men had demonstrated that the "social spirit of differentiation" which Riehl sought to foster remained vital. Some of these more traditional tendencies emanated from within the third estate itself. Even though the estate of burghers generally opposed the estatist principle, some elements of this diverse social group had displayed "healthy corporative impulses." The corporative urge had been especially pronounced among the artisans. The craft guilds and other groups formed by these men had opposed commercial and industrial freedom during the revolution; in the 1850's, Riehl pointed out, they were serving as instruments for the mutual assistance and preservation of their members by functioning as production co-operatives. Such impulses clearly indicated the basis for a policy that would encourage at least some of the "forces of social movement" to adopt conservative attitudes. If the artisans were allowed to protect themselves from the harmful effects of free trade through corporate self-regulation and if they were protected by appropriate tariffs, they too would be content to remain in their estate. "To feel proud within the necessary limitation of his social existence," Riehl wrote, "is a true virtue of the burgher." Few members of the estate possessed this pride anymore, but if statesmen adopted the correct policies, it could become widespread once again.[18]

The other force seeking social change had none of the burgher estate's redeeming virtues. "The fourth estate," which comprised the elements that had broken loose from the other three estates, was defined negatively as "the estate of estatelessness" – not only because of its origins, but also because of its desire (which appeared with especial clarity in the programs of the social democrats) to destroy the other estates completely. This estate was made up of "all those who have separated themselves or have been cast out from the grouping and stratification systems of society that have existed up till now, who consider it an insult to humanity to speak of lords, burghers, and peasants, who call themselves the 'real folk' and who thus wish that all organic differentiation of estates should be dissolved in the great mish-mash of the real folk." The fourth estate consisted of the *déclassés* from all the estates, and its members sought an end to the social order to which they no longer belonged. It had always existed, but it had only recently become aware of itself as an independent entity,

[18] *Ibid.*, 17-19, 256-258, 262, 266.

assembling "the marauders of the old society . . . under its banner as a fearful new army." [19]

Riehl insisted strongly that one ought not to use the term "fourth estate" simply to designate either wage laborers or a proletariat of the propertyless. Riehl remained somewhat vague as to where the wage laborers belonged conceptually. In his view, some but not all of them belonged to the fourth estate; and yet, particularly if they worked in factories, there was no room for these people under any of Riehl's other headings – a fact which, along with a good deal else in Riehl's work, reveals his inability to grasp the basic features of modern as opposed to traditional society. All of the second group, the propertyless proletarians, fitted into the fourth estate, but the fourth estate comprised many other groups as well. In addition to some workers, artisan journeymen, and poor farmers, it included poor aristocrats, bankrupt burghers, criminals, and young academicians.[20]

In his analysis of the fourth estate's component parts Riehl emphasized the great significance of the role played by "the proletarians of intellectual work," who were "the church militant of the fourth estate." Comprising large numbers of ambitious young state officials with doubtful prospects of promotion, schoolteachers, journalists, starving university lecturers, and artists, among others, it had, he felt, provided the most powerful impulses behind the more destructive parts of the recent social revolution. Only at the end of his discussion did Riehl turn to "the proletarians of manual labor." Their revolutionary activities and their very membership in the fourth estate seemed to stem largely from the efforts of the intellectuals, who had supposedly caused them to break away from their traditional values and thus to *feel* poor even in cases where their actual economic situation might be better than it had ever been before.[21]

Riehl did not believe, however, that the proletariat of manual laborers had been produced simply by intellectual agitation. Riehl's discussion of the practices which had undermined the existence of the naturally "healthy" estates in the earlier part of his work made that quite clear. The fostering of liberalism by the state bureaucracies, the development of industry, and the growth of cities, with their disorganizing effects on the social consciousness of the individual, had created the conditions under which destructive social theories gained widespread acceptance. The proper remedies for this predicament were implicit in Riehl's analysis

[19] *Ibid.*, 272-275.
[20] *Ibid.*, 273, 275-276, 280.
[21] *Ibid.*, 305 ff., 342 ff., 307, 355, 372.

of its causes, and we have indicated many of them already. Several aspects of his program for the fourth estate's manual laborers (the *déclassé* aristocrats and particularly the intellectual proletarians having seemingly been beyond redemption) deserve particular emphasis. Riehl hoped that a "genuine" fourth estate might be formed out of the growing numbers of wage laborers, who would become a legitimate social group at the same time that they acquired a common consciousness not only of their sufferings but also of the ways in which they could help one another to overcome those sufferings. Riehl found an exemplary form of such mutual assistance in associations for the construction of low-cost housing. Such projects were far preferable to the public works that had been undertaken in Paris, which were not only unnecessary but also demoralizing, since they made the workers aware that they were superfluous. He also approved of consumers' co-operatives. The theme he returned to in closing, however, was not so much that new forms or organization were to be encouraged as that society should be permitted to retain the older corporate structures of the past. The best policy was to allow the traditional social estates to organize themselves in such a way that a fourth estate did not become a force to be reckoned with at all. Most of the existing fourth estate would hopefully be dissolved as its component parts were reassimilated into their original estates.[22]

A number of writers echoed Riehl's plea that the social order be refounded along traditional lines through the strengthening of clearly distinguishable corporate estates. Parallels to Riehl's thinking appeared unmistakably in the work of two major publicists, Edmund Jörg and Hermann Wagener, both of whom reinforced the critique of liberalism with an even stronger emphasis on the Christian virtues of charity and resignation.[23] Jörg seemed to follow his fellow Bavarian almost to the letter when he enunciated the position of the *Historical-Political Journal for Catholic Germany* concerning the social problem, which in his view consisted essentially in the growth of an impoverished proletariat. The proletariat had arisen because the former cohesiveness of the historic estates, the nobility, the peasantry, and the burghers, had been undermined. Too many former members of these groups now wandered around aimlessly, lacking a clear social identity. The very existence of a proletariat was a sign of social illness, and attempts to improve the proletariat's condition as a group made no sense at all. The only remedy was to do

---

[22] *Ibid.*, 285-286, 290, 359-360, 383-384; see Riehl's *Land und Leute,* 91-96, on life in the cities.

[23] Fritz Wöhler, *Joseph Edmund Jörg und die sozialpolitische Richtung im deutschen Katholizismus* (Leipzig, 1929), 83; Wagener, "Vorwort," 2.

away entirely with the proletariat as such. This objective required strengthening the particular rights enjoyed by the members of the traditional estates, the most important of which was the right to determine the composition of their own membership and thus to protect themselves against inundation from without and inner decay. But such a policy alone would at best slow down or halt the dissolution of the old order: it would not eliminate the existing proletariat. Jörg therefore recommended that workers, both in the countryside and in the city, should be legally subordinated to their employers "in a service based on lifelong mutual trust." They could expect benevolent protection from above, but they would give up the right to change jobs at will. In this way, a large part of the proletariat would be incorporated into the framework of the three old estates. The rest could be controlled easily enough by the police.[24]

Wagener vigorously supported the estatist position in the North, first as editor of the reactionary *Kreuz-zeitung*, then as a collaborator on the *Berlin Review*, and later as the editor of a lengthy political and social encyclopedia. Wagener's major significance during the years immediately following the revolution lay in his having served as a leading spokesman for Prussia's "guild reaction," through which the artisans were to be afforded the possibility of helping themselves by reinstating the restrictive practices of the past. But the nobility and the peasantry also had to be protected against the "immoral and exploitative competition" which Wagener associated with the rise of industrial capitalism. Wagener's affinities with Riehl thus appeared not only in his advocacy of corporate organizations for craftsmen but also in his glowing tributes to Germany's landed elements and his numerous proposals for permitting them to regulate their own affairs, free from bureaucratic interference. Wagener came increasingly during the later part of the decade to feel that a solution to the social problem would require an active "social monarchy," one of whose tasks would be to help improve the lot of factory workers through a variety of positive measures, but the main objective he had in mind was still the preservation of the old social order. Moreover, this purpose was still to be served in large measure through corporate self-government rather than through the efforts of a central bureaucracy.[25]

---

[24] Franz Josef Stegmann, *Von der ständischen Reform zur staatlichen Sozialpolitik: Der Beitrag der Historisch-politischen Blätter zur Lösung der sozialen Frage* (Munich and Vienna, 1965), 51-52, 127-129.

[25] On Wagener, see the following: Wolfgang Saile, *Hermann Wagener und sein Verhältniss zu Bismarck: Ein Beitrag zur Geschichte des konservativen Sozialismus* (Tübingen, 1958), 44-52, 63; Shanahan, 272-280, 362 ff.; Herberger, *passim*. For the reference to competition, see Wagener, 9. See the following unsigned articles in

All of these men tried desperately to shore up a social order that was being steadily undermined by the introduction of liberal reforms and the concomitant growth of industrial capitalism. Accordingly, none of them – with the partial exception of Wagener – could offer convincing solutions for the problems that confronted the rising population of factory workers. What they did instead was to express the vain hope that these unwelcome proletarians would somehow either disappear or merge into the old structure of society. In many respects they were perceptive diagnosticians, but their positive suggestions were largely doomed to irrelevance.[26]

The advocacy of traditional corporatism as a way of reversing the process of social disintegration was countered by another set of pleas for group solidarity which pointed in a very different direction – not toward a rebuilding of the old estates but instead toward the development of co-operative associations. Some of the most notable exponents of the co-operative ideal shared a good deal of Riehl's anxiety over the loosening of traditional social ties, but they rejected his attempts to recreate the past as hopelessly anachronistic. They believed that efforts to solve the social problem by assuring special rights for the surviving elements of the old order were doomed to failure. Industrial development dictated solutions which would meet the needs not only of aristocrats, peasants, and artisans but also of urban factory workers. Co-operative associations, which could be made relevant to the needs of every social group, seemed to provide the best means for alleviating the distress of this new proletariat.

Numerous books and pamphlets by Viktor Aimé Huber presented the most extensive and articulate proposals for co-operation made by anyone in Germany during this period, proposals which were clearly designed to benefit the industrial working classes. Huber had already begun to publicize the virtues of working-class co-operatives before the revolution, having been quite favorably impressed during a trip to England in 1844 by the achievements of the famed Rochedale Equitable Pioneers Society.

the early volumes of Wagener's *Neues Conversations-Lexikon* on the various estates of society: "Ackerbau," "Adel," and "Adels-Theorie und Adels-Reform," in Vol. I (1859), 242-260, 321-373, 377-385; "Arbeit, Arbeitszeit," in Vol. II (1859), 478-488; "Bauer" and "Bauernstand," in Vol. III (1860), 367-372, 383-388; "Bourgeoisie" and "Bürger, Bürgerstand, Bürgerthum," in Vol. IV (1860), 358-366, 672-675.

[26] For further evidence of estatist thinking, see the following: Frantz, *Die Erneuerung der Gesellschaft und die Mission der Wissenschaft*, 22-34, and *Vorschule zur Physiologie der Staaten*, 301-307; Stahl, *Die Philosophie des Rechts*, II, part I, 338, 351, 374, and *Parlamentarische Reden*, 385-387.

But it was only after 1848 that he really dedicated himself to propagating the co-operative ideal.[27]

Huber, who was every bit as conservative as Riehl, Jörg, and Wagener in political matters, explicitly criticized Riehl for his lack of insight into the true character of the so-called "fourth estate," or "proletariat." Far more closely attuned than all of these other men to the emerging realities of the social problem, he perceived with much greater clarity than they did the growth of a large class of wage laborers who worked in factories. They were the true proletariat. Their needs, he argued, were only obscured if they were grouped together conceptually with all of the heterogeneous elements which made up Riehl's amorphous "estate of estatelessness." They had to be recognized as a separate social group which had come to stay.[28]

Huber strongly believed that the grievances of the industrial workers had to be remedied if the monarchical order to which he felt such deep attachment was to survive in the future. True, he did not believe that the workers were basically revolutionary, even though they would presumably have been the ones to benefit from a social revolution. Whatever part they might have played in revolutionary movements was explicable by reference to the propagandistic activities of the upper and middle classes, who had exploited the misery of the workers for their own purposes. But the workers had legitimate complaints, the growth of factories and of cities having caused considerable hardship and insecurity for those who came there to work and live. Although their demands could be fulfilled without a social revolution, Huber pointed to the distinct possibility that if no improvement in their situation were forthcoming they would once again resort to violence. It must be added here that Huber also presented his case in terms of the dictates of Christian morality. A deeply religious man with close connections to leading circles in the Protestant Church in Prussia, he was an ardent moralist, who preached as well as counselled. But the pragmatic argument that social reform was necessary to prevent social and political upheaval was always ready for those whose Christian sympathies were less lively than Huber's.[29]

Huber questioned several remedies for social distress proposed by other writers. He regarded private charity by individuals as obviously insufficient. On the other hand, he was loathe to see an increase in the responsibilities of the state, which he felt would simply lead to bureaucratic

---

[27] Ingwer Paulsen, *Viktor Aimé Huber als Sozialpolitiker* (2nd ed., Berlin, 1956), 61.

[28] Huber, review of Riehl, *Die Naturgeschichte des Volkes*, 70-79.

[29] Huber, "Arbeitende Klassen," 293-297; Paulsen, 12, 150, 197-198.

meddling in private life. Needless to say, he also rejected socialism, which he scorned both for the impracticality of its "high-flying, world-embracing" aims and for its hostility to the individual, the family, and Christianity. In his opinion, the times required a solution which relied neither on the individual nor on the state but rather on institutions lying mid-way between these two extremes, namely self-help associations.[30]

Huber was dissatisfied with a number of forms in which the associative principle had already taken shape or might be expected to take shape in the future. The old craft guild, oriented toward the needs of artisans, would have to go. A considerably more favorable attitude toward this institution appeared at various places in Riehl's work, and it was on just this score that Huber leveled some of his heaviest criticism against Riehl. The restrictive spirit of the guilds had a detrimental effect in the modern world on the dignity of the individual. In any case, factories had come to stay, and the guilds were simply irrelevant to the needs of the men who worked in them. This latter charge applied as well to the efforts of Huber's friend, Hermann Schulze-Delitzsch, the most notable figure during the period who actually organized co-operatives. Schulze-Delitzsch's efforts pointed toward the founding of credit co-operatives. These differed from guilds in that they pursued specific and limited objectives and they admitted all who wanted to join. They did not function as multipurpose social organizations, and the members did not jealously exercise the right of exclusion. Still, the credit co-operatives did share one of the guilds' defects: they could only help meet the needs of artisans and other small businessmen. Schulze-Delitzsch also had some interest in founding production co-operatives, to reduce the cost of raw materials and provide communal sales facilities for finished goods. But Huber felt that production co-operatives were even more exclusively a remedy for the problems of artisans. The workers, Huber wrote, could never accumulate the capital to build their own factories in the first place, and in any case they would be incapable of running the factories on their own. Although he admired Schulze-Delitzsch's work, he thus felt that it failed to address the needs of those groups which increasingly presented society with its greatest problems. Finally, Huber denigrated associations such as Stephan Born's Brotherhood of Workers, which had agitated for socialist goals during 1848-49. Such associations, in contrast to the craft guilds and production or credit co-operatives, were designed to serve the

---

[30] Huber: *Bruch mit der Revolution und Ritterschaft,* 40-42; *Ausgewählte Schriften,* 740; *Berlin, Erfurt, Paris,* 26. See also Paulsen, 190-195, on Huber's reluctance to make demands upon the state.

interests of factory workers, but Huber abhorred any association which incited its members to follow the path of revolution.[31]

The associations which Huber advocated were intended to provide low-cost housing and to reduce the prices of consumer goods for industrial workers. During the years immediately after the revolution, he developed quite detailed plans for co-operative settlements, which he hoped would rectify some of the most miserable aspects of working-class life. The settlements were to lie at some distance from the cities. The workers who lived there would travel to and from the urban factories by new means of public transportation. Each family would hopefully have its own small house, with enough land for a garden, but there would also be a central building for certain common needs, such as heat, light, water, baking, and bathing. Moreover, each community was to serve as the foundation for the development of further co-operation in the area of consumption, so that the cost of food and other necessities could be reduced through large-scale purchasing. Huber later placed more emphasis on consumer co-operatives than on communal housing associations, arguing that it would be better to begin with small-scale projects before trying to found co-operative settlements, but he still hoped that eventually both forms of group self-help would go hand in hand.[32]

The essential principle of the co-operative association was that the men who benefited from it were to help themselves by helping one an-other. They would not depend on outside assistance but instead would seek to improve their situation by pooling their own resources. Never-theless, Huber considered it unrealistic to expect that the workers could actually establish associations on their own. They would have to receive some help at the outset from society's aristocratic elements: the industrial-ists, large landowners, and others who possessed wealth and prestige. Huber expected the social and economic elite to recognize that associ-ations of the sort he had in mind lay in its own interests: as Huber repeatedly emphasized, co-operatives threatened no existing rights and at the same time helped to combat conditions which caused public dis-order. Another way of appealing to the upper classes was to tell them that they had to fulfill a social mission if they were to deserve either an elevated political position or the property they had received from God.

[31] Huber, review of Riehl, 74-75. Huber's criticisms of credit co-operatives were implicit, in that he never showed much interest in them. For his criticisms of production co-operatives, see his *Ausgewählte Schriften*, 824 ff. See Schulze-Delitzsch's *Assozia-tionsbuch für deutsche Handwerker und Arbeiter* (Leipzig, 1853) for a good summary of his ideas. See Huber, "Die cooperative Association in Deutschland," 78-83, for criticism of working-class militancy.
[32] Huber, *Ausgewählte Schriften*, 770-869; Paulsen, 139.

One means of fulfilling this mission would be to further the development of associations by helping with organizational and administrative tasks and by providing loans, which would obviously be required for the success of housing co-operatives. This tendency to invoke considerations of *noblesse oblige* of course revealed quite clearly Huber's strong attachment to a hierarchical organization of society. In this sense, he was every bit as much a social conservative as Riehl. He made a place for new social groups, but he did so by adding a new rung to the bottom of the old social ladder.[33]

The most interesting part of Huber's writing about co-operatives concerned not so much their basic organization or the ways in which they might come into being as the benefits he hoped their growth would bring. Quite obviously, they would help to alleviate material hardship. "The material principle of the association," Huber wrote, "is the unification of many small atomistic forces, especially proletarian atoms, . . . into a relatively large force and the most fruitful application possible of the latter. . . ." By pooling their resources, all the association's members could benefit economically. But the association was also to exert a powerful moral influence, acting "in quite a similar way in the realm of the ethical economy and in the material economy." It would make men not only more affluent but also more virtuous.[34]

Moral improvement was expected to take place in a variety of ways. It was of course to result from improvements in basic living conditions. Huber observed that poverty caused the poor to indulge in wrong-doing, and he felt that the alleviation of poverty had to precede effective practice of the Christian virtues which those who were well off so smugly enjoined upon them. Moral improvement was also to take place through further education beyond the normal end of schooling, an additional auxiliary task (besides collective buying) for which the residential association provided an effective basis. Yet another kind of moral improvement was to ensue from the harmony between the different orders of society that Huber expected to result from the benevolent assistance rendered by the aristocracy: good feelings all around would replace class hatreds. But Huber's greatest hopes for the association in the area of moral improvement lay in an aspect of the association which differed from all of these. What he repeatedly came back to with great emphasis was the idea that simply being associated was conducive to the moral end. Co-operation

[33] Huber, *Bruch mit der Revolution und Ritterschaft*, 37-45, and "Assoziation," 472-473.
[34] Huber, *Ausgewählte Schriften*, 730, 766.

itself made men better. To be not only poor but also divided and alone was a doubly demoralizing experience. "Conversely," Huber wrote, "a healthy atmosphere of the organic whole, to which the individual feels himself bound as an independent and active spirit, would raise and strengthen each individual as [a part of] a mass." Huber awaited with high hopes the development of a "collective consciousness" and of an *"esprit de corps."* These were to act as restraining forces against the temptation to indulge in vice and as sources of encouragement for positive achievement in all areas of life. This kind of morally elevating function was fully as important as any of the others that the association could fulfill. By referring to it as often and as passionately as he did, Huber forcefully underlined the gap which separated him from liberal individualism.[35]

Huber's enthusiasm for co-operative associations as a means both of reducing material hardship and of overcoming individual isolation was widely shared by other writers. Some of them were just as conservative as Huber politically and even more conservative socially. A case in point is Franz Joseph Buss, whose sympathies lay manifestly with small craftsmen rather than with factory workers. Realizing that the old corporations which had originated in the Middle Ages were no longer viable, he contended nevertheless that something had to take their place. He therefore proposed a wide range of associations dedicated to economic improvement, education, care of the poor and the sick, and the inculcation of religion, which were to combine elements of mutual help and benevolence. "Thereby," he wrote, "the spirit of division among men visible in various areas of life and the present discontent with social life which arises from it would also disappear. So many lonely and discouraged people would find in such associations elevation and honorable activity." Another conservative Catholic writer gave more direct support to Huber in a review of one of his major works in the *Historical-Political Journal,* which had already begun by the middle of the decade to modify its support for the traditionally estatist views expounded by Riehl. Nevertheless, the reviewer hoped that associations of the sort which Huber proposed would evolve into true corporations, with legal rights and responsibilities. In fact, most writers of a strongly conservative bent looked with much greater favor on the old corporations than on the newer free associations. Like Wagener and Jörg, they suspected that associations, particularly if their members were drawn from the working classes, would simply serve as a means of organizing revolutionary violence.[36]

Huber thus received more support from moderate conservatives such as Albert Schäffle and from liberals than he did from the far right. Schäffle's social thinking was perhaps closer to Huber's than that of anyone else dealt with in this study. Like Huber, he had a horror of the "atomism" which he felt had come to prevail in Germany as a result of unrestrained social and economic liberalism. The diverse corporate groups of the past had been displaced by "a mass of unorganized and isolated individuals" on the one side and the bureaucratic state with its "oppressively mechanical overgovernment" on the other. One way out presented itself: "Those groups standing mid-way between the individual and the state, which combine the higher power of a larger community with knowledge of the needs of the comrades and interest in satisfying them, must again be sought out." Not a restored guild but rather the free association was what Schäffle had in mind. He argued for the development of co-operative groups at the local level which would serve as the basis for a wide range of self-help activities. More particularly, he referred his readers to Huber's work in order to apprise themselves of the ways in which associations could enable factory workers to improve their lives without infringing upon the rights of others.[37]

The idea of association struck an especially resonant chord with many liberal intellectuals, who saw in co-operative self-help a way of introducing positive social reform along essentially liberal lines, without simply turning to the state. Writers such as Immanuel Hermann Fichte, Friedrich Gottlob Schulze, and Carl Ludwig Michelet were likely to place a greater part of their hopes for the success of associations in purely economic benefits than were men such as Huber or Buss. They were less preoccupied than the conservatives with co-operation as a path which led toward moral restraint and elevation, bringing psychic as well as economic rewards. But even though they did not share Huber's almost mystical attachment to the co-operative as a repository for the individual's loyalties and a source of his spiritual strength, they still agreed with much of what he had to say. Like Huber, they were appalled by the extent to which individual interests had displaced group interests and by the personal isolation which this development had engendered. They too expressed unease over the rapid growth of a rootless and unorganized

---

[36] Buss, *Die Aufgabe des katholischen Theils teutscher Nation in der Gegenwart*, 42-44; Stegmann, 130-131; Herberger, 40-41.

[37] Schäffle, "Abbruch und Neubau der Zunft," 37-44, and "Fabrikwesen und Fabrikarbeiter," 495.

industrial proletariat, which they feared would resort to violence in order to seek redress for its grievances. They also agreed with him that co-operative associations provided an eminently sensible means of dealing with all of these problems which Germany confronted.[38]

MODERATE PROPOSALS FOR
POSITIVE ACTION BY THE STATE

Opposition to *laissez-faire* liberalism came not only from men like Riehl and Huber, who idealized the virtues of tightly knit social groups, but also from writers who advocated active involvement by the state in promoting the social and economic well-being of its citizens. Whereas Riehl, Huber, and most of the other admirers of either the traditional estates or the newer associations distrusted the central bureaucracies and therefore questioned the advisability of the government's undertaking a positive social welfare program, other writers contended that society could not simply be left to take care of itself. Even though some of these men felt that organized associations had an important part to play in combatting social distress, they all believed that there would also have to be direct intervention by the state. We shall begin by considering several thinkers who made extremely forceful pragmatic and philosophical arguments for positive state activity, even though their specific proposals were essentially quite moderate.

The most intellectually impressive and respected advocate of state-directed social reform was Lorenz von Stein, who produced a torrent of both major works and occasional essays during these years.[39] Among his many writings, the most widely read was his revised study of the social movements in modern France, which contained his classic analysis of the dynamics of social conflict and his famous call for a social monarchy as a way of preventing the further outbreak of social revolutions such as the one which the French had experienced in 1848. Stein admitted that the work as a whole – whose heavily dialectical construction showed the clear imprint of its author's early attachment to Hegel – was difficult to penetrate, and he was not alone in this judgment.[40] The long analytic

---

[38] Fichte, *System der Ethik*, II, part II, 92-100; Schulze, *Die Arbeiterfrage*, 19-20, 138-153; Michelet, *Die Lösung der gesellschaftlichen Frage*, 38-39, 89-97.

[39] For biographical background, see Werner Schmidt, *Lorenz von Stein* (Eckenförde, 1956). For Stein's ideas, see Heinz Nitzschke, *Die Geschichtsphilosophie Lorenz von Steins* (Munich and Berlin, 1932), and Pankoke, 75-99, 126-134.

[40] See the epigraph from Rousseau on the title page of the first volume of Stein, *Geschichte der socialen Bewegung in Frankreich:* "Je ne sais pas l'art d'être clair pour qui ne veut pas être attentif." See also Ludwig Häusser's criticism of the book's "all too systematic form" in a review reprinted in Häusser's *Gesammelte Schriften*, II, 455.

introduction was the most difficult part of all, but it ought nevertheless to be regarded as one of the period's most important and influential responses by any writer to the issues which had been raised by contemporary history.

The work opened with the assertion that Stein's earlier prophecies had come true: a social revolution had indeed occurred. It had taken place necessarily, "as a result of a definite law," which was the law of social movement. This law had not just come into being in 1848-49; it was an eternal law, and it would determine the events of future centuries just as it had determined those of centuries past. Stein's work was to expound and to illustrate the operation of this law, by illuminating the ways in which changes in the social order provided the key to changes in the legal and political order.[41]

Stein laid the foundations for his system by making a distinction between two basic elements of human community: the state and society. Each helped in its own way to overcome the limitedness of individual human beings. The state was the community's "independent will," the free and conscious form of community, or "the community, elevated to a personal unity, of the will of all individuals." Its object, in principle, was to secure the free and independent life of the individuals within it, whose level of development in turn determined its own. The state's basic principle, if it was to remain true to itself, was thus to look after the welfare of its citizens. Popular freedom and welfare necessitated participation by the citizen in forming the state's will, which would heighten his personal worth and energy by elevating him above "the constraining circle of his individual life." In addition to assuring the right to such activity, or "political freedom," the state would ideally fulfill a broad range of administrative services, fostering greater personal development by providing the individual with various kinds of direction and assistance (which Stein did not spell out). It was inherent in the very nature of the state that it should perform both of these functions. If it failed to do so – if the constitution and the administration did not take account of the individual and his destiny, and the state lived for itself alone – the state would die.[42]

To explain the fact that in the real world the state did not appear in the pure form which would seem to have been dictated by its essential nature it was necessary to examine the concept and principle of society. This was the "impersonal" aspect of community, not determined by the general will but instead based on "natural life elements" and growing

---

[41] Stein, *Geschichte der socialen Bewegung*, I, ii-iii.
[42] *Ibid.,* xiii-xvii, xxxiii-xxxvii.

out of the relations among individuals that were established as a response to economic needs. The kinds and amounts of goods possessed by the individual, which determined his occupational position, exerted an enormous influence on the development of a man's outlook and personality, even though he might think of himself as being free. By the same token, variations having to do with the possession of goods governed "the order of dependence of one from the other in the human community." Every man possessed some kind of ability to work, but not everyone owned the material goods without which labor was valueless. The social order could thus be described as "the order of the dependence of those who do not possess [material goods] from those who do." Such dependence, Stein felt, was a necessary aspect of social life. Individuals in society inevitably pursued their own happiness by avoiding dependence and seeking dominion over others.[43]

The state and society consequently stood in direct opposition to one another. Whereas the principle of the state was "the elevation of all individuals to the fullest freedom, to the fullest personal development," society's principle was "the *subjection* of individuals beneath other individuals, the fulfillment of the individual through the dependence of others." The content of the life of the human community thus consisted in "a constant struggle of the state with society, of society with the state."[44]

One likely outcome of this conflict was the growth of "unfreedom," through subjection of the state to the dominant groups in society. That society's "ruling class," fearing the state's efforts to raise the lower class from its dependent position, should attempt to appropriate the state for its own ends was "the first natural law of all interaction between state and society." Its chances of success were strongly favored by the fact that the state could only act through individuals, who inevitably occupied a place in the social order. This in turn meant that it was impossible for the state to assume a position outside society: the state could not withstand the pressures which were exerted by the predominant social class. "[Although the state is] the ruler according to its true nature," wrote Stein, "it is in reality the *obeyer*. And as a result, it will naturally obey all the more emphatically and one-sidedly, the more emphatically and sharply pronounced is the rule of one social class over the others." As examples of the process by which a ruling social class organized and maintained its grip on the state, Stein pointed to property qualifications

[43] *Ibid.*, xxxviii, xxx-xxxi, xvii-xxiii, xxxix-xli.
[44] *Ibid.*, xliii, xxxi.

for voting and for the holding of public office. Having secured political power, ruling classes utilized that power in order to protect and to advance their social interests, by instituting measures which made the acquisition of property more difficult for those who did not already possess it and thus reinforced their dependence. The classic means of maintaining the existing distribution of landed property was the *Fideicommis,* or entailed estate. For capital, the corresponding instruments were guilds and monopolies – unless free competition had succeeded in asserting itself, in which case factory owners would seek to secure themselves through the legal prohibition of strikes. As these practices became more and more developed, they led to the gradual transformation of social estates into legal estates and finally into castes. When the power of a ruling class had reached this level, even individual members of the lower class could not obtain the goods which were required in order for them to rise in the social order. The power of the state, which according to its true nature was a source of freedom, would be forced simply to serve a particular social interest, and "unfreedom" would have attained its culminating point.[45]

Stein believed that these tendencies were inherent in all social development, and he found abundant indications of their presence everywhere in Europe at the time, especially in the activities of industrial capitalists. How then, he asked, could the conflict between the state and society be resolved in such a way that freedom rather than a lack of freedom was the result? What tendencies pointed in a different direction from the one he had indicated so far? [46]

The movement toward freedom had to begin with changes in the social order. Stein asserted that it could not begin with attempts to change the structure of the state, and he thus took sharp issue wih the position adopted by the political democrats. Since the effectiveness of participation in political life was determined by the distribution of goods, it followed "that any elimination of the political dependence of the ruled class is *for nought,* if it does not *rest on the possession of goods.*" Neither purely idealistic demands for freedom and equality, nor laws, nor violence could make a dependent class free unless it was "in reality already free in itself." In other words, the prerequisite for political freedom was social independence. The prerequisite for social independence was education, which fortunately could be obtained without taking anything away from the ruling class and was thus relatively easy to come by. Particularly if it had

[45] *Ibid.,* xlv-xlvi, lxviii.
[46] *Ibid.,* lxi-lxii, lxviii-lxix.

a practical bearing on economic life, education in turn might enable the men who acquired it to enhance the value of their labor and thus to increase their possession of material as well as of intellectual goods. Such a change in the balance of social power would create a contradiction between the new order of society and the traditional legal and political order, forcing changes in the latter. The changes could be undertaken in one of two ways: through political reform or through political revolution. The first grew out of a timely recognition of the need to *"confirm the legal equality of those who are already equal socially."* The second resulted when the political ruling class refused to adapt to social change and a class that was still dependent politically but already powerful socially attempted to change the existing constitution forcibly in its own interests.[47]

Neither political reform nor political revolution would succeed unless the dependent class really could increase its share of the society's economic wealth. Education had to lead not only to intellectual but also to material gain if the members of a lower class were going to be able to assert themselves politically. Unfortunately, Stein pointed out, education did not always confer economic benefits. Indeed, a dependent class would be prevented from improving itself economically by acquiring education if, as a result of earlier political revolutions, the ruling class consisted no longer of an indolent landed nobility but rather of entrepreneurial capitalists. Men who did not simply own property but also worked for their living, such as industrialists and other businessmen, would make the acquisition of economic goods by the propertyless especially difficult. In order to compete effectively against one another, they would limit wages to the level of subsistence. Under such circumstances, those who possessed no property to start with would be stymied in their efforts to rise economically by obtaining education, which would do nothing to alleviate the miseries entailed by social dependence. Education would simply make these men more aware of their subjection to the capitalists who employed them.[48]

In Stein's view, this was precisely the point where Europe stood at mid-century, a point at which the difficulties in acquiring capital encountered even by educated laborers inevitably gave rise not to political movements but to social ones. The situation was seen as one in which the lower classes were inevitably turning to communism, socialism, or social democracy. Stein heavily criticized the first two movements on a number

---

[47] *Ibid.,* lxix-lxxi, lxxvi-lxxvii, lxxx-xcvi.
[48] *Ibid.,* xcix, ci-cvi.

of grounds, most of which need not detain us. The important consideration was that they both aroused the implacable hostility of the ruling class and that accordingly none of their objectives stood any chance of realization whatsoever unless they were supported by the existing state, which both movements neglected to consider. Recognition of the fact that the lower class could not rise in society unless it received assistance from the state did appear in "the idea of social democracy," which Stein treated much more favorably than either of the first two movements. The major economic proposal of the social democrats was that the state should provide propertyless workers with the capital they needed in order to escape from dependence on their employers. The social democrats (and Stein along with them) argued that only the state could effect this redistribution of economic resources, since the employers could not do so without contradicting their own economic interests. One way in which the state might do this would be to carry out an "organization of labor," by undertaking entrepreneurial functions of its own and giving the profits to the workers. For a variety of reasons, however, Stein did not believe this course to be feasible at the time. Stein looked with greater favor on the social-democratic proposal that the state should carry out an "organization of credit," providing individual members of the working class who possessed talent and energy but no capital with interest-free loans. But the state would clearly have to take capital from those groups in society which owned it in order to provide this assistance, groups which by virtue of their economic power also monopolized political power. In the face of this dilemma the propertyless class would seek to change the basis of political power, by introducing the democratic republic with universal suffrage. If men were educated, it was inevitable that this idea would occur to them: the social democratic principle would necessarily be pushed to its ultimate conclusions. Not to recognize this necessity was sheer blindness. "For it [the idea of social democracy] is nothing," wrote Stein, "if it is not the expression and the consciousness *of the sharp inner contradiction between the idea of freedom and the order of the acquisitive society.*" Although Stein believed that effective political democracy could only follow, not precede, an amelioration of the lower class's dependent social and economic position, he also recognized that attempts to combat social democracy directly, either by means or arguments such as this one or by means of repression, were in vain.[49]

Stein contended that one of two developments would emerge in such a situation: social revolution or social reform. The first occurred when the

[49] *Ibid.*, cix-cxviii.

propertyless working-class "proletariat," aware both of its deprivation and of its solidarity, attempted to seize political power, which it would always use in order to advance its own social position. "As long as," Stein asserted, "there is a social order, any entrance of the nonpossessing class into the state constitution – be it in the name of freedom and equality . . . of power . . . of humanity, of love, of brotherhood . . . of the church, of the divinity – will always have only this and no other application of the state power as a result." For the lower classes, the state was simply a means for acquiring a share of the nation's capital. Stein's first reproach against social revolution was that it actually diminished freedom: social unfreedom persisted; the lines of dependence were simply reversed, with capital being subjected to labor. Moreover, labor inevitably squandered what it had taken freely, and the capital for which it had not worked thus did it no good in any case. Finally, the system that resulted from social revolution could only be maintained by the use of violence, since the results of universal suffrage were never in its favor. "The number of those," wrote Stein, "who have [something] to lose in a social revolution is far greater than those who gain. Experience shows that universal suffrage has *never* been suited for establishing a purely social regime." Since the working class could not rely on force indefinitely in order to thwart the rest of society, such tactics inevitably led to dictatorial re-action.[50]

The other possibility was that the state would undertake its own program of social reform. Stein wanted to show that in view of the objective conditions faced by the workers and the internal contradictions which beset any social revolution, timely reform from above provided the only means by which social freedom could conceivably be realized in a capitalist society of the sort which was rapidly emerging in western Europe. At the same time, he argued that only in this way could the state could be true to its basic principle, since, as Stein had maintained from the very start of his essay, the state's essential function was to help raise its citizens out of the dependence which society enforced upon them. Finally, social reform was obviously in the state's pragmatic interests, since it provided the only means by which the state could be sure of forestalling social revolution and maintaining public order. For all of these reasons, state-supported programs to assist the lower classes were an absolute necessity, in Germany as well as France.[51]

[50] *Ibid.,* cxviii, iv, cxix-cxxiv.
[51] *Ibid.,* cxxiv-cxli.

One problem with Stein's analysis was that although it presented a powerful case for the necessity of social reform it contained no specific suggestions. To be sure, Stein commented favorably on some of the economic programs suggested by the social democrats, but he did not really adopt them as his own. One student of Stein's thought has asserted that when Stein urged the state to adopt an active social policy he was implicitly suggesting measures such as the following: legislation which would influence wages and the length of the working day; abolition of female and child labor; social insurance; the furthering of popular education; caring for public health; and helping to provide decent housing.[52] It is quite true that Stein's later studies of public administration, published during the 1860's and 1870's, did propose many of these steps, as well as other positive measures which the state ought to undertake. But neither in his study of modern France nor in any other work which appeared during the decade after the revolutions of 1848-49 did Stein have very much to say concerning just what the state should actually do. His fundamental objective was simply to win acceptance for a basic theoretical position – namely, that the very nature of the state compelled it to aid members of the lower classes in their attempts to acquire the economic capital without which they could not become truly free men. At this point, details did not interest him.

Stein's thought also suffered from internal inconsistency. The very arguments which Stein employed in order to demonstrate the necessity of reform raised serious questions concerning the possibility of reform. How, given the fact that the state was inevitably dominated by those groups in society which possessed the greatest economic power, could the reform of society in fact be brought about?

Stein indicated two separate ways out of this dilemma, neither of which held much real promise in view of the seemingly unshakable arguments he had constructed in developing his basic analysis of the relationships between economic and political power. One way out led through an appeal to what Stein hoped would be a deeper and more comprehensive sense of self-interest on the part of the ruling class. By force of circumstances, the dominant groups in society would come to recognize the necessity of using the political power which accompanied their economic power in order to help the lower classes escape from their totally dependent position. Otherwise, they too would suffer from the effects of the lower class's deep frustration. The ruling class would necessarily sacrifice

---

[52] *Ibid.,* cxiii-cxvii; Heinrich Künne, *Lorenz von Stein und die arbeitende Klasse* (Münster, 1926), 40.

some of its narrower interests, not out of love for those who were less fortunate than they but in the realization that this was the only way to avoid the tribulations of a social upheaval. Eventually the ruling class would carry out its own social reforms and help create "the society and the republic of mutual interest." [53] Nevertheless, Stein's basic thesis that political power was unavoidably determined by the existing distribution of economic goods made this solution seem rather improbable. If its economic superiority really was the necessary and sufficient factor which enabled the ruling class to maintain a stranglehold on the state, what reason was there to expect that it would let itself be frightened into weakening its dominance just because some members of the lower class might be about to revolt, especially since lower-class revolutions were doomed to failure anyway?

Stein found another way out of the dilemma more appealing, but given his constant assertion that the state was always subjected to the interests of society's ruling class it seemed even less probable than the first one. Stein placed most of his hopes on one part of the state which he expected would stand above social interests, thus representing the good of the state alone. The part of the state which Stein had in mind was the monarchy. The king would refrain from favoring narrow social and economic interests; he would instead carry out social reform, in order to defend his larger political interests. Historically, Stein argued, the monarchs had everywhere developed their powers by supporting the lowly and the oppressed. In the future, they could maintain their power only by coming once again to the aid of the lower classes, whose support they would be able to count on as repayment for their benevolence. "Every monarchy," Stein wrote, "will henceforth become either an empty shadow or a despotism, or give way to a republic, if it does not have the high moral courage to become a monarchy of social reform." But even if Stein could demonstrate that social reform would benefit the monarchs politically, the question still remained as to how the kings would in fact be able to assert themselves against the interests of society's ruling class. Everything possible was to be done in order to safeguard their freedom of action: above all, they were not to be fettered in their reforming efforts by elected parliaments, which would inevitably reflect the dominant social and economic interests. Still, Stein's own basic theses made it difficult to see how a king could ultimately succeed in maintaining his

---

[53] Stein, *Geschichte der socialen Bewegung,* I, cxxiv-cxxxi; see also Stein, *System der Staatswissenschaft,* I, 343 ff., 418-422.

independence and having his programs administered in such a way as to accomplish a reform program.[54]

These criticisms point up certain internal difficulties in a system of thought so tightly constructed around the principle of economic determinism that it appeared to deny the possibility of the very measures of social reform which its author took the greatest pains to assert were both desirable and necessary. In summary, however, the important point is not that Stein failed to achieve perfect logical consistency. It is rather that he combined what was in many ways a profound analysis of the sources of social unrest with a clear awareness that somehow the power of the state had to be directed toward lower-class economic improvement if the causes of that unrest were to be overcome. Though lacking in specifics, the thrust and the urgency of his admonitions were unmistakable.

Stein's attempts to engage the state in an active program of social reform which would improve the conditions of lower-class life found obvious parallels in similar efforts undertaken by a number of Germany's other publicists and social theorists. The arguments these men employed were by no means identical with those developed by Stein. Some writers, such as Constantin Frantz and Hermann Wagener, both of whom seemed to echo Stein directly by calling for a "social monarchy," shared Stein's hope that a king who undertook reform from above would avert challenges to his authority from below.[55] But advocates of state action who were politically liberal – and there were a few such voices – generally showed little concern with promoting social welfare programs as a way of buttressing royal domination of government. They might seek to establish the principle of state aid to society as a way of overcoming conflict, but they did not want the monarch to remain free from parliamentary control. Nor did they necessarily focus on social conflict per se. In several cases what one encounters is less an emphasis on the need to forestall revolutionary violence than the desire to effect a conceptual

[54] Stein, *Geschichte der socialen Bewegung*, I, xxxvii-xxxviii, and III, 16 ff., 19, 49. See *ibid.*, II, 44 ff., on the relationships between parliamentary government and social exploitation in post-1830 France. It should be noted that Stein's political conservatism differed markedly from his ideas in the *Vormärz* and early in 1848, when he had held high hopes for democracy (see Pankoke, 85-90). See Erich Angermann, "Zwei Typen des Ausgleichs gesellschaftlicher Interessen durch die Staatsgewalt: Ein Vergleich der Lehren Lorenz Steins und Robert Mohls" in Werner Conze, ed., *Staat und Gesellschaft im deutschen Vormärz, 1815-1848* (Stuttgart, 1962), 181-190, for a more detailed analysis of Stein's internal contradictions.

[55] See the discussion of Frantz, *Die Staatskrankheit*, in Eugen Stamm, *Konstantin Frantz' Schriften und Leben, 1817-1856* (Heidelberg, 1907), 239-249; on Wagener, see Saile, 44-52.

synthesis of competing ideas, a synthesis which would assign each doctrine its due as a way of establishing a more persuasive theory of law or ethics. Positive action by the state could thus be recommended not simply for its pragmatic value but also for reasons more directly related to justice or morality than the ones offered by Stein. A final difference between Stein and some of these other writers arose from the fact that whereas Stein simply developed general principles they suggested at least some of what the state should do in specific practice.

Heinrich Ahrens and Immanuel Hermann Fichte, both of whom were political liberals, clearly illustrated these possibilities, each having produced lengthy studies of social thought and proposals for social reform which complemented Stein's work quite well. Surveying the recent history of European legal philosophy, Ahrens pointed out not only a basic split between "subjective" (or critical) and "objective" (or conservative) theorists but also a conflict between divergent tendencies within the tradition of subjectivism. Young Hegelianism, socialism, and communism stemmed in his view from the same critical spirit which had nourished liberalism, but their supporters rejected the liberal view that the state was simply a *Rechtsanstalt*, or institution for upholding the legal order. These newer tendencies indicated what might happen in the absence of proper constraints on the subjective will of the individual. But they were also a "*reaction* against the other extreme of the purely *negative* and formalistic legal and political theories, a *challenge* to learning, to elevate the legal and political concept above this formalism and to recognize the state as an institution which must provide social life not only with protection, but also with *positive* assistance in all essential life interests, to the extent that this is compatible with the requirements that should be made of the private activity of individuals." Ahrens regarded the state as an "organism of society," possessing a far broader purpose than merely that of forbidding transgressions against the law. If the state was to have a single purpose or goal rather than several goals, that goal could admittedly be none other than the realization of justice (*Recht*). The essential characteristic of the state was that it constituted "the legal ordering of society." But Ahrens wished to broaden the concept of law, so that it could be seen as "a basis for furthering the total well-being of humanity." It would have to encompass the mutual claims of free individuals on one another. In this light, the state – as society's legal order – appeared "not merely as a protective institution but also as a helping institution for all human life." The state would not lead the individual toward his destiny

by the hand, but it would provide the conditions which made independent development truly possible.[56]

For Ahrens, the realization of the state's goal in more specific terms
entailed such positive measures as education for all children, improvement
of the means of transportation, and protection of the public both from
natural disaster and from epidemic disease – all of which lay beyond
the capabilities of the individual. The state was also to regulate the
relationships among the various parts of the social organism, so that each
part would have its "independent life and legal sphere." Especial care
would have to be taken that there was no disturbance of the social
organism's health "through an overly great development of the one organ
and a retardation of the other." Ahrens thus warned against an over-
expansion of industrial and commercial forces, which might force "the
higher interests and intellectual goods of life" into the background.
(Ahrens did not really specify how the desired balance was to be maintained. He seemed to favor the encouragement of intellect rather than
the limitation of industry.) Within the industrial world, there was a need
for legal regulation by the state of the relations between workers and
employers.[57]

Like Ahrens, Fichte sought to present his social theory as a synthesis
of many of the ideologies articulated by his predecessors. Fichte discerned
three basic "practical ideas," or values, which had served as the main
points of reference in the debates among Europe's social and political
thinkers during the period since the middle of the eighteenth century:
individual freedom protected by law, the relationship of men to one
another in a community, and divinely prescribed order. Fichte was
especially concerned to adjudicate the conflicts which had arisen between
those who supported the first and those who supported the second of
these three values. He steadfastly opposed the "negative conception of
freedom" and the view of the state as a "mere legal and emergency
institution," which he called "the false liberalism of our time." Even
though he rejected the proposals of the French socialists and communists,
whose pursuit of an "abstract, levelling equality" threatened legitimate
individual rights, Fichte noted that they had been on the right track in
their efforts to secure greater recognition for the principle of communal
solidarity. Individual self-assertion had to be balanced by love for one's

---

[56] Ahrens, *Die Rechtsphilosophie*, ix-x, 10-15, 120-121, 126-131, 143, and *Die
organische Staatslehre*, 90-91, 239-240, 107-108.
[57] *Ibid.*, 107-117; Ahrens, *Die Rechtsphilosophie*, 146-148. Ahrens promised to
treat industrial regulation at greater length in a second volume of *Die organische
Staatslehre*, but this never appeared.

fellow man. Excessive liberalism had to be replaced by a conception of the state which accorded due recognition to *"the idea of 'beneficence,'* of *fulfilling community."* The state was not to be seen either as a mere protector of the law or as an end in itself. It was rather to be regarded as a means for maintaining the general welfare and bringing about ever greater human perfection. In the broadest sense, it was "the general vehicle for promoting all the ethical ideas." Fichte coupled this theory with a broader definition of *Recht* itself, which closely resembled Ahrens' definition. "Everyone," he wrote, "has the same claim to the free development of this genius (of the personality) in and by means of the community. Only then, when all the requirements for it are assured him through the same [the community] is the *inner justice,* the inherent (God given) right fulfilled for him; for only then does he succeed ... in becoming what ... he already *is."* Only that state was just which provided its citizens with the communal prerequisites for realizing their individual potentialities to the full.[58]

The following specific recommendations accompanied Fichte's general theoretical argument. In principle he favored guaranteeing a job to everyone who was able to work, even though he modified this demand somewhat by admitting that the state might not yet be able to fulfill it. He urged the adoption of other measures unequivocally: enacting laws to limit unrestrained competition; establishing a system of educational institutions in order to provide vocational training for workers; carrying out an "organization of commerce" by providing information about prevailing conditions of supply and demand; and limiting the length of the working day in the factories. It must of course be pointed out in conclusion that although Fichte's proposals were fairly explicit they, like the proposals made by Stein and Ahrens, did not in any way entail a radical restructuring of social and economic life.[59]

THE POSTREVOLUTIONARY ADVOCACY OF SOCIALISM

Beyond the moderates, a few scattered writers urged far more radical remedies for the social distress which they felt lay behind the mid-century revolutions, all of them expounding one or another form of socialism. None enjoyed anything like the prestige and intellectual influence which

---

[58] Fichte, *System der Ethik,* I, 14-24, x-xi, and II, part II, 211-213, 21. Fichte hoped that the spirit of love would be nourished by Christianity, with its emphasis on the brotherhood of all men. See *ibid.,* I, 819-820, and his "Die Religion und Kirche als wiederherstellende Macht der Gegenwart," 348.

[59] Fichte, *System der Ethik,* II, part II, 40, 81-91, 264-265.

accrued to writers such as Riehl, Huber, or Stein. The peripheral positions of two of the socialists, Ferdinand Lassalle and Moses Hess, are readily evident in their biographies: having attempted to encourage an uprising against the Prussian government in November of 1848, Lassalle spent several months during the early 1850's in prison, and for the remainder of the decade he confined his written advocacy of socialism to personal letters; Hess spent almost all of the decade abroad and wrote nothing that was published in Germany. In the same way that the authorities were suppressing the remnants of radical and even not so radical working-men's organizations, so too they were likely to make life difficult for socialist intellectuals, especially if they were radical politically.[60] The other two men encountered in this study who can be called socialists, Karl Rodbertus and Karl Marlo, also failed to exercise much influence over their contemporaries during these years. Nevertheless, they produced lengthy and impressive treatises on the social question – treatises in which, despite their unmistakable ties to the political left, they explicitly subordinated the pursuit of political reform to the search for a better society and set forth strong arguments for wide-ranging state control of the economy in the interests both of social stability and of social justice.[61]

A firm supporter of German unity and a member of the left center in the Prussian National Assembly during 1848, Rodbertus emerged from the revolution with a strong conviction that broadly based popular control of government was both necessary and inevitable. The opening pages of his *Social Letters to von Kirchmann* maintained that public practice would eventually have to catch up with the academic legal theories that had persistently whittled away at the basis of princely power. Just as the criticism of historical rights in the area of civil law had eventually led to personal freedom and freedom of property, so too changes in political structure would follow changes in political ideas. "Now and then," Rodbertus wrote, "a truce is attempted in this area between 'free princes' and 'free peoples,' but here too the victory of practice tends to follow the victory of scholarship; increasingly in the practice of public law ... nothing will remain valid but government by the popular will." This belief that the future direction of political change was inevitable permitted Rodbertus to assert that the great public issues to be dealt with now were

---

[60] Richard W. Reichard, *Crippled from Birth: German Social Democracy, 1844-1870* (Ames, Iowa, 1969), 99-119.

[61] See G. D. H. Cole, *A History of Socialist Thought*, II (London, 1954), 14-31, for a comparative treatment of Rodbertus and Marlo. Rodbertus and Lassalle are treated in Charles Gide and Charles Rist, *A History of Economic Doctrines*, trans. R. Richards (2nd English ed., London, 1948), 416-437.

of a different sort. Legal study had, he asserted, fulfilled its reforming mission. The role it had once played now fell to the study of economic questions.[62]

The study of economics, to which Rodbertus had already made several contributions during the *Vormärz* in the form of pamphlets which adumbrated most of his later ideas, had to yield remedies for two "very threatening phenomena" which cast their shadow over mid-nineteenth century Europe: pauperism and commercial crises. Rodbertus adduced considerable statistical evidence to the effect that these scourges of modern society had appeared suddenly after the great liberal victories around the turn of the century in the fields of private and public law and that they had become much worse in recent decades. Rodbertus summarized his basic analysis of these evils when he asserted "that the cause of pauperism and of commercial crises lies in nothing else but [the fact] that, under contemporary economic conditions, with the rising productivity of labor the wage of the working classes becomes an ever smaller portion of the national product." Even if the real incomes of the workers should increase, they would never keep pace with increases in industrial output. And in any case, there was an inevitable tendency under conditions of free competition for wages to seek a minimum level of subsistence. This decline in the workers' share of the total national product was to be condemned in and of itself. Holding to the theory that labor was the source of economic value, Rodbertus asked, "Can there be a more natural conclusion, a more just demand, than that the creators of this old and new wealth derive some advantage from this increase . . . that either their income be raised, or the time of their labor be moderated, or ever greater numbers of them enter into the ranks of those fortunate ones who are especially entitled to enjoy the fruits of labor?" But Rodbertus considered working-class poverty to be intolerable on other grounds than simply moral ones. He contended that it prevented an adequate level of demand for the increasing numbers of goods that were being produced. The imbalance between supply and demand periodically led to such a sharp decline in the marketability of industrial output that the entrepreneurs were forced to cut back their levels of production. Such cutbacks in turn increased the hardship suffered by the workers. Pauperism and commercial crises were thus mutually reinforcing. Moreover, they heightened the danger that European civilization would be completely destroyed by an oppressed and suffering class of workers. If men did not mitigate their effects by substituting "rational" laws for the "natural" ones which

---

[62] Rodbertus, *Sociale Briefe an von Kirchmann,* I, 5-6.

prevailed at the time, history would once again "brandish the whip of revolution." [63]

Rodbertus discounted several conceivable remedies for these sources of discontent, directing most of his criticism at proposed solutions for the problem of pauperism. The efforts of individuals would avail little. "The egoism which masquerades as morality," he wrote, "blames the vices of the workers as the cause of poverty." But the men who displayed such egoism failed to see "that a blind commercial power turns the prayer for work into the scourge of forced unemployment . . . that thrift is an impossibility or a cruelty." Nor could the situation be improved through the efforts of workers' associations to force the employers into granting higher wages by means of strikes when employment *was* available, since the employers could always outlast their employees. Moreover, in a letter to Hermann Schulze-Delitzsch, he expressed serious doubts about the sufficiency of associative self-help through co-operation, which he asserted had often failed when it was attempted abroad.[64]

Rodbertus offered his own solutions for pauperism and commercial crises in the fourth volume of the *Social Letters,* a work entitled *Das Kapital,* which was written at the time of the first three but published only after his death. His economic program did not actually emerge as an explicit attempt to solve these problems but rather as a means of securing a still larger objective: true freedom for the individual. His emphasis thus shifted back once again to moral and ethical considerations. Freedom entailed more for Rodbertus than independence from the will of society through the enjoyment of civil and political rights. Men were not yet free in his eyes as long as they were subjected to the wills of other individuals who could exercise control over them by virtue of the fact they owned landed and capital property. Everyone had to enjoy an equal right "to those *outer social preconditions,* which are needed by the individual in order, *according to the degree of his contribution,* to partake of the *fruits of social life.*" Without this right, the individual possessed only "an empty *legal sphere*" which lacked all content. Freedom necessitated "a civilization with a *social will,* that is, with [a] *state, centralization,* and *communism. . . . Not individualism but rather socialism concludes the series of emancipations that began with the Reformation.*"

---

[63] *Ibid.,* 6-8, 3, 72, 74-75, 79; Rodbertus, *Zur Beleuchtung der socialen Frage,* I (Berlin, 1875; a reprint, unchanged except for pagination, of the second and third of the *Sociale Briefe*), 54. On Rodbertus' pre-1848 writings, see H[einrich] Dietzel, *Karl Rodbertus,* I (Jena, 1886), 5 ff., 20-21.

[64] Rodbertus, *Sociale Briefe,* I, 6-7, 81, 43-46; F. Thorwart, *Hermann Schulze-Delitzsch* (Berlin, 1913), 78-80.

A long line of "the noblest and most perceptive men from Plato to Owen," which in recent decades also included writers such as Saint-Simon, Fourier, and Cabet, represented the intellectual tradition that pointed the way to mankind's ultimate release from bondage.[65]

Rodbertus' definition of "communism," which he used interchangeably with "socialism," was quite broad. He felt that a certain kind of communism was already inherent in the economic system that had grown out of the division of labor. There was already communal production and to some extent a communal division of the product as well. "The fact is," Rodbertus asserted, "that society begins with the limitation of the individual *through communism*, that its nature is precisely *communism*, that finally the course of history consists of nothing but the generalization of *communism*." In short, social and economic interdependence and cooperation were by their very nature communistic. The extent to which communism could be furthered depended on the existing economic structure and the social values which predominated at the time. "The degree of generalization," he wrote, "is ... conditioned by the degree of the efficacy of the division of labor, the inner strength of the ethical order, and the unanimity of the popular consciousness." His own proposal was that there should be two major changes in the structure of the economy. In the first place, the state should possess land and capital, or the means of production. Personal property was not to be eliminated, but interest-yielding property would no longer remain in private hands. In addition, wages were to be established in relation to productivity, so that the workers would receive in payment a sum equal in value to what they had created. Rodbertus did not believe that this system could be instituted immediately. Centuries would be required for its realization. For the moment, he contented himself with advocating "*a compromise among labor, landed property, and capital*," as a result of which the working classes would receive a somewhat more appropriate wage. Nonetheless, he defended the need for a prophetically utopian vision that could see this compromise as a milestone leading toward a far better future.[66]

Karl Marlo shared Rodbertus' deep concern with social questions, supported many of his views concerning the necessity of social reform, and received his high praise. Less influential on later thinkers than Rodbertus, who was to exercise considerable effect in the 1860's on Ferdinand Lassalle and in following decades on the reform-minded "socialists of

[65] Rodbertus, *Das Kapital*, 215-224. Rodbertus' explicit advocacy of "communism" – a word which he used in a much looser sense than was customary at the time – first appeared after the revolution (Dietzel, II, 41-42).

[66] Rodbertus, *Das Kapital*, 84-85, 89, 94, 115 ff., 226-228, 230.

the chair," Marlo deserves attention nevertheless as a writer who developed independently and on a much broader scale a searching critique of European society.[67] Moreover, his multivolume *Examination of the Organization of Labor* illustrates once again, even more strongly than Rodbertus' work, the ethical dimensions of much social thought during this period.

Marlo stood clearly on the political left. Having stated at the start of his work, in a preface written during 1848, that he supported republican principles, he went on in a later volume to develop a series of proposals for democratic government at every level of political life. But like Rodbertus he insisted that political matters were secondary. Indeed, he went so far as to say that these issues were irrelevant to men's true needs. The primary objectives men should be striving for were not constitutionalism and freedom of the press but measures which would improve society. The most important part of any civil order was not its constitution but rather the laws that regulated the ways men made their living. No constitutional arrangement by itself could prevent revolution if the general welfare of the citizenry had been neglected. As we have already seen in an earlier chapter, Marlo regarded the French revolution of 1848 as merely a prelude to a larger struggle for social reform. That the resolution of this struggle did not depend on the introduction of specific political forms was indicated by the agreement between the legitimist Radowitz and the democrat Louis Blanc on the necessity for an organization of labor. Economics was "an empirical science, whose results are susceptible of equal application in autocratic, aristocratic, and democratic states." He added that ". . . any admixture of political views must therefore have the double disadvantage that thereby the boundaries of various sciences are blurred and the judgment of purely economic subjects is muddied by the zeal of political parties." [68]

Marlo pointed to a wide range of economic and social problems, which affected not only the emergent working classes but also a large segment of the lower middle classes, the *Mittelstand* of small producers. Propertyless workers and their families faced ever greater poverty and demoralization because of the conditions which wage laborers had to endure in the factories and in Europe's growing cities. Hunger and the increasing absence of women from their homes contributed to rising rates of drunkenness, sexual promiscuity, and crime among this part of the population.

[67] *Ibid.*, 104-105; see Gide and Rist, 417-420, on Rodbertus' later influence.
[68] Marlo, *Programm* (appended to the first volume of the *Untersuchungen über die Organisation der Arbeit*), 1-8, and *Untersuchungen*, I, part I, 230-231, 475, 18.

Traditionally independent artisans faced the imminent prospect of sinking into the working-class proletariat or even lower. Technological development and the extension of credit primarily benefited big industrialists, who were in the process of destroying the little man's livelihood. In short, the advent of large capitalists under conditions of free competition posed a vital threat in Marlo's eyes to the welfare of most of contemporary European society.[69]

Much in the manner of academic social philosophers such as Heinrich Ahrens and Immanuel Hermann Fichte, whom we encountered in the preceding section, Marlo set forth his remedies for social distress as a unifying alternative to certain sharply conflicting doctrines espoused by other thinkers of the present and of the recent past: namely, liberalism and communism, which in his view dominated the social thought of the nineteenth century. Both of these doctrines could be regarded as forms of "panpolism": in contrast to the "monopolism" which had predominated in world history up until 1789, they emphasized equal rights for all rather than the monopoly of special privileges by the few, thus harking back to the spirit of early Christianity. But they differed from one another just as much as they differed from monopolism, the one implying equal rights to freedom while the other pointed to equality of economic goods. Both of these doctrines were woefully misleading. Even though most of the men who adhered to them were sincerely motivated by good will toward their fellow men, they lacked insight into the proper ways of achieving their own objectives. Liberals sought to enlarge the sphere of freedom, but they failed to realize that a man was free "in the most general sense of the word" only if he possessed "the power to carry out his will" and that in fact the *laissez-faire* policies which they supported removed the economic prerequisites for this capacity from an ever larger segment of the population. Liberalism ended up contradicting itself, inasmuch as it led to a new monopoly in the form of large-scale capitalism. The communists, on the other hand, did not consider the need for differential rewards as a means of inducing men to exert themselves in their work. In the event that communism was put into practice there would be an inevitable increase in compulsion to work by the state, but the total wealth of society would still decline. Wanting to make men happier, the communists would succeed only in making them poorer and more wretched.[70]

[69] Marlo, *Programm*, 1-5; W. Ed. Biermann, *Karl Georg Winkelblech (Karl Marlo)*, I (Leipzig, 1909), 113-115.
[70] Marlo, *Untersuchungen*, I, part I, 246-253, 211-215, 284-346.

Instead of liberalism or communism, Marlo called for a third form of panpolism, namely "federalism," which was to promote a maximum of personal freedom and equality for all members of society. Under the federalist system all able-bodied men would be guaranteed the right to work up to the limits of their capacities and they would be entitled to the full use of the products of their labor. In order to secure this right the state would not only set up employment agencies but also own and run all essential utilities and most other large-scale economic activities. Many forms of economic life would be left in private hands, including agriculture, small-scale production, and retail trade, but these activities would be controlled by a series of state-regulated guilds, access to which would be open to all citizens on the basis of examinations. The furtherance of public education, the establishment of a public credit system, and the creation of contributory social insurance for protection against sickness, accidents, and old age were other functions which Marlo wished the state to assume. Finally, Marlo wanted the state to regulate the right to marry, in order to check the rapid growth of population. Men would not be allowed to raise families unless they could demonstrate their ability to support them by contributing to the social insurance fund. All of these measures were regarded as being essential in order to bring about the popular well-being which had been the constant objective of the great revolutionary movements during the preceding sixty years.[71]

Marlo, like Rodbertus, supported his case for social reform by arguing that unless such reform took place another revolutionary struggle would break out. He warned that the next time around the new plutocratic nobility of wealth would be pitted in a desperate struggle against a large party of social democrats. But he also contended that social reform was a religious obligation. "All men," he wrote, "in whose breasts the last spark of religious feeling has not flickered out should dedicate their energies to socialism." Christianity dictated justice and love toward one's neighbor, and support for Marlo's program provided one way of demonstrating those qualities.[72]

What were Marlo's suggestions in the event that the upper classes lacked not only the Christian feeling but also the insight into their own best interests which would induce them to support the cause of reform, a possibility which Marlo clearly foresaw? There were points at which Marlo seemingly allied himself with the forces of revolution, suggesting that a violent upheaval might well provide the only means of instituting

---

[71] *Ibid.*, 347-383; Biermann, 119-121, 145-152; Cole, 25-27.
[72] Marlo, *Untersuchungen*, I, part I, 464, 483-485, 493, and II, 64 ff., 151.

the social and economic order which he felt was required in order to satisfy the demands of justice. He certainly went farther in this direction than Rodbertus. But basically he remained a philanthropist rather than a militant, addressing himself to humanity as a whole rather than to a revolutionary social class, and he continued to place most of his hopes in efforts to educate men to his way of thinking. The socialists' duty was "to kindle the hearts of the folk for the new idea by writing and talking." Indeed, the only real revolutionary among socialists in Germany during this period – and not a very prominent one at that – was Ferdinand Lassalle. His expressions of faith in several letters to Karl Marx (who had left Germany permanently in 1849 and was almost unknown there until the 1860's) that a future working-class revolution would surely succeed found few echoes among other writers at the time.[73]

Several points need to be made about the social thinkers in general by way of concluding this chapter. The first two are especially applicable to Marlo, but they can be abundantly documented in the writings of other men as well. Although the ideas of these writers were not always influenced by religious considerations, they did contain a distinctly more significant religious element than the ideas of most intellectuals whose primary concern lay in the area of politics. Not only conservatives such as Riehl, Jörg, Huber, and Buss, but also moderates such as Ahrens and Fichte and the democrat Marlo sprinkled their pleas for social reform with frequent references to the dictates of Christianity. Appeals to religiosity, they felt, provided an essential means of inducing men to turn away from the selfish individualism which constituted the hallmark of the liberal social order. In this regard, many of the German social thinkers participated in a broad European movement, which included the Christian socialists in England and Catholic social action groups in France. Social reformism was probably based less exclusively on religious and ethical imperatives after 1848 than it had been in the *Vormärz* (one thinks at this point of the hard-headed pragmatism revealed by many of Stein's arguments), but it still included such elements to a considerable degree. The second point is that the social thinkers revealed much more sympathy for foreigners than did any of the other groups of intellectuals. The difference in their sympathies was especially marked with regard to the French socialists, whom they usually criticized but from whom many of them derived vital stimuli nevertheless. In responding to the ideas of men like Saint-Simon and Louis Blanc as receptively as they did, they

---

[73] *Ibid.*, I, part I, 381, 231, 419; Lassalle, *Nachgelassene Briefe und Schriften*, III, 13-15, 36-37, 39-42, 52-53, 94-95.

vividly demonstrated that despite the rising tide of nationalism in general and of anti-French feeling in particular at least some German writers were still willing to learn from their counterparts across the Rhine.

A final point concerns the social thinkers' politics. Although these men came from every political camp, one cannot help being impressed by the proportion of the most important among them who were politically conservative. Rodbertus and Marlo were the only men in the whole range from the right center to the far left who deserved to be ranked in the same league with figures such as Riehl, Huber, and Stein as students of social problems and advocates of social reform. In many instances men whose politics were conservative pleaded for such reform as a way of helping to fend off liberal assaults on traditional patterns of political authority. According to this view, the great bulk of the German population would turn decisively away from efforts to undermine the political status quo as soon as their basic social and economic needs were met, thus leaving the liberals isolated. Admittedly, only a very few of the intellectuals who strongly emphasized this line of thinking held positions of much influence within any sort of an official establishment, and others (Huber being the most obvious example) openly expressed their alienation from the ruling circles in matters of social policy. Conversely, the intellectuals who enjoyed the greatest official favor, such as Friedrich Julius Stahl and Leopold Ranke, devoted at best a relatively small portion of their energies to discussing social matters. It should also be pointed out that the activities of the governments in this area were far from impressive. There was, however, particularly in Prussia, an active official effort to restore some of the privileges formerly enjoyed by the craft guilds, a policy which fulfilled many of the pleas for corporatist social reform voiced by men such as Riehl and Wagener.[74] And later in the century, after the fruits of the guild reaction had been swept away by the liberal legislation of the 1860's, the suggestions made by men like Stein found their counterpart in the conservative state socialism introduced by Otto von Bismarck. The belief, articulated by many of Germany's leading social thinkers in the aftermath of the revolution, that a close connection existed between conservative politics and social reform served again as a guiding principle of public policy.

[74] See Hamerow, *Restoration, Revolution, Reaction,* 211-218.

VI

CONCLUSION

This study has been organized around a number of different themes related to the revolution of 1848-49 and dealt with in the literature of the 1850's, but by way of summary let us review some distinctions among groups of men which were developed toward the outset. The political liberals still adhered to the ideal of national unity under constitutitional government, even though they occasionally admitted that their tactics might have to be modified in light of the defeat which the centrist elements of the Frankfurt Parliament had suffered at the hands of their enemies on the right and the left. These men retained great faith in a moderate program of reform – a program, it should be noted, which had never entailed any support for democracy or much support for social reform. They similarly believed in their own power to help realize this program through scholarly writing, particularly in the field of history. The liberals opposed and were opposed by smaller groups of men who were located at the political extremes. On the one side stood the democratic radicals. Persecuted, isolated, and frequently despondent about their immediate propects, they consoled themselves nevertheless with the belief that the achievement of political democracy had been thwarted primarily by liberal unwillingness to take the decisive step of revolution and that their cause was bound to triumph in the end. On the other side stood the conservatives. They offered the recent agitation by revolutionary democrats as proof that their own instinctive rejection not only of radicalism but also of liberalism was fundamentally sound, arguing that radical insurrection was the inevitable consequence of more limited attacks against the political status quo.

In contrast to all three of these groups, a number of men who adhered to a wide variety of political positions felt that the most pressing issues raised by the events of 1848-49 were not political but instead social. Much more far-reaching and provocative on the whole in their analyses than the predominantly political thinkers, they insisted on the importance of human relationships outside the state. Some, displaying the same faith in the power of thought which liberals revealed in their pleas for partisan historical writing, called for the development of a new *Gesellschaftswissenschaft*, or "science of society." Almost all of them detected a wide range of ills in the area of social and economic life, brought on in their view primarily by inflexible *laissez-faire* liberalism. Some advocated mutual solidarity and self-help from below, looking to groups such as the estate, the guild, or the co-operative association as the means by which the individual could escape what seemed to them to be his increasing loneliness in the modern world. Others demanded a more active role on the part of government. Rejecting both the reverent Hegelian view of the state as an end in itself and the limited liberal view of the state as a "night watchman," they focused on the wider goals and purposes which states ought to further in the interests of their citizens. They suggested various ways in which the state should render assistance to society, some rather modest, others pointing toward the establishment of state socialism.

This summary suggests a general conclusion which comprises several parts. The interpretation of the 1850's as a decade which witnessed a far-reaching process of "softening up" in intellectual life for Bismarck's successful revolution from above between 1862 and 1871 requires serious modification. Preparation of a sort for the decisive events of the 1860's did occur, but what most historians have written on this subject is in many ways both inadequate and misleading. Beyond these defects, the general view of the 1850's as a prelude to the political struggles of the following decade has been too narrowly limited. It has failed to comprehend much of what was especially interesting and vital in the intellectual life of the postrevolutionary years, most notably by disregarding what was happening in the area of social thought.

Let us begin with a crucial aspect of what occurred in men's minds which has frequently been referred to but seldom been given the emphasis it deserves. The intellectual representatives of the progressive forces did display much greater hostility than before to one another. In the *Vormärz*, intellectuals who advocated change had constituted something of a common front. As a result of the revolution, the front disintegrated into its constituent elements. The postrevolutionary liberals manifested not only continued opposition to the established powers but also a new resentment toward those who wished to pursue goals which led beyond constitutional government and national unity. Some liberals called attention to social issues, but not many. The general liberal response to the social movements and to the pursuit of political democracy was that they had grievously injured the chances of making any gains at all. Many of the democrats and the social thinkers had in turn become disillusioned with what they took to be the hesitancy and the limitations of political liberalism. To put it another way, one of the most important changes within the German intellectual community during this period was the growth of a spirit of division, which was manifested in mutual recrimination and attacks on men who before 1848 had been allies. Divisions had of course already set in during 1848-49 in the sphere of active politics, but the process of reflection on the course of recent history after the revolution deepened them. As the ideological spectrum came to mirror more nearly the tensions within German society, it also heightened those tensions. Such splits in what had formerly been a unified progressive movement greatly weakened that movement from within and hardly augured well for the future. Indeed, one of the main liabilities which saddled the opposition to Bismarck in the 1860's was precisely the gulf which separated it from the German masses. This was not simply a matter of neglecting to carry out widespread organizational efforts. Bismarck's opponents were also separated from the majority of the population by mutual distrust, which, as Heinrich von Sybel clearly recognized, would have made it difficult to stage mass demonstrations even if the liberals had tried to do so.[1] Liberal hostility toward movements associated with the interests of the lower classes and the apathy of men concerned with the social problem toward political liberalism were the most damaging legacies of the 1850's to the decade of domestic and international conflict which followed.

Heightened awareness of such splits was not, however, at all the same thing as abandonment of one's own goals and principles. An attack on a former ally was in fact a frequent substitute for criticism of oneself. Intellectuals generally felt that they had been proved right – or at least that they had been left unscathed – by what happened in 1848-49, not that they had been discredited. Very few writers decided that their earlier convictions had been invalidated in any fundamental way by the course of events. The process appears to have been one of sharpened self-definition rather than of abrupt about-face. Part of the explanation for this phenomenon doubtless lies in the fact that the intellectuals had so deeply

---

[1] Julius Heyderhoff, ed., *Die Sturmjahre der preussisch-deutschen Einigung, 1859-1870: Politische Briefe aus dem Nachlass liberaler Parteiführer*, I (Berlin, 1925), 152-153.

committed themselves through their open political involvement. Looking at the year 1848-49 alone, we discover that approximately four fifths of the seventy men included in this study sat either in the Frankfurt Parliament or another deliberative body, served in a ministry, wrote political pamphlets, worked as journalists, or participated in some other fashion in political life.[2] Men who had already committed themselves publicly were not necessarily prevented from changing their minds, but they were not quite so free to do so as they would have been under other circumstances.

There were admittedly a number of men who responded to the revolution by advocating the reinforcement of the traditional ruling powers, in order to rescue Germany from liberal folly and the radical chaos to which it had supposedly led. But they seldom did so in the spirit of atonement or self-abnegation. The men who strike one as decidedly conservative politically had almost all been conservatives before the revolution began, and while they had much to denounce they had little to renounce. Very few of the pre-1848 liberals failed to maintain their allegiance to the liberal cause. To be sure, liberals had to ask themselves many hard questions after the events of 1848-49, and in some cases they did modify their earlier priorities and expectations. A number of them came to place more emphasis on the need for unity than on the need to reorganize political life within the state. Many were also coming to feel that unification would have to be achieved in co-operation with the existing governments rather than under the aegis of a popular parliament alone. Heightened respect for material power, both as an instrument for the attainment of political ends and as a standard of value in its own right, was an unmistakable fact of intellectual life. But the magnitude of such shifts is too often exaggerated. Concern with the national issue had already been on the rise during the 1830's and 1840's. It is also important to remember that most of the liberals had never, except perhaps during the year of revolution itself, been really committed advocates of parliamentary government in the English sense of that term. They had certainly never been convinced democrats. Their failure during the post-revolutionary years to pursue democratic objectives consequently represented a return to rather than an abandonment of their earlier positions. It should also be pointed out that even men such as August Ludwig von Rochau, who employed the rhetoric of power in a particularly striking

[2] Even when we subtract several men who were included in this study in the first place simply because they had sat in the Frankfurt Parliament, over three quarters of the remaining intellectuals had been politically active.

way, had by no means given up their constitutional objectives in favor of national ones. They still regarded liberalism and nationalism as two sides of the same coin.

Continuity is also apparent in the area of general attitudes toward the public relevance of intellectual endeavour. The writers' faith in the power of thought to shape the course of public events belies the view that during the postrevolutionary decade they were moving toward the Bismarckian belief in "blood and iron" as the only means of settling the great questions of the day. We have admittedly encountered a significant thread of criticism which disputed both the political capacities of thinkers and the general efficacy of thought, but on the whole the confidence of Germany's writers in themselves and in the public value of their products remained high. Given their belief that the writings of socialists and communists had contributed heavily to what were generally regarded as the revolution's worst aspects, they could hardly deny the influence of ideas in political and social struggles.

The real crisis of German liberalism occurred in the 1860's, after the politically quiet decade of reaction had been succeeded by the New Era. This short period began when Frederick William IV's brother, Prince William, became regent in Prussia late in 1858 and replaced the autocratic Manteuffel ministry. Elsewhere too during the next few years the liberals were in the process of making fresh breakthroughs – especially in Baden, which was evolving toward ministerial responsibility to parliament, but also in Bavaria. Events seemed to confirm the liberals in their expectations that domestic political reform was inevitable.[3] International developments also raised liberal hopes. When war broke out between Austria and Piedmont in northern Italy early in 1859, few Germans, except for democratic radicals such as Arnold Ruge, Georg Gottfried Gervinus, and Ferdinand Lassalle (and the opportunistic Bismarck), openly sided with the Italians, but when the Austrians were defeated liberal satisfaction was plainly evident. Italians had set a dazzling example by taking an enormous step toward unity and at the same time had humbled the main obstacle to a *kleindeutsch* solution of the German national problem.[4] A concomitant of these domestic and foreign develop-

---

[3] For general discussion of the reawakening of political life at the end of the decade, see Theodore S. Hamerow, *The Social Foundations of German Unification, 1858-1871: Struggles and Accomplishments* (Princeton, 1972), 8ff., and Heinrich Heffter, *Die deutsche Selbstverwaltung im 19. Jahrhundert* (Stuttgart, 1950), 404 ff. See Haym, *Ausgewählter Briefwechsel*, 160 ff., and Droysen, *Briefwechsel*, II, 577 ff., for the views of two of the more important figures treated in this study.

[4] Koppel Pinson and Klaus Epstein, *Modern Germany* (2nd ed., New York, 1966), 112-114.

ments was the burgeoning of new pressure groups and parties, such as the National Union, founded in Frankfurt in 1859, and the Progressive Party, founded in Prussia in 1861.

By the middle of 1862, it was clear that the New Era had ended. Prussian liberals were now deeply enmeshed in a constitutional conflict with the government over the organization and the financing of the army, and in September Bismarck was called to the helm. The liberals struggled for several years against the iron chancellor's efforts to maintain monarchical autocracy in budgetary and military affairs. Hermann Baumgarten, writing to Heinrich von Sybel from Baden in 1863, was more radical than most intellectuals when he urged the Prussian liberals not to negotiate but instead to attack and if need be to summon the rest of the country into action. Nevertheless, a general swing to the left at this time in response to the government's challenge was unmistakable. It appeared in the columns of the *Prussian Annals* and in the sharply critical parliamentary speeches of Rudolf von Gneist, as well as in an essay written by Heinrich von Treitschke, which threatened the Prussian government with a revolution if it did not change its repressive policies.[5]

After 1864, when Prussian and Austrian forces defeated Denmark and secured German control over Schleswig-Holstein, a marked change in liberal attitudes toward the government began to set in. The liberal opposition steadily waned in the face of Bismarck's tangible success in the area of foreign policy, even though conflicts persisted regarding constitutional matters. Rudolf Haym spoke for many liberals when he wrote in April of 1866 that although he hesitated to give the Prussian government a vote of confidence he still felt obligated to support it fully, inasmuch as it was obviously pursuing the goal of national unity. The *Prussian Annals,* now edited by Treitschke, similarly declared that the national issue was paramount and urged support for Bismarck in the upcoming struggle against Austria.[6]

The reversal of earlier liberal expectations in domestic politics culminated when Prussian forces emerged victorious over Austria and her German allies after the battle of Königgrätz on July 3, 1866, the decisive event in the brief war which gave Prussia hegemony over northern Germany. Treitschke now wrote, "Liberalism should finally take a sober look at the modest extent of its power, it should reduce its aims in accord with what is attainable, and it should no longer delude itself that this

---

[5] Heyderhoff, 151-152; Heffter, 428-429; see also Hamerow, 149 ff.

[6] Haym, 245; Hans Rosenberg, ed., *Die nationalpolitische Publizistik Deutschlands: Vom Eintritt der neuen Ära in Preussen bis zum Ausbruch des deutschen Krieges* (Berlin, 1935), II, 960-962.

Prussia, in whose evolving political structure the crown, the army, and the local self-government are the strongest pillars, will simply allow itself to be made over in the form of an English-Belgian model." The most notorious declaration of a change of heart appeared in a famous essay written for the *Prussian Annals* by a former radical, Hermann Baumgarten. The essay, entitled "German Liberalism: A Self-criticism," asserted that Bismarck's opponents had been discredited by history. Liberal intellectuals were no match in his view for the Prussian Junkers when it came to the practical task of attaining concrete political successes. At about the same time, on September 25, most of the liberals in the Prussian Diet signaled their agreement with these views by voting in favor of an indemnity bill which absolved Bismarck from any charges of having acted illegally in his expenditure of public funds without parliamentary approval. Many of the liberals thus took a decisive step toward acquiescing in autocratic rule. But this attitudinal change resulted more from Bismarck's spectacular diplomatic and military successes than from a crisis of confidence caused by earlier liberal failures. Previously, the liberals had been able to console themselves with the thought that whatever their own faults might have been their adversaries had not acquitted themselves with much distinction either, but that was certainly no longer the case by 1866.[7]

A still more important conclusion is that the revolution of 1848-49 and the intellectuals' continued confidence in the power of the written word during the 1850's produced a considerable outpouring of serious thinking which deserves attention completely apart from the matter of how Germany came to be unified. Like any major disruption of political and social life, the revolution provided men with food for thought, and that food was by no means left untouched. There occurred in fact a highly productive reorientation in German intellectual life. In short, it is not the thought of the 1850's which suffers from sterility or narrowness but instead our historical comprehension of it.

Two areas of German intellectual life were especially stimulated by the revolution. One was history. Not only was academic historical study in the narrow sense on the rise; in addition, a number of men advocated historical perspectives in such fields as economics and philosophy. Similarly, men were turning away from speculative theory and toward historical empiricism in the area of political discourse. The liberals and some

---

[7] Heffter, 454; Hermann Baumgarten, "Der deutsche Liberalismus: Eine Selbstkritik," *PJ*, XVIII (1866), 455-515, 575-628; see also Karl-Georg Faber, "Realpolitik als Ideologie: Die Bedeutung des Jahres 1866 für das politische Denken in Deutschland," *HZ*, Vol. 203 (1966), 1-45.

democrats, such as Gervinus, expressed a strong belief that the goals they sought were necessary not only from a moral but also from a historical viewpoint. The legitimacy of their programs was based in their eyes to a considerable degree on what they considered to be historical inevitability. Philosophers at the time and intellectual historians with strong leanings toward German idealism might regard these changes both as an abdication of responsibility and as a decline in quality, but to an intellectual historian whose sympathies for the idealist tradition are less fervent it simply represents a reorientation.

The other especially vital area was marked out by the social thinkers – men like Lorenz von Stein and Wilhelm Heinrich Riehl, both of whom produced classics of nineteenth-century social analysis in the immediate aftermath of the revolution. Their writings clearly reveal the inadequacy both of the general stereotype which assumes the period's barrenness and of the tendency which has prevailed in most scholarship to treat the intellectual history of the 1850's simply in terms of attitudes toward politics. Such an emphasis is quite understandable in view of the fact that the 1850's were immediately followed by a decade in which the struggle of monarchical and bureaucratic versus popular and parliamentary power and the question of how Germany was going to be unified assumed paramount importance in German public life. But reading history backwards in this way seriously impairs our comprehension of the full range of problems which occupied men during the years before the great events of the 1860's. The thought of the decade between the revolution and the end of the reaction not only addressed political issues but also demonstrated an increased sensitivity to and sophistication about social and economic issues among a substantial number of Germany's leading scholars and other writers. These men developed new ways of studying society and presented solutions for social problems which they felt had been inexcusably neglected. Although their work did not bear directly on most of the disputes which commanded public attention during the period between 1859 and 1871, it mattered a great deal to the intellectual life of the time in which it was written. The social thinkers had something new and important to tell their contemporaries. Although their specific recommendations often diverged sharply, these men confronted mid-century Germans with a perceptive and forceful criticism of the intellectual assumptions and public policies which had subordinated the concern for social welfare to preoccupation with political institutions. Moreover, their significance extends beyond the 1860's. They provided important antecedents for such later nineteenth-century phenomena as the historical school of economics, which flourished under the leadership of Gustav Schmoller, the full elaboration of academic sociology by figures such as Ferdinand Tönnies and Max Weber, the social reformism championed by the *Verein für Sozialpolitik,* and the practical successes of the various co-operative movements. The emergence of a heightened social consciousness after a revolution which many German thinkers rightly regarded as having been not only politically but also socially motivated was the real event in postrevolutionary intellectual life.

THE MEN AND THEIR WORKS

Intellectual historians who treat more than a handful of writers seldom make explicit their criteria of selection. They provide few clues as to how they assembled the rosters of thinkers whose ideas they discuss. This habitual preference for covering one's tracks is fully consistent with the tendency of most intellectual historians to think of themselves as more akin to humanists than to social scientists, but it demands much of the reader and gives him too little in return. On the one hand, it asks him to accept the results of an investigation without being privy to the reasons behind some of the most important decisions which preceded and accompanied its execution. On the other, it often prevents him from arriving at any very clear notions about the extent to which the ideas he has encountered can be generalized beyond the individuals who are under consideration. For these reasons, I have decided to depart from the custom of silence when it comes to explaining the "mechanics" of intellectual history. The following few pages articulate the criteria and the methods I employed in accumulating the names of the men and the titles of the books and articles dealt with in this study. Short biographical notes on these men and listings of the works by them that proved germane to my research follow these preliminary remarks on methodology.

At an early stage in my investigation of the postrevolutionary decade, I constructed a preliminary roster of 189 men, almost all of whom were historians, jurists, political scientists, economists, or philosophers; or publicists who were clearly writing at a level which transcended current events of only passing interest. Clerics and theologians, philologists, experimental psychologists, natural scientists, geographers, purely imaginative writers, and statesmen were not considered. Some of those who were excluded may well have had interesting views on the issues discussed in this study, but it seemed plausible to me that in assessing the impact of the revolution on the intellectuals it would make most sense to focus on men whose professional activity involved them in the analysis of political or social questions. Moreover, I excluded Austrians, as well as (with a very few exceptions) men who emigrated from Germany during or immediately after the revolution and then stayed out of the country permanently. By and large, the men on my roster spent most of the decade in the area which was to become the German Empire, or they returned to it in the course of the 1860's.

The most important single source of names was the fifteen-volume *En-*

cyclopedia of the Social Sciences, ed. Edwin R. A. Seligman and Alvin Johnson (New York, 1930-35), an internationally collaborative work whose authors apparently tried to record all the major figures in the history of the various disciplines of greatest relevance to the study of society. They also treated a great many political and social publicists. As a repository of this kind, it is unequalled. Some men do seem to be listed more because of their interest to subsequent thinkers than because of the attention they attracted when they were writing, but few thinkers of any great repute among their contemporaries (at least in the 1850's) appear to be omitted. Noting the names of all Germans who were born in 1835 or earlier and who were still alive after the end of the revolution, subject to the conditions outlined above, I came up with a list of 124 men. Supplementing this source with the second volume of Wilhelm Windelband's standard *History of Philosophy* (trans. James H. Tufts, New York, 1901), I added another fifteen names. In addition, I used the two editions of the *Verzeichniss der Abgeordneten zur ersten deutschen Nationalversammlung in Frankfurt am Main* (Frankfurt a. M., 1848-49) and Max Schwarz, *MdR: Biographisches Handbuch der Reichstage* (Hannover, 1965), to compile a list of the professors and other university teachers from non-Austrian areas at the Frankfurt Parliament – intellectuals who had been involved in the revolution in an obviously direct and personal way. After applying the disciplinary criteria explained above, I added thirty-four new names from this list to my larger one, over a dozen academicians from the Frankfurt Parliament having already been noted in my other sources. Finally, I used a variety of general histories of the disciplines, histories of Germany, and special studies as a check on the major sources. In this way, I added sixteen more names, bringing the total to 189.

I checked all of these names in the catalogues of the Widener Library at Harvard University, the British Museum, and the Bavarian State Library, as well as in Christian Gottlob Kayser's standard *Vollständiges Bücher-Lexikon*. In addition to works published during the period 1849-59, I noted memoirs, correspondence, and collections of reprinted essays. I then checked for articles by these men in a number of periodicals and other collaborative works: the *Allgemeine Monatsschrift für Wissenschaft und Literatur* (published 1850-54); the *Deutsche Vierteljahrs Schrift*; the *Deutsches Staats-Wörterbuch* (ed. Johann Caspar Bluntschli and Karl Brater, 11 vols., Stuttgart and Leipzig, 1857-70); *Die Gegenwart: Eine encyclopädische Darstellung der neuesten Zeitgeschichte für alle Stände* (ed. August Kurtzel, 12 vols., Leipzig, 1848-56); *Germania: Die Vergangenheit, Gegenwart und Zukunft der deutschen Nation* (ed. Ernst Moritz Arndt, 2 vols., Leipzig, 1851-52); the *Historisch-politische Blätter für das katholische Deutschland*; the *Historische Zeitschrift* (first published in 1859); the *Preussische Jahrbücher* (first published in 1858); the third edition of *Das Staats-Lexikon: Encyklopädie der sämmtlichen Staatswissenschaften für alle Stände* (ed. Karl von Rotteck and Karl Welcker, 14 vols., Leipzig, 1856-66) and the *Zeitschrift für die gesammte Staatswissenschaft*. In all of these publications, I also noted anonymous items and items by men not on my list which dealt with topics of particular interest. I subsequently looked at everything I had noted which was at all likely to comment in more than a purely reportorial fashion on one or another of those problems which seemed to me to be of central importance for tracing the impact of the revolution on the intellectuals: the public functions of scholarly intelligence, recent political and social history, or broad political and social questions of continuing importance during the 1850's. Only such writings are listed below.

The biographical notes indicate the main lines of professional activity and any evidence which I have been able to find of participation in politics before, during, or after the revolution. They usually do not go beyond the 1850's. Further information about most of these men can be obtained from either the *Allgemeine Deutsche Biographie* or the *Neue Deutsche Biographie*. Entries on most of them also appear in the original *Encyclopedia of the Social Sciences*. A few works on individuals which were especially useful are listed in various parts of the secondary bibliography. At the end of this appendix is a list of over 100 men whom I checked in the course of my research without discovering any items that were more than marginally relevant to my purposes.

AHRENS, Heinrich (1808-74). Jurist, with specialty in legal philosophy. Taught at Göttingen in the early 1830's, then fled to Belgium after participating in the uprising of 1831. In Belgium, taught philosophy and was active in political life until 1848. Sat on the left center and worked on the constitutional committee at the FP. Was called to Leipzig after teaching in Austria during the 1850's.

"Freiheit, Freiheitsrechte," in *DSW*, III (1858), 730-745.

Juristische Encyclopädie, oder organische Darstellung der Rechts- und Staatswissenschaft auf Grundlage einer ethischen Rechtsphilosophie. Vienna, 1855.

Die organische Staatslehre auf philosophisch-anthropologischer Grundlage. Vienna, 1850 (Vol. II of *Die Philosophie des Rechts und des Staates*).

Die Rechtsphilosophie, oder das Naturrecht, auf philosophisch-anthropologischer Grundlage (1838). 4th ed., Vienna, 1852 (as 4th ed., Vol. I of *Die Philosophie des Rechts und des Staates*).

Rede, gehalten am 26. April beim Antritt des Lehramtes der Rechtsphilosophie (1850; reprinted at the end of *Die organische Staatslehre*).

ARND, Karl (1788-1877). Economist and journalist. Worked in government service as an engineer.

Die naturgemässe Volkswirtschaft, mit besonderer Rücksicht auf die Besteuerung und die Handelspolitik (1845). 2nd ed., Frankfurt a. M., 1851.

Die Staatsverfassung nach dem Bedürfniss der Gegenwart. Frankfurt a. M., 1857.

ARNDT, Ernst Moritz (1769-1860). Historian and publicist. Taught history at Bonn, 1818-20. Was subsequently arrested (though neither convicted nor acquitted) because of his nationalism. Returned to political writing in the 1830's and to a professorship of history at Bonn in 1840. Sat on the right center at the FP. Retired in 1854.

Ein Lebensbild in Briefen, ed. Heinrich Meisner and Robert Geerds. Berlin, 1898.

"Einleitung," in *Germania,* Vol. I (1851).
Pro populo Germanico. Berlin, 1854.

BAMBERGER, Ludwig (1823-99). Publicist, with legal training. A Jew, was active in 1848-49 as a popular orator and democratic organizer. Fled to Switzerland in 1849 after participating in the uprising in the Palatinate. Studied economics and worked in banks in London, Rotterdam, and Paris during the 1850's and 1860's. Returned to Germany in 1866.
Erinnerungen. Berlin, 1899.
Erlebnisse aus der pfälzischen Erhebung im Mai und Juni 1849. Frankfurt a. M., 1849.

BAUER, Bruno (1809-82). Theologian, publicist and historian. Taught at Berlin and Bonn in the 1830's and early 1840's, but was prevented from teaching after that because of his left-wing Hegelianism.
Die bürgerliche Revolution in Deutschland seit dem Anfang der deutschkatholischen Bewegung bis zur Gegenwart. Berlin, 1849.
De la dictature occidentale. Charlottenburg, 1854.
Russland und das Germanenthum. 2 vols. Charlottenburg, 1853.
Der Untergang des Frankfurter Parlaments: Geschichte der deutschen constituirenden Nationalversammlung. Berlin, 1849.

BAUMGARTEN, Hermann (1825-93). Publicist and historian. Finished his university studies in 1847 after much difficulty because of his radical politics. Edited the *Deutsche Reichszeitung* from 1848 to 1852, supporting moderate liberalism, then turned back to radicalism during the reaction. Worked as a research assistant to Gervinus. In 1861, took a post at the technical institute in Karlsruhe.
Gervinus und seine politischen Ueberzeugungen (anon.). Leipzig, 1853.

BAUMSTARK, Eduard (1807-89). Economist and political scientist. Taught at Greifswald starting in 1848. In 1848, was active in the Prussian National Assembly. Sat in the Erfurt Parliament and, later in the 1850's, in the Diet of the German Confederation.
Zur Geschichte der arbeitenden Klasse. Greifswald, 1853.

BERNHARDI, Theodor von (1802-85). Historian, economist, publicist, and diplomat. In 1834, entered Russian government service. After 1851, worked in Germany as a private scholar. Wrote for the *Preussische Jahrbücher.*
Aus dem Leben Theodor von Bernhardis, Vol. II: *Unter Nikolaus I. und Friedrich Wilhelm IV.: Briefe und Tagebuchblätter aus den Jahren 1834-1857.* Leipzig, 1893.
"Unsere Verfassung im Sinn der extremen und im Sinn der gemässigten Parteien" (1858), in *Vermischte Schriften,* Vol. II. Berlin, 1879.

BIEDERMANN, Karl (1812-1901). Historian and publicist. Taught philology and political science at Leipzig starting in 1838. Edited the *Deutsche Monatschrift* and served on Leipzig's municipal council in the 1840's. Was prevented from lecturing after 1845 because of his support for Prussian leadership in German unification. In the FP, sat on the left center. Attended the Gotha assembly. Lost his professorship in 1853 because of legal proceedings arising out of his editorship of the *Deutsche Annalen* (which appeared only briefly). In 1855, began editing a government-owned newspaper in Weimar.

"Demokratie, demokratisches Princip," in *SL*, Vol. IV (1860).

"Die Entwickelung des parlamentarischen Lebens in Deutschland," in *Germania*, Vol. I (1851).

"Die Entwickelung des Staatswesens in Deutschland, England und Frankreich," in Friedrich von Raumer, ed., *Historisches Taschenbuch*. Leipzig, 1859.

Erinnerungen aus der Paulskirche. Leipzig, 1849.

Frauen-Brevier: Kulturgeschichtliche Vorlesungen. Leipzig, 1856.

"Die Versuche zur Einigung Deutschlands seit der Auflösung des Reichs," in *Germania*, Vols. I-II (1851-52).

BLUNTSCHLI, Johann Caspar (1808-81). Jurist. Taught at Zürich and served on the city council until 1848. Then emigrated to Munich, where he quickly began to teach, specializing in German private and public law. Briefly published a newspaper during the revolution. Wrote many articles for the *Deutsches Staats-Wörterbuch* (11 vols., Stuttgart, 1857-70), which he edited with Karl Brater. In 1859, he and Brater founded the *Süddeutsche Zeitung*.

"Absolute Gewalt," in *DSW*, Vol. I (1857).

Allgemeines Staatsrecht, geschichtlich begründet. Munich, 1852.

"Bürgerstand," in *DSW*, Vol. II (1857).

"Civilisation," in *DSW*, Vol. II (1857).

"Demokratie," in *DSW*, Vol. II (1857).

Denkwürdiges aus meinem Leben. 3 vols. Nördlingen, 1884.

"Doktrinarismus," in *DSW*, Vol. III (1858).

"Dritter Stand," in *DSW*, Vol. III (1858).

"Eigenthum," in *DSW*, Vol. III (1858).

BÖCKH, August (1785-1867). Classical philologist and historian. Held a professorship at Berlin starting in 1810 and held other high positions at the university in subsequent years. Was an active member of an electoral club in 1848.

"Ueber die Einheit der Preussischen Monarchie und über die Einheit Deutschlands" (1849), in *Reden*, ed. Ferdinand Ascherson. Leipzig, 1859.

"Ueber die Pflichten der Männer der Wissenschaft gemäss der bisherigen Entwickelung und dem gegenwärtigen Standpunkt derselben" (1855), in *Reden*.

"Ueber die Umbildung der Deutschen Universitäten" (1850), in *Reden*.

"Ueber die Wissenschaft, insbesondere ihr Verhältniss zum Praktischen und Positiven" (1853), in *Reden*.

BÖHMERT, Victor (1829-1918). Publicist and editor of commercial newspapers in the 1850's. Later taught at the technical institute in Dresden.

Freiheit der Arbeit! Beiträge zur Reform der Gewerbegesetze. Bremen, 1858.

BUSS, Franz Joseph (1803-78). Jurist. Taught at Freiburg starting in 1836 and sat for several years during the 1840's in the lower chamber of Baden's diet. Was a Catholic and opposed bureaucracy in favor of the Church, but urged protection of workers. In 1848, presided at the first German *Katho-likentag* in Mainz, sat on the far right at the FP. Later attended the Erfurt Parliament. Defended the Church in the struggle over schools in Baden during the 1850's.

Die Aufgabe des katholischen Theils teutscher Nation in der Gegenwart, oder der katholische Verein Teutschlands. Regensburg, 1851.

"Die deutsche Einheit und die Preussenliebe" (1849), in Ludwig Bergsträsser, ed., *Der politische Katholizismus,* Vol. I. Munich, 1921.

DAHLMANN, Friedrich Christoph (1785-1860). Historian. In the 1830's, taught politics and history at Göttingen, was elected to Hanover's diet. His *Die Politik, auf den Grund und das Mass der gegebenen Zustände zurückgeführt* (Göttingen, 1835) was an influential expression of moderate liberalism. Was dismissed from Göttingen in 1837 after protesting the revocation of the Hanoverian constitution. Went to Bonn in 1843. Worked on the constitutional committee at the FP, where he helped lead the right center. Attended the Gotha assembly. Sat in the upper chamber of the Prussian Diet, 1849-50, and in the Erfurt Parliament, then returned to academic work.

Briefwechsel zwischen Jakob und Wilhelm Grimm, Dahlmann und Gervinus, ed. Eduard Ippel. 2 vols. Berlin, 1885-86.

DROYSEN, Johann Gustav (1808-84). Historian. Taught at Kiel before the revolution. Was one of the founders of the "Prussian" school of historiography. Was active behind the scenes in the FP, sitting on the right center. Later attended the Erfurt Parliament. In 1851, went to Jena; in 1859, to Berlin.

Briefwechsel, ed. Rudolf Hübner. 2 vols. Berlin and Leipzig, 1929.

Geschichte der preussischen Politik, Vol. I: *Die Gründung.* Berlin, 1855.

"Grundriss der Historik" (1858, as manuscript), in *Historik: Vorlesungen über Enzyklopädie und Methodologie der Geschichte,* ed. Rudolf Hübner. Munich and Berlin, 1937.

"Preussen und das System der Grossmächte" (1849), in *Politische Schriften,* ed. Felix Gilbert. Munich and Berlin, 1933.

"Zur Charakteristik der europäischen Krisis" (1854), in *Politische Schriften.*

DUNCKER, Maximilian (1811-86). Historian. Was imprisoned for six months in 1837 because of activities in a *Burschenschaft* at Bonn. Started teaching at Halle in 1839. At the FP, sat on the right center. Attended the Gotha assembly. Sat in the Prussian Diet and in the Erfurt Parliament, 1849-50. Because his moderate views were unpopular at conservative Halle, left for Tübingen in 1857. In 1859, became director of the Prussian government's press office.

Feudalität und Aristokratie. Berlin, 1858.

"Die neuere Geschichte Frankreichs" (anon.), *PJ,* III (1859), 288-299.

"Die Politik der Zukunft" (anon.), *PJ,* II (1858), 27-43.

Politischer Briefwechsel aus seinem Nachlass, ed. Johannes Schultze. Leipzig, 1923.

Vier Wochen auswärtiger Politik. Berlin, 1851.
Zur Geschichte der deutschen Reichsversammlung in Frankfurt. Berlin, 1849.

EISELEN, Johann (1785-1865). Economist and political scientist. Starting in 1829, taught at Halle. Served on Halle's city council in the 1830's.
Preussen und die Einheitsbestrebungen in Deutschland. Halle, 1850.

ERDMANN, Johann Eduard (1805-92). Philosopher. Started teaching at Berlin in 1834 after several years as a pastor in his native Latvia. In 1836, went to Halle. Belonged to the right wing of the Hegelian school. In 1848, wrote several pamphlets and gave lectures on political philosophy.
Philosophische Vorlesungen über den Staat. Halle, 1851.
Versuch einer wissenschaftlichen Darstellung der Geschichte der neuern Philosophie, Vol. III, part II: *Die Entwicklung der deutschen Speculation seit Kant.* Leipzig, 1853.

FALLMERAYER, Jakob Philipp (1790-1861). Historian and publicist. Taught in a Bavarian secondary school, 1826-34, then turned to journalism. Lost a professorship which he had held at Munich since March of 1848 because of membership in the FP, where he sat on the left center. Continued to write for the *Augsburger allgemeine Zeitung* after the revolution.
"Gegenwart und Zukunft" (1852-55), in *Gesammelte Werke,* Vol. II: *Politische und culturhistorische Aufsätze,* ed. Georg Martin Thomas. Leipzig, 1861.
"Die Lage" (1852), in *Gesammelte Werke,* Vol. II.

FICHTE, Immanuel Hermann (1796-1879). Philosopher. Began teaching at Berlin, but was later forced to teach in a *Gymnasium* because of suspected sympathies for the *Burschenschaften.* Went to Bonn in 1837, then left for Tübingen because of dissatisfaction with the conservatism of the Prussian Cultural Ministry. In 1847, organized the first in what was intended to be a series of yearly meetings of German philosophers, but these were cut short by the revolution. Gave an address at the FP on the constitution.
"Die Religion und Kirche als Wiederherstellende Macht der Gegenwart" (1852), in *Vermischte Schriften,* Vol. II. Leipzig, 1869.
System der Ethik, Vol. I: *Die philosophischen Lehren von Recht, Staat und Sitte in Deutschland, Frankreich und England, von der Mitte des achtzehnten Jahrhunderts bis zur Gegenwart.* Leipzig, 1850.
System der Ethik, Vol. II, part II: *Die Lehre von der rechts-sittlichen und religioesen Gemeinschaft, oder die Gesellschaftswissenschaft.* Leipzig, 1853.

FORTLAGE, Carl (1806-81). Philosopher. Taught at Jena starting in 1846.
Genetische Geschichte der Philosophie seit Kant. Leipzig, 1852.
"Ueber den Unterschied von Staat und Gesellschaft," *Allgemeine Monatsschrift für Wissenschaft und Literatur* (1853), 775-785.

FRANTZ, Constantin (1817-91). Publicist and social-political theorist. Worked in the Prussian Cultural Ministry during the 1840's. Travelled widely and wrote on philosophical subjects and current politics both before and during

the revolution. Performed diplomatic service in Spain in the 1850's, then
returned to private life in 1858.

Die Constitutionellen (anon.). Berlin, 1851.

Die Erneuerung der Gesellschaft und die Mission der Wissenschaft
(anon.). Berlin, 1850.

Louis Napoleon (anon.). Berlin, 1852.

Die Staatskrankheit (anon.). Berlin, 1852.

Unsere Politik (anon.). Berlin, 1850.

Unsere Verfassung (anon.). Berlin, 1851.

Von der deutschen Föderation (anon.). Berlin, 1851.

Vorschule zur Physiologie der Staaten. Berlin, 1857.

FREYTAG, Gustav (1816-95). Publicist, imaginative writer, and historian.
After teaching philology for several years at Breslau, left the university in
1847 to pursue a literary career. In 1848, became co-editor of *Die Grenzboten.* Ties to nationalism and liberalism were strengthened through association with and employment by Grand Duke Ernst II of Sachsen-Coburg
and Gotha in the 1850's.

Bilder aus der deutschen Vergangenheit (1859). 2 vols. 2nd ed., Leipzig,
1860.

Debit and Credit (1855), trans. L. C. C. New York, 1858.

Erinnerungen aus meinem Leben. Leipzig, 1887.

Gesammelte Werke, Vol. XV: *Politische Aufsätze.* 2nd ed., Leipzig, 1897.

GERVINUS, Georg Gottfried (1805-71). Historian. Was dismissed from Göttingen for political reasons in 1837, then went to Heidelberg. His widely
read *Geschichte der poetischen National-Literatur der Deutschen* (5 vols.,
Leipzig, 1835-42) located literature in a social context and called for political
activity. Founded the *Deutsche Zeitung* in 1847. Sat on the right center at
the FP, but was not active and left in July, 1848. His major work after the
revolution was the *Geschichte des neunzehnten Jahrhunderts seit den Wie-
ner Verträgen* (8 vols., Leipzig, 1855-66). It dealt mainly with the century's
early decades, but the introductory volume which preceded it led to his being
dismissed from Heidelberg. Was acquitted of charges of high treason but
not allowed to teach again. For correspondence, see above, under Dahlmann.

Einleitung in die Geschichte des neunzehnten Jahrhunderts. Leipzig, 1853.

G. G. Gervinus Leben, von ihm selbst: 1860. Leipzig, 1893.

Shakespeare, Vol. I. Leipzig, 1849.

GIESEBRECHT, Wilhelm von (1814-89). Historian. Taught in a Prussian
Gymnasium in the 1840's and early 1850's, then went to Königsberg in 1857.
Joined the Historical Commission of the Bavarian Academy of Sciences in
1858, then replaced Sybel at Munich in 1861. Had participated in a political club which supported the monarchy during the revolution.

"Die Entwicklung der modernen deutschen Geschichtswissenschaft," *HZ,*
I (1859), 1-17.

GNEIST, Rudolf von (1816-95). Jurist. Taught at Berlin starting in 1839
and served as an assistant judge, 1841-50. Advocated jury trials. Was elected

to Berlin's municipal assembly in 1848, but was defeated in efforts during 1848-49 to win a seat in the Prussian National Assembly. Won a seat in the Prussian Diet in 1858.

Berliner Zustände: Politische Skizzen aus der Zeit vom 18. März 1848 bis 18. März 1849. Berlin, 1849.

Das heutige englische Verfassungs- und Verwaltungsrecht. 2 vols. Berlin, 1857-60.

HÄUSSER, Ludwig (1818-67). Historian. Taught at Heidelberg starting in 1840. Helped Gervinus found the *Deutsche Zeitung* in 1847. Was at the Pre-Parliament preceding the FP and sat in the upper chamber of Baden's diet in 1848 and 1850. Supported Prussia at the Erfurt Parliament.

"Baden vor den Ereignissen von 1848" (anon.), in *Gegenwart,* Vol. II (1849).

Denkwürdigkeiten zur Geschichte der Badischen Revolution. Heidelberg, 1851.

"Macaulay's Geschichte Englands" (1849-52), in *Gesammelte Schriften: Zur Geschichts-Literatur,* Vol. II. Berlin, 1870.

"Das Ministerium Bekk in Baden," in *Germania,* Vol. I (1851).

"Die Revolution in Baden seit dem Septemberaufstande 1848 bis zum Ende der Katastrophe von 1849" (anon.), in *Gegenwart,* Vol. III (1849).

HAGEN, Karl (1810-68). Historian. Taught at Heidelberg starting in 1836. In the 1840's, did some work as a political publicist. Sat on the far left at the FP, then lost his university position. Taught at Bern starting in 1855.

Geschichte der neuesten Zeit vom Sturze Napoleon's bis auf unsere Tage. 2 vols. Braunschweig, 1850-51.

"Ueber die verschiedenen Richtungen in der Behandlung der Geschichte" (1855), in *Reden und Vorträge.* Bern and Solothurn, 1861.

HAYM, Rudolf (1821-1901). Philosopher, historian, and publicist. Failed to habilitate at Halle in 1845 because of his sympathy for left-wing Hegelianism. At the FP, sat on the right center. Attended the Gotha assembly. In 1848, edited the *Nationalzeitung;* in 1850, the *Constitutionelle Zeitung,* until forced to leave Berlin by the government. Taught at Halle during the 1850's. In 1858, founded the *Preussische Jahrbücher.*

"Aufruf zur Begründung der Preussischen Jahrbücher" and "Rundschreiben des Herausgebers an die Mitarbeiter der Preussischen Jahrbücher" (1857), in Otto Westphal, *Welt- und Staatsauffassung des deutschen Liberalismus.* Munich and Berlin, 1919.

Aus meinem Leben. Berlin, 1902.

Ausgewählter Briefwechsel, ed. Hans Rosenberg. Berlin and Leipzig, 1930.

Die deutsche Nationalversammlung. 3 vols. Frankfurt a. M. and Berlin, 1848-50.

Hegel und seine Zeit: Vorlesungen über Entstehung und Entwickelung, Wesen und Wert der Hegel'schen Philosophie. Berlin, 1857.

"Die Literatur des ersten deutschen Parlaments," *Allgemeine Monatsschrift für Literatur,* I (1850), 132-153.

"Sybel's historische Vierteljahrsschrift" (anon.), *PJ,* II (1858), 105-106.

"Vorwort," *PJ,* III (1859), 1-15.
Wilhelm von Humboldt. Berlin, 1856.

HESS, Moses (1812-75). Philosopher and publicist. Wrote for Young Hegelian periodicals in the 1840's. Lived in Geneva and Paris in the 1850's. Returned to Prussia in 1861.
Briefwechsel, ed. Edmund Silberner. The Hague, 1959.
Jugement dernier du vieux monde social (1851), partly reprinted in German translation in *Ausgewählte Schriften,* ed. Horst Lademacher. Cologne, 1962.

HUBER, Viktor Aimé (1800-69). Publicist and social reformer, with special interest in co-operative associations. Taught modern languages and history at Rostock and Marburg, 1832-42, representing the latter university in Kurhessen's diet. Taught at Berlin, 1843-51. Edited the journal *Janus* for the Prussian government, 1845-48. Edited the journal *Concordia* for a building society in Berlin, 1849-50, then became disillusioned with the society's lack of concern for the working classes and quit. General disappointment with Prussian conservatism led to departure from Berlin for Wernigerode in 1852. Travelled widely in western Europe to observe working-class life.
"Arbeitende Klassen," in *DSW,* Vol. I (1857).
"Assoziation," in *DSW,* Vol. I (1857).
Ausgewählte Schriften über Socialreform und Genossenschaftswesen, ed. K. Munding. Berlin, 1894.
Berlin, Erfurt, Paris. Berlin, 1850.
Bruch mit der Revolution und Ritterschaft. Berlin, 1852.
"Die cooperative Association in Deutschland," *DVS* (1855), II, 51-107.
Review of Wilhelm Heinrich Riehl, *Die Naturgeschichte des Volkes,* in *Göttingische gelehrte Anzeigen* (1856), I, 33-86.
Suum cuique in der deutschen Frage. Berlin, 1850.

JÖRG, Joseph Edmund (1819-1901). Publicist and historian. Studied theology, then worked as a research assistant to Ignaz Döllinger. In 1849, was active as a conservative orator in Bavarian election campaigns. Did more historical research after the revolution. Gained a post in the Bavarian civil service and became editor of the *Historisch-politische Blätter für das katholische Deutschland* in 1852. Wrote many articles, none of which were signed.

KNIES, Karl (1821-98). Economist. Taught at Marburg, 1846-51, then left to teach in Switzerland because of political differences with the government of Hesse-Kassel. Went to Freiburg in 1855.
"Der Deutsche Bund bis zur Epoche von 1830" and "Der Deutsche Bund seit 1830 bis zur Auflösung des Bundestags im Jahre 1848" (anon.), in *Gegenwart,* Vols. I-II (1848-49).
Die politische Oekonomie vom Standpunkte der geschichtlichen Methode. Braunschweig, 1853.
"Die Wissenschaft der Nationalökonomie seit Adam Smith bis auf die Gegenwart" (anon.), in *Gegenwart,* Vol. VII (1852).

LASAULX, Ernst von (1805-61). Philologist and philosopher of history.

Taught at Munich starting in 1844, but lost his post temporarily during the revolution because of conflicts with the government. Sat on the far right, worked on the constitutional committee at the FP. Was in the Bavarian Diet during the 1850's.

"Grundstein zu einem Denkmal für das deutsche Parlament in der Paulskirche," *HPB*, XXIII (1849), 703-704.

Neuer Versuch einer alten, auf die Wahrheit der Thatsachen gegründeten Philosophie der Geschichte. Munich, 1856.

Studien des classischen Altherthums: Akademische Abhandlungen, Mit einem Anhange politischen Inhaltes. Regensburg, 1854.

LASSALLE, Ferdinand (1825-64). Social philosopher, publicist, and socialist labor leader (during the 1860's). Academic training was in the area of philosophy. Spent several months in prison because of his activities in the revolution of 1848.

Nachgelassene Briefe und Schriften, ed. Gustav Mayer, Vols. II-III. Stuttgart and Berlin, 1923 and 1922 (*Lassalles Briefwechsel von 1848 bis zum Beginn seiner Arbeiteragitation* and *Der Briefwechsel zwischen Lassalle und Marx*).

LAUBE, Heinrich (1806-84). Novelist, playwrite, and publicist. Was regarded as a member of Young Germany and was imprisoned for membership in a *Burschenschaft* and for his political writings in the *Vormärz*. Was elected to the FP from a constituency in Austria. Sat on the left center. Attended the Gotha assembly. Returned to literary and theatrical work afterwards.

Das erste deutsche Parlament. 3 vols. Leipzig, 1849.

MARLO, Karl (pseudonym for Karl Georg Winkelblech; 1810-65). Economist. Taught chemistry at the technical institute in Kassel starting in 1837. Began to study social questions early in the 1840's. Sat in Kurhessen's diet and was active at artisan congresses in 1848.

Untersuchungen über die Organisation der Arbeit, oder System der Weltökonomie. 3 vols. Kassel, 1850-59.

MICHELET, Carl Ludwig (1801-93). Philosopher. Taught at Berlin starting in 1826. Belonged to the left wing of the followers of Hegel. Did some writing on politics during 1848. Was active before and after 1848 in a philanthropic organization.

Die Geschichte der Menschheit in ihrem Entwickelungsgange seit dem Jahre 1775 bis auf die neuesten Zeiten. 2 vols. Berlin, 1859-60.

Die Lösung der gesellschaftlichen Frage. Frankfurt a. M. and Berlin, 1849.

Wahrheit aus meinem Leben. Berlin, 1884.

MOHL, Robert von (1799-1875). Jurist and political scientist. Travelled widely in Europe and America during his early years. Taught first at Tübingen, then went to Heidelberg in 1847. An influential early work was *Die Polizei-Wissenschaft nach den Grundsätzen des Rechtsstaates* (3 vols., Tübingen, 1832-34). In 1844, started the *Zeitschrift für die gesammte Staatswissenschaft*. Sat in Württemberg's diet briefly in the mid-1840's. In the FP, sat on the left center, also served as imperial minister of justice. Attended the Gotha assembly.

"Drei deutsche Staatswörterbücher" (anon.), *PJ*, II (1858), 243-267.

Encyclopädie der Staatswissenschaften. Tübingen, 1859.

"Die erste deutsche Reichsversammlung und die Schriften darüber" (anon.), *DVS* (1850), II, 1-75.

Die Geschichte und Literatur der Staatswissenschaften. 3 vols. Erlangen, 1855-58.

"Gesellschafts-Wissenschaften und Staats-Wissenschaften," *Zeitschrift für die gesammte Staatswissenschaft,* VII (1851), 3-71.

Lebenserinnerungen. 2 vols. Stuttgart and Leipzig, 1902.

"Neuere deutsche Leistungen auf dem Gebiete der Staatswissenschaften" (anon.), *DVS* (1854), III, 1-77.

"Das Repräsentativsystem, seine Mängel und die Heilmittel: Politische Briefe eines Altliberalen" (anon.), *DVS* (1852), III, 145-235.

NEBENIUS, Karl Friedrich (1785-1857). Economist. Was Baden's minister of the interior in the 1840's. Retired from active service in 1849 to devote himself to academic work.

Baden in seiner Stellung zur deutschen Frage. Karlsruhe, 1850.

OPPENHEIM, Heinrich Bernhard (1819-80). Publicist. Belonged to a Jewish banking family. Taught political science and international law at Heidelberg in the early 1840's, but soon abandoned his academic career in favor of politics. Edited *Die Reform* in 1848 with Arnold Ruge. Was defeated in elections for the FP. In 1849, engaged in revolutionary activities in Baden.

"Zur Kritik der Demokratie" (1850), in *Vermischte Schriften aus bewegter Zeit*, Vol. I. Stuttgart and Leipzig, 1866.

PFIZER, Paul Achatius (1801-67). Publicist and government official. Wrote the influential *Briefwechsel zweier Deutschen* (Stuttgart and Tübingen, 1831), an important early expression of support for Prussian leadership in German unification. During the revolution, was in a reform ministry in Württemberg and sat on the right center in the FP.

Deutschlands Aussichten im Jahr 1851. Stuttgart, 1851.

Politische Aufsätze und Briefe, ed. Georg Küntzel. Frankfurt a. M., 1924.

"Preussen und Oestreich in ihrem Verhältniss zu Deutschland" (anon.), in *Germania,* Vol. I (1851).

PHILLIPS, George (1804-72). Jurist. Taught at Munich, 1834-47. Sat on the far right at the FP. Moved to Austria in 1850.

"Kirche oder Revolution?" (1853), in *Vermischte Schriften,* Vol. II. Vienna, 1856.

"Ueber den Geschichtsunterricht" (1851), in *Vermischte Schriften,* Vol. I. Vienna, 1856.

PRINCE-SMITH, John (1809-74). Publicist. Was born in England, moved to Germany in 1830. Taught languages in a *Gymnasium,* then devoted himself to writing. Sat on Berlin's municipal council, 1848-50. Ran for the Prussian Diet in 1849 but failed to be elected. Helped found the Congress of German Economists in 1858.

"Kommissions-Bericht über das Gewerbegesetz vom 9. Februar 1849" (1849), in *Gesammelte Schriften,* ed. Karl Braun-Wiesbaden, Vol. III. Berlin, 1880.

RANKE, Leopold (1795-1886). Historian. After 1825, spent his scholarly career at Berlin. Edited a semiofficial *Historisch-politische Zeitschrift* in the 1830's. In 1841, was named official historian of the Prussian state. In 1854, lectured privately to King Maximillian II of Bavaria and became a member of the Privy Council in Prussia.

*"Aufsätze zur eigenen Lebensgeschichte" (1888), in *Weltgeschichte,* Vol. IV. 2nd ed., Leipzig, 1896.

Das Briefwerk, ed. Walther Peter Fuchs. Hamburg, 1949.

Neue Briefe, ed. Hans Herzfeld. Hamburg, 1949.

"Politische Denkschriften aus den Jahren 1848-1851," in *Werke,* Vols. 49-50. Leipzig, 1887.

Ueber die Epochen der neueren Geschichte (unpublished lectures from 1854). Leipzig, 1888 (Vol. IX, part II, of the *Weltgeschichte*).

RAUMER, Friedrich von (1781-1873). Historian. Taught political science as well as history at Berlin starting in 1819. In the FP, sat on the right center. Was elected to the upper chamber of the Prussian Diet in 1849. Attended the Gotha assembly.

Briefe aus Frankfurt und Paris, 1848-1849. 2 vols. Leipzig, 1849.

"Briefe über gesellschaftliche Fragen der Gegenwart" (1850), in *Vermischte Schriften,* Vol. I. Leipzig, 1852.

RIEHL, Wilhelm Heinrich (1823-97). Social theorist, cultural historian, and publicist. After studying theology in the 1840's, was active as a conservative newspaper editor during the revolution. Worked for several years on the *Augsburger allgemeine Zeitung* in the early 1850's, then was given a position on the official government newspaper in Munich and an honorary professorship in the university's faculty of political economy. Became a full professor in 1859.

Die bürgerliche Gesellschaft (1851). 5th ed., Stuttgart and Augsburg, 1858 (Vol. II of *Die Naturgeschichte des Volkes als Grundlage einer deutschen Social-Politik* after the first edition).

Land und Leute (1854). 4th ed., Stuttgart and Augsburg, 1857 (Vol. I of *Die Naturgeschichte des Volkes*).

"Die Volkskunde als Wissenschaft" (1858), in *Culturstudien aus drei Jahrhunderten.* Stuttgart, 1859.

ROCHAU, August Ludwig von (1810-73). Publicist. Was trained in history, law, and political science. Was sentenced to life imprisonment after an attack on a guard house in Frankfurt in 1833 but escaped to France. Sent many reports back to German newspapers, then returned to Germany in 1848. Was expelled from Berlin during the reaction because of his articles in the *Constitutionelle Zeitung.* In 1859, became editor of the *Wochenschrift des Nationalvereins.*

"Absolutismus: Nachtrag," in *SL,* Vol. I (1856).

"Die deutsche Kleinstaaterei und ihre Folgen," in *Germania,* Vol. I (1851).

Geschichte Frankreichs vom Sturze Napoleons bis zur Wiederherstellung des Kaiserthums, 1814-1852. 2 vols. Leipzig, 1858.

Grundsätze der Realpolitik, angewendet auf die staatlichen Zustände Deutschlands (anon.), Stuttgart, 1853.

"Die verfassunggebende deutsche Reichsversammlung," *DVS* (1849), III, 129-310.

RODBERTUS, Johann Karl (1805-75). Economist. Studied law and held legal posts in Prussian local government during the 1820's. After studying economics, bought an estate in Pomerania and turned to farming. Prestige among other landowners based on the good management of his estate led to local office. Wrote several pamphlets on economic and social issues during the 1830's and 1840's. In 1848, was a leader of the left center in the Prussian National Assembly and served briefly as minister of education and culture. Ran for the Prussian Diet in 1849, but withdrew after the three-class suffrage was introduced.

Das Kapital: Vierter socialer Brief an von Kirchmann (written in 1851), in *Aus dem literarischen Nachlass,* ed. Theophil Kozak. Berlin, 1884.

"Mein Verhalten in dem Conflict zwischen Krone und Volk" (1849), in *Kleine Schriften,* ed. Moritz Wirth. Berlin, 1890.

Sociale Briefe an von Kirchmann. 3 vols. Berlin, 1850-51.

RÖSSLER, Constantin (1820-96). Philosopher and publicist. Taught at Jena in 1848, then abandoned his academic career to work on *Die Grenzboten.* After the revolution, returned to Jena, but then left again to take up freelance journalism in 1860.

System der Staatslehre. Leipzig, 1857.

ROSCHER, Wilhelm (1817-94). Economist. Taught history and political science in the 1840's at Göttingen. An important early work was his *Grundriss zu Vorlesungen über die Staatswirthschaft, nach geschichtlicher Methode* (Göttingen, 1843). Went to Leipzig in 1848.

"Der gegenwärtige Zustand der wissenschaftlichen Nationalökonomie und die notwendige Reform desselben," *DVS* (1849), I, 174-190.

Die Grundlagen der Nationalökonomie (1854). 3rd ed., Stuttgart and Augsburg, 1858 (Vol. I of *System der Volkswirthschaft*).

RUGE, Arnold (1802-80). Publicist and political philosopher. Spent five years in prison because of his activities in a *Burschenschaft,* then taught ancient philosophy at Halle, 1832-36. Founded the *Hallische Jahrbücher für deutsche Wissenschaft und Kunst* in the late 1830's and joined with Karl Marx to edit the *Deutsch-französische Jahrbücher* in 1844. Sat on the far left in the FP. Moved to London in 1849 (returning to Germany occasionally after 1865). Continued to write on political and literary subjects for German journals.

Arnold Ruges Briefwechsel und Tagebuchblätter aus den Jahren 1825-1880, ed. Paul Nerrlich. 2 vols. Berlin, 1886.

Die Gründung der Demokratie in Deutschland, oder der Volksstaat und der social-demokratische Freistaat. Leipzig, 1849.

SCHÄFFLE, Albert (1831-1903). Economist, social theorist, and publicist. Had abandoned theological study to join in the radical uprising in Baden in 1849, but quickly became disillusioned with the revolutionaries' demagoguery. Became professor of political science at Tübingen in 1860.

"Abbruch und Neubau der Zunft" (1856), in *Gesammelte Aufsätze,* Vol. I. Tübingen, 1885.

Aus meinem Leben. 2 vols. Berlin, 1905.

"Fabrikwesen und Fabrikarbeiter," in *DSW,* Vol. III (1858).

"Gewerbe, Gewerbefreiheit, Gewerbeordnung," in *DSW,* Vol. IV (1859).

"Der moderne Adelsbegriff" (1856), in *Gesammelte Aufsätze,* Vol. I.

"Vergangenheit und Zukunft der deutschen Gemeinde" (1856), in *Gesammelte Aufsätze,* Vol. I.

SCHMIDT, Julian (1818-86). Literary historian and publicist. Abandoned secondary school teaching in 1847 for journalism. In 1848, took over *Die Grenzboten* with Gustav Freytag.

Geschichte der deutschen Literatur seit Lessing's Tod (1853). 3 vols. 4th ed., Leipzig, 1858.

Geschichte der französischen Literatur seit der Revolution 1789. 2 vols. Leipzig, 1858.

SCHMIDT, Wilhelm Adolf (1812-87). Historian. Taught at Berlin starting in 1840. Edited the *Zeitschrift für Geschichtswissenschaft,* which appeared for several years in the 1840's. Also wrote on the social question. Sat on the left center in the FP and wrote newspaper articles during the revolution. Went to Zürich in 1851, to Jena in 1860.

Geschichte der preussisch-deutschen Unionsbestrebungen seit der Zeit Friedrich's des Grossen. Berlin, 1851.

Preussens deutsche Politik: Die Dreifürstenbünde, 1785. 1806. 1849. Berlin, 1850.

SCHOPENHAUER, Arthur (1788-1860). Philosopher. Taught at Berlin in the 1820's, then retired to private life. His major work, *Die Welt als Wille und Vorstellung,* appeared in 1819. Continued to write, but ideas changed little in succeeding years.

Arthur Schopenhauer: Mensch und Philosoph in seinen Briefen, ed. Arthur Hübscher. Wiesbaden, 1960.

Parerga und Paralipomena: Kleine philosophische Schriften (1851), ed. Arthur Hübscher. 2 vols. Wiesbaden, 1946-47 (Vols. V-VI of *Sämmtliche Werke*).

SCHULZ-BODMER, Wilhelm (1797-1860). Publicist. Was imprisoned twice for his writings in the *Vormärz,* then went to Zürich. Continued to write there, contributing many articles to the *Staats-Lexikon.* Returned to Germany in 1848, sat on the far left in the FP. Then went back to Zürich.

"Anarchie: Nachtrag im Rückblicke auf die Ereignisse des letzten Jahrzehnts," in *SL,* Vol. I (1856).

"Communismus und Socialismus seit 1848," in *SL,* Vol. III (1859).

Die Rettung der Gesellschaft aus den Gefahren der Militärherrschaft. Leipzig, 1859.

Schulze, Friedrich Gottlob (1795-1860). Economist. Taught at Jena starting in 1819. Also headed an agricultural institute and helped to set up local agricultural associations.

Die Arbeiterfrage, nach den Grundsätzen der deutschen Nationalökonomie, mit Beziehung auf die aus Frankreich nach Deutschland verpflanzten Systeme des Feudalismus, Merkantilismus, Physiokratismus, Socialismus, Communismus und Republikanismus. Jena, 1849.

Nationalökonomie, oder Volkswirthschaftslehre, vornehmlich für Land-, Forst- und Staatswirthe. Leipzig, 1856.

Stahl, Friedrich Julius (1802-61). Jurist and political theorist. Was much interested in ecclesiastical affairs. After a number of years in Bavaria, started teaching at Berlin in 1840. Was elected to the Prussian Diet's upper chamber in 1848, sitting on the far right. Remained there in the 1850's. Also sat in the Erfurt Parliament. Wrote many articles during the 1850's for the *Kreuzzeitung.*

Parlamentarische Reden, ed. J. P. M. Treuherz. Berlin, 1856.

Die Philosophie des Rechts, Vol. II: *Rechts- und Staatslehre auf der Grundlage christlicher Weltanschauung,* part I: *Die allgemeinen Lehren und das Privatrecht* (1837). 3rd ed., Heidelberg, 1854.

Die Philosophie des Rechts, Vol. II, part II: *Die Staatslehre und die Principien des Staatsrechts* (1837). 3rd ed., Heidelberg, 1856.

Der Protestantismus als politisches Princip. Berlin, 1853.

Die Revolution und die constitutionelle Monarchie (1848). 2nd ed., Berlin, 1849.

Was ist die Revolution? Berlin, 1852.

Stein, Lorenz von (1815-90). Social philosopher. Lived in Paris during the early 1840's. His *Der Socialismus und Communismus des heutigen Frankreichs* (Leipzig, 1842) was widely read. Taught legal history at Kiel starting in 1843 while working for several newspapers. During the revolution, represented Schleswig-Holstein's provisional government in Paris and sat as a moderate liberal in the diet. Was dismissed from Kiel in 1850 by the Danes because of his support for local independence. After working in Munich as a journalist in 1854, joined the faculty of political science at Vienna in 1855.

"Demokratie und Aristokratie" (anon.), in *Gegenwart,* Vol. IX (1854).

"Das Gemeindewesen der neueren Zeit" (anon.), *DVS* (1853), I, 22-84.

Geschichte der socialen Bewegung in Frankreich von 1789 bis auf unsere Tage. 3 vols. Leipzig, 1850.

"Der Socialismus in Deutschland" (anon.), in *Gegenwart,* Vol. VII (1852).

System der Staatswissenschaft, Vol. I: *System der Statistik, der Populationistik und der Volkswirthschaftslehre.* Stuttgart and Tübingen, 1852.

System der Staatswissenschaft, Vol. II: *Der Begriff der Gesellschaft und die Lehre von den Gesellschaftsklassen.* Stuttgart and Augsburg, 1856.

"Das Wesen des arbeitslosen Einkommens und sein besonderes Verhält-niss zu Amt und Adel" (anon.), *DVS* (1852), IV, 139-190.

STRAUSS, David Friedrich (1808-74). Theological critic. Taught at a semi-nary in Tübingen in the early 1830's but lost his post in the storm over his book, *Das Leben Jesu* (2 vols., Tübingen, 1835-36). Barely missed being elected to the FP, but was elected to the diet in Württemberg, where he supported moderate conservatism.

Ausgewählte Briefe, ed. Eduard Zeller. Bonn, 1895.

Briefwechsel zwischen Strauss und Vischer. 2 vols. Stuttgart, 1952-53.

SYBEL, Heinrich von (1817-95). Historian. Spent the 1840's at Bonn and Marburg. Attended the Pre-Parliament in 1848, but failed in an effort to be elected to the FP. Did serve in 1848 in the Hessian Diet. Criticism of reactionary government there in a newspaper in 1850 led to prosecution, but he was not convicted. Was a delegate at the Erfurt Parliament. In 1856, went to Munich. Founded the *Historische Zeitschrift* in 1859.

"Die christlich-germanische Staatslehre: Ihre Bedeutung in der Gegen-wart, ihr Verhältniss zum geschichtlichen Christen- und Germanenthum," in *Germania*, Vol. II (1852).

Geschichte der Revolutionszeit von 1789 bis 1795, Vols. I-II (1853-54). 2nd ed., Düsseldorf and Stuttgart, 1859.

Ueber den Stand der neueren deutschen Geschichtschreibung. Marburg, 1856.

"Vorwort," *HZ*, I (1859), iii-v.

TREITSCHKE, Heinrich von (1834-96). Historian. Studied under Dahlmann and Roscher in the 1850's, worked on the editorial staff of the *Preussische Jahrbücher*. Started teaching at Leipzig in 1859.

Briefe, ed. Max Cornicelius. 4 vols. Leipzig, 1913-20.

Die Gesellschaftswissenschaft: Ein kritischer Versuch. Leipzig, 1859.

"Die Grundlagen der englischen Freiheit" (anon.), *PJ*, I (1858), 366-381.

TRENDELENBURG, Adolf (1802-72). Philosopher. Taught at Berlin, where he held a variety of important university positions. Was secretary of the philo-logical-historical division of the Prussian Academy of Sciences, 1847-71. Sat in the Prussian Diet, 1849-51.

Die sittliche Idee des Rechts. Berlin, 1849.

VISCHER, Friedrich Theodor (1807-87). Philosopher. Taught at Tübingen starting in 1835. Was suspended for two years in the mid-1840's for defend-ing the ideas of D. F. Strauss. In the FP, first sat on the left center, then moved farther left. Wrote articles during the revolution for the *Schwäbische Merkur*. After further governmental harassment, went to Zürich in 1855. For correspondence, see above, under D. F. Strauss.

"Die Religion und die Revolution," *Deutsche Monatsschrift für Politik, Wissenschaft, Kunst und Leben,* II, part II (1851), 32-40.

WAGENER, Hermann (1815-89). Publicist. Studied law at Berlin and worked in Prussia as a legal official in the *Vormärz*. Edited the conservative *Kreuz-zeitung*, 1848-54. Was elected to the Prussian Diet in 1853. Edited the

Neues Conversations-Lexikon: Staats und Gesellschafts-Lexikon (23 vols., Berlin, 1859-67).

Erlebtes: Meine Memoiren aus der Zeit von 1848 bis 1866 und von 1873 bis jetzt, Vol. I. Berlin, 1884.

"Vorwort" and "Einleitung," in *NCL*, Vol. I (1859).

WAITZ, Georg (1813-86). Historian. Taught at Kiel, 1840-48, after that at Göttingen. Having represented the university in the diet before the revolution, joined the provisional government of Schleswig-Holstein in 1848, serving as envoy to Berlin. Sat on the right center and worked on the constitutional committee at the FP. Attended the Gotha assembly. Wrote some pamphlets on the Schleswig-Holstein question in the 1850's.

"Falsche Richtungen," *HZ*, I (1859), 17-28.

"Das Wesen des Bundesstaates," *Allgemeine Monatsschrift für Wissenschaft und Literatur* (1853), 494-530.

WELCKER, Karl Theodor (1790-1869). Jurist and political theorist. Taught at several universities in the early part of his career. Was dismissed from Freiburg in 1832 and prosecuted for writing newspaper articles critical of the political status quo but was acquitted. Then devoted himself to political life (having been elected to Baden's diet in 1831) and to editing the *Staats-Lexikon*, which began to appear in 1834. At the FP, sat on the right center. Sat in Baden's diet again in 1850. In the 1850's, edited a third edition of the *Staats-Lexikon*.

"Abc, politisches, und das politische A und O," in *SL*, Vol. I (1856).

"Deutsche Geschichte, deutsche Kaiser und deutsche Grundgesetze," in *SL*, Vol. IV (1859).

"Vorwort zur dritten Auflage des Staats-Lexikon: Ueber den gegenwärtigen Standpunkt Deutschlands in dem politischen Entwickelungskampf des Jahrhunderts," in *SL*, Vol. I (1856).

WIRTH, Max (1822-1900). Economist and publicist.

Die deutsche Nationaleinheit in ihrer volkswirthschaftlichen, geistigen und politischen Entwickelung. Frankfurt a. M., 1859.

Grundzüge der National-Oekonomie. Cologne, 1856.

WUTTKE, Heinrich (1818-76). Historian. Taught at Leipzig starting in 1841. Did some writing on politics in the 1840's and was active with Robert Blum as a leader of Saxony's liberal opposition. Sat on the left center at the FP and wrote many newspaper articles during the revolution.

Der Stand der deutschen Verfassungsfrage. Leipzig, 1850.

To give a more complete picture of the range of my investigations, I have appended the following lists of additional names. I checked almost all of them in all of the catalogues, periodicals, and other works referred to on p. 194 but did not discover enough of interest to warrant including them in the group of men listed above. An asterisk indicates that a man sat in the Frankfurt Parliament.

ECONOMISTS

Braun, K. (1822-93)
Dietzel, K. A. (1829-84)
Gossen, H. H. (1810-58)
Hagen, K. H. (1785-1856)
Hanssen, G. (1809-94)
Haxthausen, A. (1792-1866)
Helferich, J. A. R. (1817-92)
*Hermann, F. B. W. (1795-1868)
Heyd, W. (1823-1906)
*Hildebrand, B. (1812-78)

Kraemer, A. (1832-1910)
Meitzen, A. (1822-1910)
Nasse, E. (1829-90)
Neumann, F. J. (1835-1910)
Rau, K. H. (1792-1870)
Soetbeer, A. G. (1814-92)
*Stahl, F. W. (1812-73)
Thünen, J. H. (1783-1850)
Wagner, A. (1835-1917)

HISTORIANS

Arnold, W. (1826-83)
Curtius, E. (1814-96)
Friedländer, L. (1824-1909)
*Gfrörer, A. F. (1803-61)
Gregorovius, F. (1821-91)
Grimm, H. (1828-1901)
Güdemann, M. (1835-1918)
Hegel, K. (1813-1901)
Hillebrand, K. (1829-84)
Janssen, J. (1829-91)
Klopp, O. (1822-1903)

*Kutzen, J. R. (1800-77)
Leo, H. (1799-1878)
Lipsius, J. (1834-1920)
Marquardt, K. J. (1812-82)
Mommsen, T. (1817-1903)
Nitzsch, K. W. (1818-80)
Pertz, G. H. (1795-1876)
Schlosser, F. C. (1776-1861)
*Schubert, F. W. (1799-1868)
*Sepp, J. N. (1816-1909)
*Stenzel, G. A. (1792-1854)

JURISTS AND POLITICAL SCIENTISTS

*Albrecht, W. E. (1800-76)
*Arndts, L. (1803-78)
Bähr, O. (1817-95)
*Behr, W. J. (1775-1851)
Bekker, E. I. (1827-1916)
Berner, A. F. (1818-1907)
*Beseler, G. (1809-88)
Brinz, A. (1820-87)
Bruns, K. G. (1816-80)
*Cucumus, C. (1792-1861)
Dahn, F. (1834-1912)
Degenkolb, H. (1832-1909)
*Deiters, P. F. (1804-61)
Dernburg, H. (1829-1907)
*Edel, C. (1806-90)
Eichhorn, K. F. (1781-1854)

Endemann, W. (1825-99)
Ficker, C. J. (1826-1902)
Fitting, H. H. (1831-1918)
Gerber, K. F. W. (1823-91)
Goldschmidt, L. (1829-97)
Hälschner, H. (1817-89)
Hänel, A. (1833-1918)
Heffter, A. W. (1796-1880)
Holtzendorff, F. (1829-89)
Homeyer, K. G. (1795-1874)
Jhering, R. (1818-92)
*Jordan, S. (1792-1861)
Keller, F. L. (1799-1861)
Leist, B. W. (1819-1906)
Maurer, G. L. (1790-1872)
Maurer, K. (1823-1902)

*Michelsen, A. (1801-81)
*Mittermaier, K. (1787-1867)
*Müller, H. M. (1803-76)
Planck, G. (1824-1910)
Planck, J. J. W. (1817-1900)
*Poezl, J. (1814-81)
Savigny, F. K. (1779-1861)
*Simson, E. (1810-99)

*Tellkampf, J. L. (1808-76)
*Temme, J. (1798-1881)
*Thöl, J. H. (1807-84)
Windscheid, B. (1817-92)
*Zachariae, H. A. (1806-75)
Zachariae von Lingenthal, K.
(1812-94)
*Fischer, G. (1803-68)

PHILOSOPHERS

Beneke, F. E. (1798-1854)
Büchner, L. (1824-99)
Dilthey, W. (1833-1911)
Drobisch, M. (1802-96)
Dühring, E. (1833-1921)
Feuerbach, L. (1804-72)
Fischer, K. (1824-1907)
*Kapp, C. (1798-1874)
*Knoodt, P. (1811-89)
Köppen, F. (1775-1858)
Lange, F. A. (1828-75)

Lotze, R. H. (1817-81)
Prantl, C. (1820-88)
Rosenkrantz, W. (1821-74)
Rosenkranz, K. (1805-79)
Schelling, F. W. J. (1775-1854)
Strumpell, L. (1812-99)
Ulrici, H. (1806-84)
Weisse, C. (1801-66)
Zeller, E. (1814-1908)
Ziller, T. (1817-82)

PUBLICISTS AND MISCELLANY

Baer, A. (1834-1908)
Dietzgen, J. (1828-88)
*Grimm, J. (1785-1863)
Grün, K. T. F. (1817-87)
Kirchmann, J. H. (1802-84)

Lagarde, P. (1827-91)
*Rümelin, G. (1815-88)
Stirner, M. (1806-56)
Twesten, K. (1820-70)
*Venedey, J. (1805-71)

SECONDARY BIBLIOGRAPHY

In none of the sections below are the listings in any way exhaustive. Occasionally an item which was only marginally useful has been included by virtue of its being a standard work. Generally, however, I have listed only works which I have cited in the text or have found to be of some value in developing my own conception of German thought during the middle of the nineteenth century. I have been especially selective in listing works which treat individuals. Moreover, except in a few cases, I have not listed the various books and articles which have informed my understanding of the political and social realities to which the German intellectuals were responding. The main exceptions have been a few general works on nineteenth-century Germany and on the revolution of 1848-49, which combine political, social, and intellectual history. These are listed in Section I.

I. WORKS OF GENERAL RELEVANCE FOR THE STUDY OF MID-NINETEENTH-CENTURY GERMAN INTELLECTUAL HISTORY

A. POLITICAL AND SOCIAL BACKGROUND

Bechtel, Heinrich. *Wirtschaftsgeschichte Deutschlands im 19. und 20. Jahrhundert*. Munich, 1956. Several chapters treat social and economic thought.

Droz, Jacques. *Les révolutions allemandes de 1848*. Paris, 1957.

Eyck, Frank. *The Frankfurt Parliament, 1848-1849*. London and New York, 1968.

Griewank, Karl. "Ursachen und Folgen des Scheiterns der deutschen Revolution in 1848," *HZ*, Vol. 170 (1950), 495-523.

Hamerow, Theodore S. "History and the German Revolution of 1848," *American Historical Review*, LX (1954), 27-44.

—. *Restoration, Revolution, Reaction: Economics and Politics in Germany, 1815-1871*. Princeton, 1958.

—. *The Social Foundations of German Unification, 1858-1871*. 2 vols. Princeton, 1969-72.

Heffter, Heinrich. *Die deutsche Selbstverwaltung im 19. Jahrhundert: Geschichte der Ideen und Institutionen*. Stuttgart, 1950.

Holborn, Hajo. *A History of Modern Germany, 1840-1945.* New York, 1969.

Huber, Ernst Rudolf. *Deutsche Verfassungsgeschichte seit 1789,* Vols. II-III. 2nd ed., Stuttgart, 1963-68.

Schnabel, Franz. *Deutsche Geschichte im neunzehnten Jahrhundert,* Vols. II-IV. Freiburg im Breisgau, 1933-36.

Srbik, Heinrich Ritter von. *Deutsche Einheit: Idee und Wirklichkeit vom Heiligen Reich bis Königgrätz,* Vol. II. Munich, 1935.

Stadelmann, Rudolf. *Soziale und politische Geschichte der Revolution von 1848.* Munich, 1948.

Treitschke, Heinrich von. *History of Germany in the Nineteenth Century,* trans. Eden and Cedar Paul, Vols. V and VII. New York, 1919.

Valentin, Veit. *Geschichte der deutschen Revolution von 1848-49.* 2 vols. Berlin, 1930-31.

Walker, Mack. *German Home Towns: Community, State, and General Estate, 1648-1871.* Ithaca and London, 1971.

B. HIGHER EDUCATION, JOURNALISM, AND PUBLISHING

Engelsing, Rolf. *Massenpublikum und Journalistentum im 19. Jahrhundert in Nordwestdeutschland.* Berlin, 1966.

Goldfriedrich, Johann. *Geschichte des deutschen Buchhandels,* Vol. IV. Leipzig, 1913.

Griewank, Karl. *Deutsche Studenten und Universitäten in der Revolution von 1848.* Weimar, 1949.

Haacke, Wilmont. *Die politische Zeitschrift, 1665-1965,* Vol. I. Stuttgart, 1968.

Kirchner, Joachim. *Das deutsche Zeitschriftenwesen: Seine Geschichte und seine Probleme,* Vol. II. Wiesbaden, 1962.

Koszyk, Kurt. *Deutsche Presse im 19. Jahrhundert.* Berlin, 1966.

Lexis, Wilhelm, ed. *Die deutschen Universitäten.* 2 vols. Berlin, 1893.

O'Boyle, Lenore. "The Image of the Journalist in France, Germany, and England, 1815-1848," *Comparative Studies in Society and History,* X (1968), 290-317.

——. "Klassische Bildung und soziale Struktur in Deutschland zwischen 1800 und 1848," *HZ,* Vol. 207 (1968), 584-608.

Paulsen, Friedrich. *Geschichte des gelehrten Unterrichts auf den deutschen Schulen und Universitäten vom Ausgang des Mittelalters bis zur Gegenwart,* Vol. II. 3rd ed., Berlin and Leipzig, 1921.

Ringer, Fritz K. *The Decline of the German Mandarins: The German Academic Community, 1890-1933.* Cambridge, Mass., 1969. Contains a useful overview of developments in the nineteenth century.

C. THE HISTORY OF IDEAS

Angermann, Erich. *Robert von Mohl, 1799-1875: Leben und Werk eines altliberalen Staatsgelehrten.* Neuwied, 1962. Treats the ideas of many of Mohl's contemporaries.

Kohn, Hans. *The Mind of Germany.* New York, 1960.

Lamprecht, Karl. *Deutsche Geschichte,* Vol. XI, part I. Berlin, 1908.

Löwith, Karl. *From Hegel to Nietzsche: The Revolution in Nineteenth-century Thought,* trans. David E. Green. New York, 1964.

Marcuse, Herbert. *Reason and Revolution: Hegel and the Rise of Social Theory.* 2nd ed., New York, 1963.

Meinecke, Friedrich. "Drei Generationen deutscher Gelehrtenpolitik," *HZ,* Vol. 125 (1922), 248-283.

Schuder, Werner, ed. *Universitas Litterarum: Handbuch der Wissenschaftskunde.* Berlin, 1955. Brief articles on the histories of the disciplines.

Sieburg, Heinz-Otto. *Deutschland und Frankreich in der Geschichtsschreibung des neunzehnten Jahrhunderts.* 2 vols. Wiesbaden, 1954-58. Treats the general intellectual background to German conceptions of the history of France and vice-versa.

Ziegler, Theobald. *Die geistigen und socialen Strömungen des neunzehnten Jahrhunderts.* Berlin, 1899.

II. WORKS DEALING WITH THE HISTORIES OF INDIVIDUAL ACADEMIC DISCIPLINES

A. PHILOSOPHY

Randall, John Herman. *The Career of Philosophy,* Vol. II: *From the German Enlightenment to the Age of Darwin.* New York and London, 1965.

Rosenberg, Hans. "Zur Geschichte der Hegelauffassung," in Rudolf Haym, *Hegel und seine Zeit.* 2nd ed., Leipzig, 1927.

Simon, Walter. *European Positivism in the Nineteenth Century.* Ithaca, 1963.

Windelband, Wilhelm. *A History of Philosophy,* Vol. II: *Renaissance, Enlightenment, Modern,* trans. James H. Tufts. New York, 1901.

B. HISTORY

Engel, Josef. "Die deutschen Universitäten und die Geschichtswissenschaft," *HZ,* Vol. 189 (1959), 223-378.

Gooch, G. P. *History and Historians in the Nineteenth Century.* rev. ed., Boston, 1959.

Iggers, Georg G. *The German Conception of History.* Middletown, 1968.

McClelland, Charles E. *The German Historians and England: A Study in Nineteenth-Century Views.* Cambridge, Eng., 1971.

Srbik, Heinrich Ritter von. *Geist und Geschichte vom deutschen Humanismus bis zur Gegenwart.* 2 vols. Munich, Salzburg, and Vienna, 1950-51.

C. THE SOCIAL SCIENCES

Braunreither, Kurt. "Zur Geschichte des staatswissenschaftlichen Faches an der Humboldt-Universität zu Berlin im ersten Halbjahrhundert ihres Bestehens," *Wissenschaftliche Zeitschrift der Humboldt-Universität zu Berlin,* IX (1959-60), 429-473, 621-678.

Eisermann, Gottfried. *Die Grundlagen des Historismus in der deutschen Nationalökonomie.* Stuttgart, 1956.

Gide, Charles, and Charles Rist. *A History of Economic Doctrines,* trans. R. Richards. 2nd English ed., London, 1948.

Gilbert, Felix. "Lorenz von Stein und die Revolution von 1848: Ein Beitrag zur Entstehung der deutschen Gesellschaftswissenschaft," *Mitteilungen des Österreichischen Instituts für Geschichtsforschung,* L (1936), 369-387.

Maus, Heinz. "Geschichte der Soziologie," in Werner Ziegenfuss, ed., *Handbuch der Soziologie.* Stuttgart, 1956.

Oberschall, Anthony, *Empirical Social Research in Germany, 1848-1914.* Paris and The Hague, 1965.

Schumpeter, Joseph A. *History of Economic Analysis,* ed. Elizabeth Boody Schumpeter. New York, 1954.

Small, Albion W. *Origins of Sociology.* Chicago, 1924.

Stieda, Wilhelm. *Die Nationalökonomie als Universitätswissenschaft.* Leipzig, 1906.

Stintzing, Roderich, and Ernst Landsberg. *Geschichte der deutschen Rechtswissenschaft.* 3 vols. Munich and Berlin, 1880-1910.

III. WORKS DEALING WITH PARTICULAR CURRENTS OF POLITICAL AND SOCIAL THOUGHT

A. *LIBERALISM, RADICALISM, AND NATIONALISM*

Birtsch, Günter. *Die Nation als sittliche Idee: Der Nationalstaatsbegriff in Geschichtsschreibung und politischer Gedankenwelt Johann Gustav Droysens.* Cologne, 1964.

Brazill, William J. *The Young Hegelians.* New Haven, 1970.

Bussmann, Walter. "Zur Geschichte des deutschen Liberalismus im 19. Jahrhundert," *HZ,* Vol. 186 (1958), 527-557.

Dorpalen, Andreas. *Heinrich von Treitschke.* New Haven, 1957.

Droz, Jacques. *Le libéralisme rhénan, 1815-1848.* Paris, 1940.

Faber, Karl-Georg. "Realpolitik als Ideologie: Die Bedeutung des Jahres 1866 für das politische Denken in Deutschland," *HZ,* Vol. 203 (1966), 1-45.

Gagel, Walter. *Die Wahlrechtsfrage in der Geschichte der deutschen liberalen Parteien, 1848-1918.* Düsseldorf, 1958.

Gilbert, Felix. *Johann Gustav Droysen und die preussisch-deutsche Frage.* Munich and Berlin, 1931.

Heller, Hermann. *Hegel und der nationale Machtstaatsgedanke in Deutschland.* Leipzig and Berlin, 1921.

Hook, Sidney. *From Hegel to Marx: Studies in the Intellectual Development of Karl Marx.* rev. ed., Ann Arbor, 1962. Useful background on the Young Hegelians.

Kaehler, S. A. "Realpolitik zur Zeit des Krimkrieges: Eine Säkularbetrachtung," *HZ,* Vol. 174 (1952), 417-478.

Kaltenbach, Anneliese. *Orientation et définition du patriotisme allemand chez un historien de l'Allemagne du Sud: Le Palatin-Badois Ludwig Haeusser, 1818-1867.* Paris, 1965.

Krieger, Leonard. *The German Idea of Freedom: History of a Political Tradition.* Boston, 1957.

Mommsen, Wilhelm. *Grösse und Versagen des deutschen Bürgertums: Ein Beitrag zur politischen Bewegung des 19. Jahrhunderts, insbesondere zur Revolution 1848/49.* 2nd ed., Munich, 1964.

Meinecke, Friedrich. *Machiavellism: The Doctrine of Raison D'état and Its Place in Modern History,* trans. Douglas Scott. New Haven, 1962.

—. *Weltbürgertum und Nationalstaat,* ed. Hans Herzfeld. Munich, 1962.

O'Boyle, Lenore. "The Democratic Left in Germany, 1848," *Journal of Modern History,* XXXIII (1961), 374-383.

Rosenberg, Hans. *Rudolf Haym und die Anfänge des klassischen Liberalismus.* Munich and Berlin, 1933.

—. "Theologischer Rationalismus und vormärzlicher Vulgärliberalismus," *HZ,* Vol. 141 (1930), 497-541.

Sell, Friedrich C. *Die Tragödie des deutschen Liberalismus.* Stuttgart, 1953.

Thomas, R. Hinton. *Liberalism, Nationalism, and the German Intellectuals, 1822-1847: An Analysis of the Academic and Scientific Conferences of the Period.* Cambridge, Eng., 1951.

Westphal, Otto. *Welt- und Staatsauffassung des deutschen Liberalismus: Eine Untersuchung über die Preussischen Jahrbücher und den konstitutionellen Liberalismus in Deutschland von 1858 bis 1863.* Munich and Berlin, 1919.

Witzmann, Georg. *Die Gothaer Nachversammlung zum Frankfurter Parlament im Jahre 1849.* Gotha, 1917.

Zehntner, Hans. *Das Staatslexikon von Rotteck und Welcker.* Jena, 1929.

B. CONSERVATISM

Hahn, Adalbert. *Die Berliner Revue: Ein Beitrag zur Geschichte der konservativen Partei zwischen 1855 und 1875.* Berlin, 1934.

Martin, Alfred von. "Der preussische Altkonservativismus und der politische Katholizismus in ihren gegenseitigen Beziehungen," *Deutsche Vierteljahrsschrift für Literaturwissenschaft und Geistesgeschichte,* VII (1929), 489-514.

Neumann, Sigmund. *Die Stufen des preussischen Konservatismus.* Berlin, 1930.

Schoeps, Hans-Joachim. *Das andere Preussen: Konservative Gestalten und Probleme im Zeitalter Friedrich Wilhelms IV.* 2nd ed., Honnef/Rhein, 1957.

Vierhaus, Rudolf. *Ranke und die soziale Welt.* Münster, 1957.

C. SOCIAL CRITICISM AND THE PURSUIT OF SOCIAL REFORM

Alexander, Edgar. "Church and Society in Germany: Social and Political Movements and Ideas in German and Austrian Catholicism, 1789-1950," in Joseph N. Moody, ed., *Church and Society: Catholic Social and Political*

Thought and Movements, 1789-1950. New York, 1953.

Andler, Charles. *Les Origines du socialisme d'état en Allemagne*. Paris, 1897.

Angermann, Erich. "Zwei Typen des Ausgleichs gesellschaftlicher Interessen durch die Staatsgewalt: Ein Vergleich der Lehren Lorenz Steins und Robert Mohls," in Werner Conze, ed., *Staat und Gesellschaft im deutschen Vormärz*. Stuttgart, 1962.

Biermann, W. Ed. *Karl Georg Winkelblech (Karl Marlo): Sein Leben und sein Werk*. 2 vols. Leipzig, 1909.

Cole, G. D. H. *A History of Socialist Thought*, Vols. I-II. London, 1953-54.

Conze, Werner. "Vom 'Pöbel' zum 'Proletariat': Sozialgeschichtliche Voraussetzungen für den Sozialismus in Deutschland," *Vierteljahrsschrift für Sozial- und Wirtschaftsgeschichte*, XLI (1954), 333-364.

Dietzel, H. *Karl Rodbertus: Darstellung seines Lebens und seiner Lehre*. 2 vols. Jena, 1886-88.

Geramb, Viktor von. *Wilhelm Heinrich Riehl: Leben und Wirken, 1823-1897*. Salzburg, 1954.

Herberger, Karl Valerius. *Die Stellung der preussischen Konservativen zur sozialen Frage, 1848-62*. Meissen, 1914.

Jantke, Carl. *Der vierte Stand: Die gestaltenden Kräfte der deutschen Arbeiterbewegung im XIX. Jahrhundert*. Freiburg, 1955.

Lichtheim, George. *The Origins of Socialism*. New York and Washington, 1969.

Mehring, Franz. *Geschichte der deutschen Sozialdemokratie*, Vols. I-II. 6th and 7th eds., Stuttgart, 1919.

Müssiggang, Albert. *Die soziale Frage in der historischen Schule der deutschen Nationalökonomie*. Tübingen, 1968.

Nitzschke, Heinz. *Die Geschichtsphilosophie Lorenz von Steins*. Munich and Berlin, 1932.

Pankoke, Eckart. *Sociale Bewegung – Sociale Frage – Sociale Politik: Grundfragen der deutschen 'Socialwissenschaft' im 19. Jahrhundert*. Stuttgart, 1970.

Paulsen, Ingwer. *Viktor Aimé Huber als Sozialpolitiker*. 2nd ed., Berlin, 1956.

Reichard, Richard W. *Crippled from Birth: German Social Democracy, 1844-1870*. Ames, Iowa, 1969.

Rohr, Donald G. *The Origins of Social Liberalism in Germany*. Chicago and London, 1963.

Schmidt, Kurt. *Die Genossenschaft: Ihre Geschichte, ihr Wesen und Recht und ihre Entwicklung in Deutschland*. Berlin, 1949.

Schmidt, Werner. *Lorenz von Stein: Ein Beitrag zur Biographie*. Eckenförde, 1956.

Shanahan, William O. *German Protestants Face the Social Question*, Vol. I: *The Conservative Phase, 1815-1871*. South Bend, Indiana, 1954.

Stegmann, Franz Jozef. *Von der ständischen Sozialreform zur staatlichen Sozialpolitik: Der Beitrag der Historisch-Politischen Blätter zur Lösung der sozialen Frage*. Munich and Vienna, 1965.

Wöhler, Fritz. *Joseph Edmund Jörg und die sozialpolitische Richtung im deutschen Katholizismus*. Leipzig, 1929.

INDEX OF NAMES